Planetary Social Thought

# Planetary Social Thought

The Anthropocene Challenge to the Social Sciences

Nigel Clark and
Bronislaw Szerszynski

polity

First published in 2021 by Polity Press

Polity Press
65 Bridge Street
Cambridge CB2 1UR, UK

Polity Press
101 Station Landing
Suite 300
Medford, MA 02155, USA

ISBN-13: 978-1-5095-2634-5
ISBN-13: 978-1-5095-2635-2 (pb)

Cover image:
Akiyama Yō, Japanese, born in 1953
Untitled MV-1019 from the Metavoid series
Japanese, Heisei era, 2010
Stoneware
Ceramics: 20.3 x 32.1 cm (8 x 12 5/8 in.)
Museum of Fine Arts, Boston
Stanley and Mary Ann Snider Collection
2012.632

A catalogue record for this book is available from the British Library.

Typeset in 10 on 12pt Sabon
by Fakenham Prepress Solutions, Fakenham, Norfolk NR21 8NL
Printed and bound in Great Britain by TJ Books Limited

For further information on Polity, visit our website:
politybooks.com

To our mothers, Elaine Clark (1931–2019) and Sylvia May Szerszynski (1929–2020), who both passed during the writing of this book.

# Contents

# Detailed Contents

# Acknowledgements

We find ourselves trying to finish off *Planetary Social Thought* in the midst of a global crisis that is raising deep, perturbing questions about the very point of thinking and writing, while also offering profound reminders of our total dependence on the labour and the gifts of other people – most of whom will remain anonymous and distant. In its own little way, the book is intended as a kind of tribute to the vast and largely irrecoverable chain of bodies, knowledges and practices that have got us this far – through all the previous upheavals of the Earth – ultimately gifting us with the luxury of thinking and writing time. So too do we take inspiration from those younger generations who are currently doing their utmost to keep our planet in a liveable state.

Many, many encounters, prompts and borrowings contributed to *Planetary Social Thought*, and we thank all those who helped us along the way, while taking responsibility for whatever twists and distortions we folded into the mix. One or other or both of us gave talks based on parts of this book at the conference 'Narratives of Scale in the Anthropocene: Imagining Human Responsibility in an Age of Scalar Complexity', University of Vechta, held at the Haus der Kulturen der Welt, Berlin, 11–13 September 2019; to the Vienna Anthropocene Network, University of Vienna, 4 October 2019; to the Institute for Advanced Sustainability Studies, Potsdam, 5 November 2019; at the seminar 'After Progress: Plural Potentialities', Goldsmiths University of London, 29 November 2019; at the 'New Earth Histories Conference', University of New South Wales, Sydney, 4–6 December 2019; and to the UNSW Arts and Social Sciences Faculty, New Earth Histories Research

Program, 11 December 2019. Thanks to the organizers of these events for the opportunity to share our ideas-in-the-making, and to the participants for some very helpful comments.

We held an online seminar on a draft of the book on Academia.edu, and received very useful feedback from Miguel Alexiades, Ahmed Mousa Badawi, Fionn Bennett, Daniel Duhart, Peter Haff, Serpil Oppermann, Hazel Medd and Robert Chris. Thanks are due to Lesley Green for helping us with some important references for chapter 6, and to Yasmin Gunaratnam and Kathryn Yusoff for conversations and collaborations that fed into chapter 5 – along with Stephanie Wakefield and Nora K. Jemisin for the conversation at The New School, New York, 20 April 2018, that was also an inspiration for this chapter.

Many thanks are also due to the timely and insightful advice of our anonymous referees; to Jonathan Skerrett, Senior Commissioning Editor at Polity, for helping us steer the book as it became 'other to itself' through various transformations; to Karina Jákupsdóttir, Assistant Editor at Polity, for keeping us on track throughout the project and for helping us with the cover design; and to Fiona Sewell for her speedy mid-COVID copy-editing of our manuscript.

Etymological derivations are generally from https://www.etymonline.com/.

Finally, we would like to thank ceramic artist Akiyama Yō for permission to use the work *Untitled MV-1019* (2010) from the Metavoid series on the cover.

# Introduction: What Planet Are You On?

## The Day before Tomorrow

A lot has happened since we started writing this book: massive outbreaks of wildfire, widespread drought, locust plagues, a pandemic, global economic crisis and a rush of what we might call de-globalization. What has also been happening – and what continues to happen despite temporary restrictions on gathering in public spaces due to COVID-19 – is that a new generation of activists across the world have been demanding that political and economic leaders put climate change at the top of their agendas. Even before they are old enough to vote, school-age campaigners have helped recruit sympathetic politicians, taken their governments to court, and called for radical changes in their own educational curricula.

Although earlier generations have confronted planet-scaled threats, this is arguably the first global cohort to come to a clear understanding that, no matter what, the world they are inheriting will be significantly less hospitable to human and nonhuman life than that of their parents. For young protesters, informed by the connections that the physical sciences have established between the combustion of fossil hydrocarbons and climatic destabilization, what is at stake is not simply the direction the future will take but whether there will be a future at all. As one student's banner in a recent protest in South Africa put it 'You'll die of old age. I'll die of climate change.' Or, as another asked, 'Why the actual f\*\*\* are we studying for a future we won't have!' (Shoba et al. 2019).

In the light of current climate science, these are hardly exaggerations. Even in the unlikely scenario that internationally agreed-upon targets for emissions reductions are met, we are still heading towards a global mean temperature increase this century of an estimated 2.7–3.0 °C (Anderson 2015). This is well above the 2 °C limit that has often been considered a planetary 'guardrail' that should not be overstepped. But as climatologists Kevin Anderson and Alice Bows sum up the state of their field:

> There is now little to no chance of maintaining the rise in global mean surface temperature at below 2°C, despite repeated high-level statements to the contrary. Moreover, the impacts associated with 2°C have been revised upwards sufficiently so that 2°C now more appropriately represents the threshold between dangerous and extremely dangerous climate change. (2011: 41)

What defines 'extremely dangerous' climate change – and even merely 'dangerous' climate change – is a high risk of passing over thresholds or 'tipping points' in the global system that would result in runaway, self-reinforcing shifts such as the break-up of the West Antarctic ice sheet, loss of tropical coral reefs, melting of permafrost, or die-back of the Amazon rainforest (New et al. 2011; Lenton et al. 2008). Overflowing the pages of scientific reports, such projections are now the stuff of mass-media documentaries, daily newsfeeds and social media memes. And this means that there is now a cohort of young people – those who are putting themselves on the front line of climate activism – who have no memory of a world that was not already heading towards a significant systemic threshold beyond which living conditions are effectively unknowable.

Like others who are unfairly and disproportionately exposed to changing climate – an uncompletable list that includes inhabitants of arid zones, atolls and deltas, polar regions and urban heat islands – these young activists raise charges that demand a response: an *urgent* response. After decades of 'sluggish, litigious, uneven, and generally unimpressive' efforts to contain the climate problem (Roberts and Parks 2007: 225), there is now widespread agreement that zero-carbon targets must be reached within the lifetime of the majority of the global population. For the first time in twenty years of UN international climate change conferences, delegates to the Paris 2015 gatherings agreed that the vast majority of proven fossil fuel reserves must never be extracted and combusted. Pressing home this decision, making sure that subterranean hydrocarbons actually stay in the ground is one of the foremost tasks that today's climate campaigners have taken upon themselves.

But just as our planet sways to many beats, pulses and cycles, so too does collective human action move to a range of rhythms and temporalities. Matters of great urgency such as getting greenhouse gas emissions under control play a vital role in bringing people together, rewriting political agendas, expanding the frame of what feels thinkable and doable. However, every situation troubling enough to spark controversy, every problem that cries for a decisive response, also opens up questions with other temporal horizons: tempos that are slower, deeper, longer-range, iterative or resurgent. And these other considerations rarely sit it out on the sideline while more immediate issues are dealt with; sooner or later they surface, intrude, irrupt – revealing their unavoidable embroilment in the landscape of pressing concerns.

While climate action rightly makes headlines, the idea of the Anthropocene has emerged as a key vehicle for opening up broader matters of concern about human relationships with the Earth. A proposed geological epoch defined by human impact on Earth systems and on the rocky strata that make up the planet's crust, the Anthropocene extends and multiplies the notion that the global climate might be pushed over a tipping point into a new operating state. In this regard, it has become closely associated with efforts to bring into visibility a whole range of possible limits or thresholds in the Earth system, each of which would have drastic implications for the capacity of the Earth to sustain the kind of human life and nonhuman worlds that we are familiar with.

More than just putting new causes for alarm on the agenda, we argue in this book, the Anthropocene offers incitements for thinking about our planet across a range of timescales, fields of vision and trajectories. Such provocations, we propose, can and ought to prompt us to ask some far-reaching questions. What kind of planet is this on which we find ourselves? What has our planet done in the past and what might it be capable of doing in the future? And closely associated with these 'planetary' themes, we also need to ask: what kind of creature or being are we? How have 'we' inhabited and made use of this planet in the past, and what might we find ourselves doing with the Earth and all its shifting, changeable processes in the future? This is what we refer to as *planetary social thought*.

To give a sense of what we mean, let's return to the vital issue of ensuring that fossilized hydrocarbons never leave their subsurface reservoirs – this time with a slightly different spin. Very quickly, any insistence upon 'carbon descent' raises questions about how staying comfortable, producing the things we want or moving from place to place might otherwise be powered. Many of us will be familiar with associated debates about renewable energy, infrastructural transition, changing patterns of demand and so on. But the increasingly incontrovertible evidence that combusting matter-energy from beneath the surface of our planet is transforming the very operation of Earth systems raises another set of questions. How did so much carbon get to be sequestered deep in the Earth in the first place, and what are the implications of this deep storage for the way the Earth works? And, further, how did we, as a being or species, come to be capable of setting things on fire? How did we, or at least some of us, become so proficient at traversing the Earth's geological strata in search of utilizable energy and materials?

Having considered these issues, we might ask yet another set of questions. If we were to desist from digging deep in search of hydrocarbons to combust, then what else might we do with fire? And what else might we do with the subterranean Earth, and all the capabilities we have developed for exploring, understanding and negotiating 'the very thickness of the planet'? (Virilio 1994: 39).

The aim of *Planetary Social Thought* is not so much to resolve these issues, or to identify clear pathways out of the current predicament, as it is to broaden the terms of engagement of the social sciences and humanities with knowledge about how our planet works. For us, as it is for educational theorist Jasmine Brooke Ulmer (2019), 'the Anthropocene is a question, not a strategic plan'. The lived experience of people on the front line of climate crisis or Earth system change is a vital point of departure for such questioning. But to really do justice to their suffering, their indignation, their demands for action, we argue, the questions need to keep on coming. We need to pursue these issues beyond the conventional terrain of the social, through the contact zone of human and nonhuman processes, and deep into the times and spaces of the Earth itself. If the fundamental question of the political is how we could live our lives otherwise, we argue in this book, so too is it timely to ask how a planet becomes other than it is. If we are interested in or excited by questions of how to collectively do things differently, so too should we be concerned and curious about how the Earth, over time, has discovered how to do things differently. As we propose in *Planetary Social Thought*, these are questions that can no longer be kept separate. Or rather, they never should have come apart.

## The Coming of the Anthropocene

For growing numbers of people, everyday experience and longer-term cultural memory confirm that something is amiss with the global climate. But for many of us, it is science that is providing the grammar to frame and speak of such experiences. While scientific terminology is often uninviting to nonspecialist audiences, the notion of the Anthropocene has played a pivotal role in expressing the idea that our home planet is undergoing fundamental and irreversible change. First dropped into a conference discussion rather spontaneously by atmospheric chemist Paul Crutzen in 2000, the Anthropocene has emerged as one of the scientific concepts – if not *the* scientific concept – of the new millennium.

'Anthropocene' is a fusion of the Greek *anthropos*, meaning 'human' and *kainos*, meaning 'new'. Crutzen stumbled on the term as a way of saying that the Earth may no longer be in the Holocene, the relatively stable 11,700-year-old epoch that follows the end of the last Pleistocene glacial episode. The Holocene is considered by geologists, in most regards, to be a fairly unremarkable interglacial phase, one of dozens of brief warmer spells that punctuate the generally much colder two and a half million years of so of the Pleistocene epoch. What makes it special is really only that the Holocene is the geological interval in which some members of our own species, with accelerating speed, have done a lot of new things: settled into more sedentary lifestyles, domesticated significant numbers of plant and animal species, agglomerated into ever larger assemblies with more extensive built infrastructures, turned continents, seas and eventually the entire globe into an interconnected sphere of operations. But the Anthropocene idea goes a step further. Rather than just suggesting that our species has left marks or traces on the Earth's surface, it proposes that we have become geologic or geophysical agents: that we have impacted upon the working of the Earth as a whole.

Crutzen's use of the Anthropocene to signify the end of the Holocene attracted attention for the way in which it provided a shorthand term for a raft of transformations that human activities are effecting in the outer layers of our planet. Climate, insist Earth and life scientists, is an issue of immense importance. In vital ways, the rhythms and pulses of the global climate bring together many of the other things that are happening on or near the surface of the Earth. But climate change is far from the only problem we face. The loss of biological diversity, the acidification of oceans caused by rising carbon dioxide concentration, the thinning of the stratospheric ozone layer, changes to the global cycles of key elements such as nitrogen and phosphorus, high levels of particulate or 'aerosol' pollution of the atmosphere, the extensive transformation of the landform and ecologies of the terrestrial Earth, and irreversible changes to the way fresh water pools and flows across the planet's surface are amongst the other extremely serious global environmental challenges that scientists have assembled into the Anthropocene concept (see Steffen et al. 2004; 2015a; Rockström et al. 2009).

Writing lists – whether they are shopping lists or global challenge inventories – has a way of helping us feel that we are getting on top of things. But in the case of global environmental changes, we most emphatically are not. We've already touched upon the immense risks that are associated with adding carbon dioxide to the Earth's atmosphere.

Current estimates of sea-level rise suggest that some 275 million people worldwide are now living on land that with 3 °C of warming will eventually be inundated (Holder et al. 2017). With regard to threats to biological diversity, which has long been considered a localized or regional problem, some ecologists now believe that 'the plausibility of a future planetary state shift seems high' (Barnosky et al. 2012: 55). If such a global transition were to occur, they suggest, it would be comparable to the 'Big Five' mass extinction events that have occurred in the Earth's history – currently identified at 443, 359, 251, 200, and 65 million years ago (Barnosky et al. 2012: 53). With regard to the Earth's global nitrogen cycle, at risk largely from agrochemical fertilizer use, researchers suggest we would need to go back 2.5 *billion* years to find changes of comparable magnitude (Lewis and Maslin 2015: 172).

By bringing all these transformations together into the single figure of a planet exiting a familiar geological epoch and entering a new one, the Anthropocene offers a way to get our heads around changes that might otherwise seem separate, detached or just too abstract. But it's not simply the bundling together of a whole range of changes that gives the Anthropocene its clout. It's the way that it offers us a language or grammar for thinking about the Earth as a system that – in its entirety – is capable of going through a transition, and doing this *rapidly*.

Already in the 1980s, there was mounting evidence that in the past climate change has happened abruptly rather than gradually (Broecker 1987). The idea that Earth's entire climate system might pass suddenly and irreversibly over a threshold – like a capsizing canoe or bursting balloon – prompted a search for other Earth processes with 'tipping points'. By the time that Crutzen made his 2000 'Anthropocene' interjection, there was already a gathering sense amongst Earth scientists that there were numerous potential tipping points or thresholds in the Earth system – and a rumbling fear that passing over one threshold might trigger abrupt changes elsewhere in the system.

Along these lines, as the Anthropocene thesis took shape, it came to encapsulate the possibility that the Earth system as a whole – by virtue of the way that it functions as a single integrated system – might be capable of rapid transition from one operating state to another. As palaeontologist and Anthropocene Working Group chair Jan Zalasiewicz puts it: 'the Earth seems to be less one planet, rather a number of different Earths that have succeeded each other in time, each with very different chemical, physical and biological states' (cited in Hamilton 2015: 6).

As its scientific exponents clearly intend, the Anthropocene concept works at once as a diagnosis of the current state of the planet and as a warning cry, a planetary alarm, a call for action. As a scientific hypothesis, the Anthropocene is still under review. At the time of writing, evidence for the novel geological epoch is being evaluated by the disciplinary bodies who preside over the official geological timescale. Whatever decision is made, however, the Anthropocene idea has gained considerable traction beyond the world of the natural sciences and seems unlikely to go away in the foreseeable future. An Earth with the potential to turn into a planet that is new and strange to its inhabitants is a storyline – it would appear – that none of us can afford to ignore. But it is not as straightforward as this, as social scientists and humanities scholars have been quick to point out.

## The Challenge for Social Thought

For many of us social thinkers, the Anthropocene is at once a compelling and an unsettling idea. It grasps us because it feels important to understand what is happening to the only planet upon which human social life – and life as we know it – exists. It is troubling because the Anthropocene gives a prominent place to the activities of human actors – and the question of what humans do, collectively, what they are and what they might be capable of is *our* speciality, not that of the natural sciences. Who speaks – which is almost always a question of speaking on behalf of others – is important to social thinkers. It matters a great deal to us who has the opportunity, the wherewithal, the power to talk on behalf of society, to speak for all humanity, and to be the voice of Earth processes.

In diagnosing human activities as a force of geological or planetary significance, natural scientists have stretched and expanded the conventional terrains of scientific research. In assuming responsibility for voicing the current climatic or planetary predicament, many scientists have taken a step further. All this means that questions of what defines natural science, what it is good for, what it ought to do next, are under negotiation.

But if we are to conceive of ourselves as we once envisaged glaciation, meteor impacts or tectonic plate movement, this is a problem for social thought – because these are precisely the kinds of forces we formerly believed to be outside of society, indifferent to the striving of social actors and, as such, not in need of our consideration. This is why, as science studies scholar Bruno Latour puts it, in reflecting on the meaning of the Anthropocene for social thinkers, '[w]hat the New Climatic Regime calls into question is not the central place of the human; it is its composition, its presence, its figuration' (2018: 85). We simply do not have to hand stories, theories or concepts fit for the task of explaining what it means for human agents to find themselves behaving like Earth or cosmic forces. It's worth recalling that at an earlier moment literary theorist Gayatri Chakravorty Spivak called upon fellow social thinkers to 'imagine ourselves as planetary subjects rather than global agents, planetary creatures rather than global entities' (2003: 73). But so too should we note how long it has taken most of us to really begin answering this call.

Our sense is that the encounter with geological forces – whether human or inhuman – is as much an opportunity for social thought as it is a threat. Our concern in this book is with what social scientists and humanities scholars could make of both the Anthropocene idea and the broader developments in Earth and life science from which the Anthropocene hypothesis emerged. Rather than analysing the event of 'the Anthropocene', or figuring how social thinkers might reclaim from natural scientists their privilege of asking and answering questions about social being, we want to confront *ourselves* as social scientists with some difficult questions.

What might it mean for those of us schooled in the social sciences and humanities to view the Anthropocene as an incitement, a provocation to think social life *through* the Earth: to ask, curiously and insistently, what planet we are on, and what kind of 'planetary creatures' we are? In particular we want to think through the idea that ours is a planet with a propensity for reorganizing its own component parts, for lurching or leaping from one operating state to another. The term we give to this understanding of a planet that is capable both of self-transformation and of being nudged into change by outside forces is *planetary multiplicity*. This is our way of conceiving of an Earth that has the capacity – at every scale, from the microscopic to the entire Earth system – to become other to itself, to self-differentiate.

So we seem to be at a *planetary* juncture, at which confronting what the Earth is capable of doing, and developing theoretical and methodo-logical tools to investigate how this enables and conditions social life, feels like a matter of urgency. However, we are also at a *historical* juncture, one at which the global predominance of Western knowledge claims, whether in the human or the natural sciences, is being strongly contested. In a globalized world in which many Indigenous or traditional ways of knowing have been suppressed, marginalized and overwritten by knowledge practices that more or less emerged from a single region, the authority of Western science is under contestation.

This raises pressing questions of how the multiplicity of the planet relates to the multiplicity that is so much a part of human beings as planetary creatures. The challenge of thinking through the Earth in ways that are open to 'modern' science but also to a world of other knowledge practices and ways of life is one that will accompany us, animate us, unsettle us, throughout this book. How does the Earth's own capacity to be other than it is – its planetary multiplicity – relate to the otherness, the difference, the alterity that is so constitutive of human life? These questions do not just orbit around our idea of planetary social thought – they are at its molten core.

It is not possible to ask what planet we are on without also asking about the different ways this planet is engaged with, experienced, known and imagined. The term we give to the way that different human groups or collectives respond to the multiplicity that inheres in our planet is *earthly multitudes*. As we will explain in more detail, for us an earthly multitude is a shared way of responding to the challenges raised by the changeability of the Earth and the opportunities opened up by planetary self-ordering and variation.

Our planetary social thought, then, is more than an immediate response to the predicament signalled by the Anthropocene. Our twinned concepts of planetary multiplicity and earthly multitudes are intended to offer a more generalized way of understanding the connections between human self-making, plurality and diversity and the inherent change-ability of the Earth at every scale. Through linking planetary multiplicity with earthly multitudes, we seek to show how human difference and social 'otherness' are bound up with the capacity of the Earth to self-differentiate or become other to itself. And in this way we have found that one of the most important consequences of the Anthropocene problematic is to feel ourselves drawn into engagement with earlier geological intervals, earlier moments in human and Earth history.

## Planetary Thought in the Making

Whether we conceive of it as Western civilization, industrial modernity or global capitalism, there is a growing doubt as to whether a world order reliant on the combustion of fossil fuels has any long-term future. Insisting that coal, oil and gas stay in the ground is an effective way of putting this system under pressure and revealing where its fault-lines lie. And identifying and defying vested interests that are intent on perpetu-ating carbon- and mineral-intensive production in the face of all the evidence pointing to its perils is another necessary step towards any new order. But for all their political probity, neither saying no to fossil fuels nor staging tribunals for the most suspect parties in the current environmental crisis takes us far in the direction of remaking dominant Earth–society relations.

To begin opening up alternative possibilities we need to consider how 'we' arrived at the current conjuncture, to ask how different social formations came to acquire their force and impact. This is an obvious question for those constituencies or groupings whose actions weigh most heavily upon the Earth, but it is just as important wherever the planet has been peopled. 'Fossil capital' and 'petro-states' may have left their mark on the Earth system (see Malm 2016; Huber 2013: 5–6), but Amazonian and West African communities have generated their own soil strata (Fraser et al. 2014), while skilled use of fire in the Australian context 'allowed the Aborigine to move a continent' (Pyne 1997b: 31).

As we will be arguing, this is never simply a matter of inscribing a social or cultural power on a waiting landscape, but always an active conjoining of powers from across the different parts of the Earth: human, more-than-human, fully inhuman. It is about the making of ourselves as we make over land and life. 'The question concerns the forces that make up man', writes philosopher Giles Deleuze: 'with what other forces do they combine, and what is the compound that emerges?' (1988b: 88). And as we will see in chapter 3, in no uncertain way, this question also concerns the forces with which *women* have combined. As geographer Kathryn Yusoff makes clear, what is at stake in the context of the Anthropocene is more than the problematic of 'social relations with fossil fuels' or any other elemental form or force. It is no less than 'the contemplation of the social as composed through the geologic' (2013: 780); or as we would put it in our terms, the thinking of earthly multitudes as composed with and through planetary multiplicity.

To inquire how, when, to what degree different kinds of social beings have joined forces with different geological formations or geophysical fluxes, we are suggesting, is to cast a glimmer of light on the question of what other powers of the Earth we might yet turn towards or turn back to. What kinds of earthly multitudes might we yet become? The more we can find out about sociocultural processes of composing or compounding with the geologic, the more we can excavate or recuperate or just simply notice, the more options we have for engaging otherwise with our planet. Writing in response to the COVID-19 pandemic, but also speaking to analogous complex and cascading events, epidemiologist David Waltner-Toews and his colleagues insisted that '[u]nder post-normal conditions, the knowledge base should be pluralised and diversified to include the widest possible range of high-quality potentially usable knowledges and sources of relevant wisdom' (2020). This resonates closely with our own intent to look deeply and widely for companionable, insightful modes of planetary social thought.

Viewed both as a species and as a heterogeneous ensemble of lineages and collectives, humankind has a vast amount of experience of living with and through the dynamism of the Earth. Our notion of earthly multitudes is intended to convey something of the great diversity of ways in which humans engage with and elaborate upon planetary self-differentiation, and what is at stake in acquiring this experience and knowledge. As we will see, learning how to live on a fickle and sometimes fast-moving planet takes time, and the task is never finished. And even time-honoured wisdom needs to start somewhere. For all that humans are arguably 'overwhelming the other great forces of nature' (Steffen et al. 2007), this does not mean we can simply impose our will on these forces. For as science writer John McPhee (1989) has pointed out, to manipulate other dynamic geological forces – rivers, lava flows, mud slides – necessarily involves learning to 'think' like them, and forming more-than-human alliances.

Planetary thought and practice is a messy, inexact art. Trial and error implies coping with experiments that fall short, go awry or succeed too well. And this means that what is in the making is likely to be more than just new arts and technics of mediating the Earth's inconstancy. What must also be thought up, improvised, relearned are ways of dealing with failure and loss – our own and others'. For a planet that has the capacity to become other to itself is also one on which humans and our fellow creatures are likely to become unsettled or estranged. Such challenges are incessant. And this is why we think of planetary social thought as a work in progress, a collaborative task, an open-ended and interminable journey.

## Structure of the Book

In the opening chapter, 'Earth at the Threshold', we seek to understand what is at stake in the scientific concept of the Anthropocene by contextualizing it in various developments in the Earth and life sciences that emerged in the 1960s and 1970s. We look at how these new paradigms destabilized the gradualist consensus about geohistory and reintroduced the idea that the Earth can itself generate sudden and drastic change – and in this way opened up what we see as the challenge of thinking with and through a dynamic, self-organizing planet.

Chapter 2, 'Who Speaks *through* the Earth?', addresses the reaction of social scientists and humanities scholars to the dominant scientific narrative of the Anthropocene. Many critical social thinkers argue that we need to *socialize the Anthropocene*, introducing questions about power, knowledge and social difference. But we make the case for an equally necessary counter-move of *geologizing the social*. The 'human' acquisition of geological agency, we contend, needs to be viewed not only as a manifestation of social power, but as an expression of those powers and properties of the Earth with which we have joined forces.

In chapter 3, 'Planetary Social Life in the Making', we use a case study of the domestic chore of ironing clothes to begin to show what it means to reimagine the social through the lens of a dynamic planet. By tracking both the use of high heat and the weaving of fabric from their contemporary conjunction on the ironing board back to their deepest historical roots, we show how a mundane practice, pushed far enough, opens out into the dynamics and structures of the Earth itself. And in the process, we catch sight of how a conventional social category like gender can also be seen to have significant geologic or planetary dimensions.

Chapter 4, 'What is Planetary Social Thought?', takes stock of the journey so far and explains our own approach in more detail. Coming back to the question of what planets are and what they can do, we track key moments at which our own planet has undergone reorganization and learned to do things it couldn't do before. This leads into a discussion of what we mean by 'planetary multiplicity' and the kinds of methods we think are needed to make sense of a far-from-equilibrium, self-organizing planet. We then tease out the twin concept of 'earthly multitudes' – our way of understanding how different social practices relate to the dynamism and self-differentiation of the Earth itself.

In chapter 5, 'Inhuman Modernity, Earthly Violence', we use the concepts of planetary multiplicity and earthy multitudes to revisit the classic social science question of how to make sense of the modern world. Here, we contend that eighteenth- and nineteenth-century European encounters with a catastrophic deep time played a significant role in the racialized reimagining of a world of non-European 'others' as remaining mired in nature. Drawing together ideas from decolonizing thought, Black studies and science fiction, we go on to suggest that white colonialism involved the positioning of a 'stratum' of black and brown bodies to absorb the shocks of a volatile Earth. But so too, we argue, can such enforced exposure to unfamiliar geological and ecological conditions spark the emergence of new 'subterranean' earthly multitudes.

Chapter 6, 'Terra Mobilis', offers an extended case study of the increasing mobility of resources, artefacts and human beings. We set out from the example of the Yamnaya, central Asian nomadic herders who around 3,000 BCE fashioned a new pattern of life that involved moving in new ways, on horseback and using ox-drawn wagons. This was a socio-technical assemblage that was to spread and slowly transform the human world – but would also establish one of the preconditions for the later Anthropocene explosion of powered transport. We situate this story within the larger story of the 'mobility revolutions' of the Earth, through which the planet learned to move solid objects in new ways – and end with an exploration of how this mode of analysis might expand our ideas about the future of human mobility.

Chapter 7, 'Grounding Colonialism, Decolonizing the Earth', picks up on the issue of decontextualizing and moving matter from the previous chapter and works it through in the context of mineral phosphate extraction and the growing problem of impacting the global phosphorus cycle. We follow critics from Pacific extractive colonies who have denounced phosphate-enriched pastoral farming in Aotearoa New Zealand, Australia and elsewhere for scattering the ancestral spirit of their peoples. This opens up the more general question of how to negotiate between the secularized visions of Western science and the more 'enspirited' knowledge practices of Indigenous or traditional peoples, which we approach through the boundary-traversing figure of the aerial topdressing plane.

Chapter 8, 'Earthly Multitudes and Planetary Futures: Ten Questions', closes the book by signalling further opportunities for thought, research and practice. The questions that we pose point to possible contributions of planetary social thought to present and near-future challenges, ranging from the fate of the current global social order, through the relationship between human earthly multitudes and other living things, to the resonance between planetary multiplicity and a cosmos replete with other, diverse astronomical bodies.

# 1

# Earth at the Threshold

## Introduction: Points of No Return

> Edges, Borders, Boundaries, Brinks and Limits have appeared like a
> team of trolls on their separate horizons. Short creatures with long
> shadows, patrolling the Blurry End. (Roy 1997: 3)

So writes Arundhati Roy at the outset of *The God of Small Things*, a
novel about demarcations and thresholds, and about the lasting consequences of passing through or over them. It is also a story in which the
small things of the title turn out to have big repercussions, where the
echo of seemingly modest events resounds through time and space.

In both spoken and unspoken ways, borders and the issue of who
will be permitted to cross them loom large in the imagining of ecological
catastrophe. Global environmental change joins a long list of other
problems, challenges and lures that propel some people into mobility
while prompting others to erect and police boundaries. Whenever there
is talk of a major transition in the global climate or the Earth system,
the question of some great acceleration of movement across the Earth's
surface is never far away. But whatever the trigger for trans-boundary
mobility, the point of transition – the portal or passage from one world
to another – tends to be loaded with meaning for those concerned.
'Thresholds', observes geographer Clive Barnett (2005: 16), 'are ...
scenes for the drama of responsiveness, hospitality and responsibility.'

The drama of the threshold goes back a long way. So far, in fact, that
we have lost track of when it was first performed or scripted. With its

reference to threshing – the work of separating valuable grain from the dispensable husk or chaff – the term 'threshold' takes us back to a deep agrarian past. At a certain point, now unrecoverable, the meaning of 'threshold' shifted from the floor where cereals were threshed and began to denote the entrance to the room – with its raised doorstep to keep in the precious grains (Liberman 2015). From there it burgeoned into the point of admission to any important site or state of being.

But future genealogists of the threshold may well find themselves with another semantic leap to decipher. In recent decades we have witnessed an irruption of new uses of the threshold metaphor: a jump that takes us from sociocultural contexts to ecological cases, and from there – rapidly – to the entirety of the Earth. The identification of 'thresholds' in the Earth system – and the proposal to set up and patrol boundaries around these potential transition points – is perhaps the most important practical application of the Anthropocene concept to date. As sustainability scientist Johan Rockström and his interdisciplinary team put it in a paper promoting the idea of protective boundaries at the planetary scale, '[t]ransgressing one or more planetary boundaries may be deleterious or even catastrophic due to the risk of crossing thresholds that will trigger non-linear, abrupt environmental change within continental-to planetary-scale systems' (Rockström et al. 2009: 1).

Like other thresholds, limits in the Earth system appear in the discourse of the Anthropocene as points of no return. 'We have passed the exit gate of the Holocene', announce historians Christophe Bonneuil and Jean-Baptiste Fressoz. 'We have reached a threshold' (Bonneuil and Fressoz 2016: xiii). In the planetary boundaries literature, once a threshold in the Earth system or subsystems has been breached, change is expected to be rapid, cascading and – for the foreseeable future – irreversible. Earth system scientist Will Steffen and his multidisciplinary co-authors have recently cautioned that our species may be on 'a one-way trip to an uncertain future in a new, but very different, state of the Earth System' (Steffen et al. 2011b: 756). For this reason, collectively identifying and patrolling no-go zones at the threshold of the Earth's 'safe operating space' is fast emerging as one the most pressing political issues of our time.

We should not underestimate the magnitude of the change entailed not just when the reach of the political extends to the Earth in its entirety but when the object of governance shifts from movements of people and things across the surface of the planet to the dynamics of Planet Earth itself. That we ourselves are situated at this brink makes it too soon to be sure what the Anthropocene might come to mean, too early to fully diagnose its significance and consequences. What we are emphasizing is that the 'event' of the Anthropocene thus far – its primary provocation to thought and action – hinges on a novel understanding of an Earth with the capacity to pass over thresholds and to become something *other than it is*. That we humans are the hypothetical trigger of this threshold transition is crucial; but to understand ourselves as capable of pushing the Earth system past a point of no return requires us to appreciate how a planet can be capable of becoming otherwise, and how it can make its transitions with speed and finality.

In this chapter, we look at the science of the Anthropocene and the broader set of developments in the Earth and life sciences that have made it possible to think of a planet with a propensity for astronomically scaled self-differentiation. We explore the scientific origins of 'planetary multiplicity' and open up the question of what it means to inhabit a planet that not only responds to novel human pressures but also has its own history of working out how to do entirely new things.

## Identifying a New Geological Epoch

Naming is important to social scientists and humanities scholars. Names, we believe, convey sociocultural values, they express power relations, they encapsulate how some of us get to define and depict the world at the expense of others. Which is why social thinkers have proposed a slew of alternatives to the term 'Anthropocene' – Anthrobscene, Chthulucene, Gynocene, Capitalocene – counter-terms that have clamoured and jostled over the last decade without coming close to toppling the title Paul Crutzen apparently conjured up in a couple of seconds during his celebrated conference interjection.

Earth scientists are meticulous when it comes to identifying the divisions between geological time periods that concern them. As Jan Zalasiewicz and his colleagues remind us, '[t]he Geological Time Scale is held dear by geologists and it is not amended lightly' (Zalasiewicz et al. 2010: 2228). Geoscientists too take naming seriously. Their choice of titles for geological time may indicate sites at which signals of change are particularly conspicuous, commemorate life forms prominent in an epoch, or foreground characteristics that distinguish the interval from those around it. The name for the Pleistocene is ancient Greek for 'mostly new' while that for the Holocene means 'wholly new'; the Ordivician period is named after an obscure Welsh tribe, and the name of the Hadean eon – the seething, lifeless first 600 million years of Earth history – is Greek for 'hellish'. What geologists are not especially interested in, however, is attributing culpability for epochal shifts (see Davies 2016: 69–70); the prospect of the 'Anthropocene' being interpreted by social critics as a monolithic judgement on every member of our species seems not to have been a big concern of the scientists who rallied around the 'epoch of humans' designation.

Geoscientists have been generous in acknowledging predecessors in the identification of a novel human-inflected time unit. When informed that ecologist Eugene Stoermer had previously deployed the term 'Anthropocene', Crutzen invited him to co-author an introductory piece on the proposed epoch (Crutzen and Stoermer 2000). Further precedents came to light: American science writer Andrew Revkin's 'Anthrocene' age introduced in the early 1990s, Russian geochemist Vladimir Vernadsky's 1930s championing of a reason-dominated 'noösphere', Italian geologist Antonio Stoppani's positing of an 'Anthropozoic era' in the 1870s, and, as far back as the 1780s, French naturalist Comte de Buffon's musings on a human imprint across the face of the Earth (Zalasiewicz et al. 2011; Davies 2016: 43; Bonneuil and Fressoz 2016: 4).

Mounting evidence that the idea of humankind transforming the Earth was not particularly novel encouraged efforts to distinguish what was original about its most recent incarnation. Philosopher Clive Hamilton and science historian Jacques Grinevald (2015) are among those who claim that it is only with the coming of age of the interdisciplinary field of Earth system science that the mechanisms of changing Earth processes can be understood well enough to properly gauge a *systemic* human influence – as opposed to simply registering incremental changes. Through its definitive concern with globally integrated biogeochemical cycles, Earth system science demonstrates how it is possible for the planet to generate its own transformations at every scale – from the localized ecosystem right up to the planetary level. A formative influence on Earth system science was the idea that life itself has played a key role in planetary dynamics for billions of years, as proposed in the Gaia hypothesis (Steffen et al. 2004: 3). But it is important to keep in mind that the field came of age focusing on 'contemporary global change' – which is to say, transformations triggered primarily by our own species (Zalasiewicz et al. 2017: 85).

However, as the Anthropocene intuition graduated into a testable hypothesis, Earth system science came to rely upon other modes of geoscientific inquiry to substantiate its point about anthropogenic impacts. In 2008, a dedicated Working Group was convened by the Subcommission of Quaternary Stratigraphy to assess the available data and present a case to the 'higher' geological authorities about the proposed epochal shift. In order to satisfy the stringent requirements of the International Commission on Stratigraphy and its parent body, the International Union of Geological Sciences, it is necessary to link any proposed amendment to the Geological Time Scale to forensic evidence from the Earth's rocky strata (see Davies 2016: 64). Consequently, much of the responsibility for making the case for the Anthropocene passed from Earth system science to the older, more 'mainstream' discipline of geology: to stratigraphers and palaeontologists whose definitive concern is 'with ancient, pre-human rock and time' (Zalasiewicz et al. 2017: 85).

It is notable, however, that the composition of the Anthropocene Working Group included Earth system scientists, the first time they had joined any panel dealing with the definition of a geological time unit. As the Working Group itself contends, one of the signal achievements of Anthropocene science thus far has been the way that it has brought these two formerly distinct geoscience fields together – in particular to collaborate over the question of what traces human-triggered transformations in the present Earth system will be likely to leave in the lithic strata of the distant future (Zalasiewicz et al. 2017; Steffen et al. 2016).

To attain formal recognition for the Anthropocene, 'the "geological signal" currently being produced in strata now forming must be sufficiently large, clear and distinctive' (Anthropocene Working Group 2019). Not only must this 'footprint' be an effectively permanent addition to the lithic composition of the Earth's crust, it also needs to be geosynchronous – that is, distributed across the planet's surface at approximately the same time. To make this case, human influence on the Earth system and its associated imprint in the strata were to be treated as having no fundamental difference from any other biological or geological agency: a kind of ontologically democratic approach many scientists are quite familiar with from researching the global climate and many other forms of environmental change.

The status and timing of numerous geological intervals have been and still are hotly contested. Even amidst this fractious discursive field, it soon became clear that the Anthropocene offered exceptional grounds for controversy. Even supporters of the idea of an epochal shift acknowledge the 'somewhat arbitrary' nature of attempts 'to assign a specific date to the onset of the "Anthropocene"' (Crutzen and Stoermer 2000: 17), not least because working on timescales of centuries or decades poses methodological problems for a geological toolkit geared to thousands or millions of years (Edgeworth et al. 2019). Moreover, because the formative processes of the proposed epoch are current and ongoing, researchers cannot simply work from existing rocks, fossils and other 'solid' evidence. They must orient themselves towards the lithographic signals that may or may not be discernible to a hypothetical observer far in the future, bringing a strongly speculative element into the debate. Stratigraphers find themselves in the novel predicament of attending to contemporary or recent activities in order to predict which will be the best candidates for long-term fossilization (Clark 2016; Szerszynski 2012: 169).

For many geoscientists, what added to the Anthropocene's already considerable list of contentious features was the threat posed by its obvious 'interestedness' to conventional standards of objectivity. The Anthropocene, Working Group members readily professed, 'has the capacity to become the most politicized unit, by far, of the Geological Time Scale – and therefore to take formal geological classification into uncharted waters' (Zalasiewicz et al. 2010: 2231). This has indeed turned out to be the case, though as we will see in the next chapter, the degree and direction of the proposed epoch's politicization have failed to satisfy many critical social thinkers.

Even amongst adherents to the Anthropocene hypothesis, there are major disagreements about the historical moment at which a geosynchronous signal was or will be laid down in the rocks. While most researchers initially favoured fossil-fuelled industrialization from the late eighteenth century, an 'early Anthropocene' minority focused on the Pleistocene extinction of megafauna by human hunters or the Neolithic spread of agriculture, while others proposed the cataclysmic post-1492 encounter between Europeans and the Indigenous peoples of the Americas as the turning point (Crutzen 2002; Ruddiman 2003; Lewis and Maslin 2015). The juncture that was (non-unanimously) chosen by the Anthropocene Working Group for its submission to the International Commission on Stratigraphy in 2016 was a set of changes associated with economic and technological globalization and population growth in the post-World War II decades. By this reasoning, it was only with the so-called 'Great Acceleration' of the 1950s and 1960s – and the atom-bomb tests of those decades – that the stratigraphic trace of human activities is likely to be fully global rather than regional (Steffen et al. 2007; Zalasiewicz et al. 2015). At the time of writing, the evidence is still under consideration by the Commission.

## Provocations of the Anthropocene

To meet the exacting demands of the International Commission on Stratigraphy, the case made for a new geological epoch by the unfunded Anthropocene Working Group involved the sifting and collating of mountainous geochronological evidence. But neither 'the forensic examination of rock strata' by stratigraphers (Zalasiewicz 2008: 19) nor the immensely complex global data sets assembled by Earth system scientists are obvious crowd-pleasers – raising questions about why exactly the Anthropocene concept is proving such an effective way of expressing and publicizing the current planetary predicament. What exactly is it about the proposed passage out of one geological epoch and into another, we need to ask, that has made the Anthropocene arguably the most influential scientific idea of the new millennium? And how is it that the departure from the Holocene has come to be so significant, when so many nonspecialist audiences would previously have struggled to date, characterize or even name the current geological interval?

For several decades now, various approaches to the social study of science have been unsettling any assumption that scientific ideas gain acceptance purely on merit or weight of evidence, alerting us instead to the complicated and often unpredictable processes by which some truth claims rather than others become widely adopted. When it comes to the case for the end of the Holocene, many commentators, especially those whose disciplinary backgrounds lie in understanding social life, have focused on interrogating the details of the pre-eminent role of (some) humans in bringing forth the new epoch. As Bonneuil and Fressoz pose the question: '[w]hat does it mean for us to have the future of the planet in our hands?' (2016: xiii). Or as human ecologists Andreas Malm and Alf Hornborg argue, to make sense of the Anthropocene 'we should dare to probe the depths of social history' (2014: 66).

Others, from across a range of disciplines, see in the Anthropocene idea a new or renewed emphasis on the need to position humans within the much more ancient history of the Earth. For historian Dipesh Chakrabarty, the Anthropocene issue contextualizes social and historical processes within geological timescales and spaces that radically exceed any measure of the human. Climate change and the broader Anthropocene predicament, writes Chakrabarty, call 'for thinking on very large and small scales at once, including scales that defy the usual measures of time that inform human affairs' (2014: 3). Along similar lines, and resonating with our figure of the threshold, literary theorist Jeremy Davies (2016: 11) cites poet Don McKay's claim that the Anthropocene for us provides 'an entry point into deep time'. In a related sense, but in advance of the Anthropocene concept, Gayatri Chakravorty Spivak alludes to 'a planetarity ... inaccessible to human time' (2003: 88).

In showing how the Anthropocene beckons us into realities that profoundly overreach our familiar horizons, these theorists help us to see how – alongside its gloomy forebodings – the very idea might also serve to excite imaginations. But what is to be found if we set out on this passage into the deep history of the Earth? One important turn that has taken place in the natural sciences over recent decades is the receding of the idea of an Earth that changes only slowly and incrementally. Gradualism has been usurped by an image of rapid or 'catastrophic' shifts: the vision of a planetary body with the capacity to lurch out of its current condition into a completely different operational state. What we are being offered, in short, is an Earth replete with its own thresholds.

As a scientific hypothesis, abrupt or nonlinear change in Earth systems precedes the Anthropocene concept. In 1987 Wallace Broecker, the climatologist credited with coining the term 'global warming', published a paper in the journal *Nature* entitled 'Unpleasant surprises in the greenhouse?' in which he summarized evidence recently extracted from polar ice cores, ocean sediments and bog beds. 'What these records indicate', Broecker observed, 'is that Earth's climate does not respond to forcing in a slow and gradual way. Rather, it responds in large jumps which involve large-scale reorganization of Earth's system' (1987: 123). While Broecker spared us an estimate of the timescale of these 'flips' in the Earth system, later research suggested they could take place in as little as a decade or even a few years (Alley 2000: 115–22).

Although the possibility of 'sudden drastic switches to a contrasting state' was already well known to scientists doing research at much smaller scales (Scheffer et al. 2001: 591), the idea that such leaps could occur at the planetary scale came as one of the greatest shocks of modern science. As climatologist Richard Alley puts it, the notion that the global climate can jump to an entirely different mode of operation in a handful of years has 'revolutionised our view of Earth' (2000: 13).

Behind the thesis of thresholds in the global climate was a nascent sense that the very interconnectedness of the Earth's key components – what Broecker referred to as 'the joint hydrosphere–atmosphere–biosphere–cryosphere system' – could itself be a source of change (1987: 123). Or to put it another way, out of oneness and unity could come rupture and difference. Effectively, the Anthropocene picks up this insight and takes it to its logical conclusion by proposing that not only climate but all the Earth's subsystems may be susceptible to switches to an alternative state – and that such changes would be likely to resound through the whole integrated system.

Whether we are talking of climate or the overall Earth system, there are really two different things going on here that have progressively – and momentously – converged. One is the idea that the Earth has an inherent potential to shift from one state to another and to do this quickly. The other is the claim that our own species acting collectively has attained the power to function as a driver or forcing agent of such planetary transformations. It should be stressed, however, that these are not equivalent or symmetrical propositions. It requires multiple possible operating states for humans to be able to trigger Earth system change, but the existence of this capacity for state-shifting precedes the emergence of our species by billions of years – and is in this sense fundamentally independent of *our* existence.

As we have seen, the revolutionizing of our view of the Earth that some would attribute to the Anthropocene is justifiably attributed by

Alley to earlier accounts of climate change. Its origins, however, go back further still. As historian John Brooke reminds us, the paradigm shift away from the gradualism that had dominated Earth and life science since the nineteenth century has been gathering momentum for over half a century. Brooke points out that the years 1966–73 alone saw the emergence of four major new perspectives on the dynamics of the Earth: (1) the full confirmation and development of the theory of plate tectonics; (2) a new appreciation of the role of extraterrestrial impacts in shaping Earth history; (3) the thesis that evolution is punctuated by catastrophic bursts linked to major geophysical events; and (4) the beginnings of the idea that the different components of the Earth function as an integrated system – first expressed in the Gaia hypothesis that saw life and the nonliving components of the Earth as tightly coupled (2014: 25–36). While the last of this list contributed most directly to the emergence of Earth system science, all four developments paved the way for the idea that the Earth is at once unified and capable of self-differentiation, that it is both singular and multiple.

We will shortly look more closely at these developments. But the preliminary point we take from Brooke's typology is that none of the four perspectives he identifies centres upon or requires human presence. The new understanding of the Earth that crystallized in the latter half of the twentieth century was in no way focused on the force or influence of our own species.

The Anthropocene is still a relatively new hypothesis, and as we have suggested it is both highly contested within the sciences and subject to multiple interpretations in its wider reception. To make our own position clear, we view the issue of human imprints on the Earth system and in the geological strata as nested within the broader set of questions about the kind of planet we inhabit. For us, primary among the many provocations of the Anthropocene is the emerging scientific consensus that the Earth has the potential to shift between different operating states – an aspect of what we are referring to as 'planetary multiplicity'. Only by thinking with and through the multiplicity inherent in the Earth, we would add, can we begin to make sense of the (uneven) capacity of our species to make a significant intervention in Earth processes.

This dawning sense that our Earth is replete with otherness, that a new planet might suddenly be visited upon us, we suggest, informs the mix of horror and fascination that imbues the broad reception of the Anthropocene thesis. In particular, it is the notion of Earth system *thresholds*, which evoke the passage from familiar to unknown worlds, that at once seems to haunt and lure contemporary imaginations. For all that the mechanism of Earth systems shifting might be novel, the idea of portals, transitional moments, points of no return, has an ancient resonance. How to situate the figure of the human at this juncture – we who are at once victims, witnesses and perpetrators (Michaels 1997: 140) – will be explored in more depth in the next chapter. For now, we turn in more detail to the question of how it came to be for many scientists that our astronomical body, in Zalasiewicz's words, 'seems to be less one planet, rather a number of different Earths that have succeeded each other in time'.

## The Making of Planetary Multiplicity

In its various guises, the sociological study of science encourages us to inquire into the social, cultural and historical context from which new ideas or paradigms emerge. There is an exemplary body of research that positions crucial developments in the understanding of the Earth as an integrated and dynamic system within the deepening rift between the superpowers in the post-war era. But the best of this work permits the discoveries in question to exceed their immediate circumstances – to have both origins and consequences that exceed their sociohistorical framings. Cultural historian Mike Davis speaks of a 'scientific culture incubated within Cold War militarism and technological triumphalism', but quickly adds that 'it is also the contemporary home of luminous and, dare I say, revolutionary attempts to rethink the Earth and evolution' (Davis 1996: 50; see also Haraway 1991a: 173).

The irony has often been noted that it took a fearsomely divided humanity to nurture scientific and social visions of planetary oneness. Cold War military planning, maintains anthropologist Joseph Masco, 'encapsulated the earth in military, command, control, and surveillance systems', but in the process 'it also created new understandings of the earth, sea, and sky, and of the biosphere itself as an integrated ecological space' (2010: 29). Nuclear weapons testing provided a motivation to advance scientific knowledge about the way that various flows and circulations connected up different components of the Earth system. As historian of science Paul Edwards notes, it also proffered the medium: atmospheric and undersea detonations producing clouds of radioactive debris that could be followed along their circuits through the atmosphere, hydrosphere and biosphere (2010: 209–10; see also Masco 2010: 12). But tracing radioactivity along planetary pathways was only one aspect of a broader suite of explorations prompted by superpower rivalry. Much of the geological evidence that culminated in the confirmation of the plate tectonics hypothesis in the early to mid-1960s, Masco reminds us, emerged directly from Cold War efforts to detect distant nuclear weapon tests (Masco 2010: 15).

Neither Edwards nor Masco, however, would have us see scientists simply as servants of their respective power blocs. A pivotal moment in the envisioning of the Earth as a single, dynamic system was the International Geophysical Year of 1957–8, a transnational initiative involving 20,000 scientists from sixty-seven nations distributed across 4,000 scientific stations (see Lövbrand et al. 2009). While the International Geophysical Year in many ways reflected its Cold War milieu, it also intentionally set out to bridge geopolitical differences in the interests of inclusive planetary monitoring. In doing so, as we will see, it not only advanced the idea of integrated planetary thinking but also located geoscience concerns in a greater extraterrestrial context.

Retrospectively, it is tempting to see post-war science moving relentlessly towards the Earth systems approach to complex, nonlinear planetary dynamics. But as Brooke's typology reminds us, it was old-school geology that was 'utterly reorganized' by confirmation of the theory of plate tectonics – aided by the 'Cold War' discovery of sea-floor spreading at mid-ocean ridges (Brooke 2014: 23). These submarine ranges turned out to be the sites at which crust-forming magma pumped out of the planet's interior. Subsequent research established that liquid rock welled up at these deep-ocean spreading centres, forming new oceanic crust whose ultimate fate was to be forced underground once again by the pressure of new crustal formation (Colling et al. 1997: 114–15).

The new global tectonics provided a unifying schema through which localized geological processes were recontextualized within the continuous cycling of the planet's entire lithosphere. In the process, geologists came to see earthquakes, volcanoes, submarine landslides and other upheavals less as exceptions to a prevailing state of quiescence, and more as routine expressions of the Earth's crustal dynamics or what Zalasiewicz refers to as 'normal catastrophes' (Zalasiewicz 2008: 34; see also Westbroek 1991: 47–54). In this way, some time before Earth system science arrived at its vision of a state-shifting planet, mainstream 'hard rock' geology was already realigning itself around a narrative in which planetary unity and fracturing, continuity and catastrophe were two sides of the same coin.

For all that plate tectonics set the lithosphere into graunching motion, the gradualism of the preceding century and a half endured in the image of a centimetres-per-annum creep of crustal slabs and their incremental contribution to the formation of rock strata. As Davis (1996) notes, it was the burgeoning interest in the effects of meteor or 'bolide' impacts – the second of Brooke's new perspectives – that posed a greater challenge to gradualist orthodoxy. While the thesis that a massive meteor hit had devastated terrestrial life at the Cretaceous and Tertiary (K–T) boundary some 65 million years ago was announced by physicist Luis Alvarez and geologist Walter Alvarez in a 1980 paper, the idea had been gestating since the early 1970s, when traces of an anomalous mineral stratum in the stratigraphic record had been detected (Brooke 2014: 46).

Along with advances in the understanding of the irregular orbits of near-Earth objects, gathering evidence of the planet-wide effects of incoming projectiles lent new credence to the idea that Earth history was punctuated by sudden violent events. This resonated closely with the third of Brooke's insurgent approaches, the thesis that biological evolutions did not simply follow the gradual, linear trajectory of Darwinian orthodoxy, but periodically surged into episodes of rapid, nonlinear macro-evolution (Brooke 2014: 29–30). Lively conversations soon ensued between 'punctuated equilibrium' evolutionary thinkers such as Stephen Jay Gould and Niles Eldridge and the extraterrestrial impact theorists over the possibility that meteor strikes in the Earth's past were responsible for cataclysmic bouts of extinction followed by bursts of accelerated evolution (Brooke 2014: 25; Davis 1996: 75–6).

The predecessors of Earth system thinking, Brooke's fourth new perspective, were not immediately implicated in the burgeoning neo-catastrophist turn in geological and evolutionary thought. In the late 1960s, scientist–inventor James Lovelock hatched the idea that biological life played a key role in regulating the overall state of the Earth. Developed by Lovelock in collaboration with evolutionary biologist Lynn Margulis during the 1970s, what became known as the 'Gaia hypothesis' proposed that living organisms, atmospheric conditions and tectonic geology interacted to form a single system that served to maintain the Earth's outer envelope in a state conducive to life (Lovelock 1979).

Initially controversial, as were the other three of Brooke's new perspectives, the Gaia hypothesis helped draw the previously lagging component of life into the vision of interconnected spheres of air, water, ice and rock that the International Geophysical Year programme and its successors had begun to work up. While credit would later be given to important predecessors of the Gaia idea, especially amongst Russian scientists, it was the Lovelock–Margulis version that gave the vital push to the idea of tight coupling of the subsystems of the Earth. As Earth system science developed, however, the earlier Gaian emphasis on stabilizing or self-regulating relationships between system components was increasingly supplemented by concerns about how interconnectivity within complex systems could also amplify disturbances, resulting in runaway destabilization (see Crutzen 2004: 72; Schellnhuber 1999). And, in this way, Earth system thinking began its own move in the direction of the new catastrophism, where it would eventually burgeon into the most urgent and encompassing vision of abrupt, nonlinear change at the planetary scale.

Well before this way of thinking was elevated to the level of the planet, examples of rapid rather than gradual transition had been observed by field ecologists in a variety of real-world ecological systems, ranging from the eutrophication of lakes to the algal colonization of coral reefs (Scheffer et al. 2001). Ecosystems appeared to absorb stresses or shocks up to a point, but once that limit was crossed, the system in its entirety would lurch into rapid, irreversible change. This sense that 'sudden, drastic switches to a contrasting state' (Scheffer et al. 2001: 591) were the norm in many ecosystems found resonance with observations of rapid changes of state in other complex systems of varying kinds and scales, which emerged as a unifying theme in the interdisciplinary field of complexity studies that came of age in the 1980s.

The key to both self-regulation and rapid, runaway change, as complexity theorists would have it, is the propensity of densely networked connections to organize themselves into feedback loops. Feedback loops involve the recursive cycling of inputs or effects through a system, and tend to absorb and dampen down perturbations or stress. But once a certain point is passed, feedbacks have a habit of switching from a stabilizing or 'negative' function to a 'positive' amplification of pressures for change. And it is this passage over a threshold into self-augmenting change that can tip a system into a relatively speedy reorganization into a new operating state (Scheffer et al. 2001).

The technical term frequently used by complexity theorists for such a transition in a system of any type or scale is a 'catastrophic shift'. This meaning of catastrophe, originating in mathematics, refers simply to the dynamical process in which the switch between feedbacks takes place, and is not intrinsically linked to the magnitude of changes or the severity of their repercussions. In this regard, the catastrophic shifts in ecosystems and other observable systems and the kind of massive upheavals that concerned neo-catastrophist geologists and biologists were initially relatively distinct concepts. But as neo-catastrophists increasingly worked notions of complexity and self-organization into their theories, and as systems scientists scaled up their study of nonlinear shifts to continental or planetary levels, the two conceptual framings of catastrophe quickly converged. In neither of its two original meanings, nor in their initial convergence – it should be clear by now – did the term catastrophe have any necessary association with human triggers or the impact of changes on our species.

It was the evidence unearthed from polar ice cores and other proxies of past climate that indicated that what could happen to a pond, reef or forest could also happen to an entire planetary system. By the late

1980s, as we saw earlier, there was growing awareness that the global climate could 'flip'. From around this time, Earth system science took it upon itself to explore the possibility that 'sudden, drastic switches to a contrasting state' might be the norm throughout the Earth system. Maturing over the course of the ambitious International Geosphere-Biosphere Programme (1987 to 2015), Earth system science emerged as the pre-eminent voice of concern over what Hans Joachim Schellnhuber would describe in 1999 as the 'perhaps irreversible transgression of critical thresholds' at the planetary scale (1999: C23). It was the following year that Schellnhuber's colleague, International Geosphere-Biosphere Programme vice-chair Paul Crutzen, would launch the term 'Anthropocene' on its meteoric ascent.

With increasing reference to the Anthropocene, Earth system science research has continued to probe the possibility of passing over thresholds in major Earth subsystems, as summarized in the planetary boundaries literature. The risk of abrupt system reorganization has been identified and estimated in the case of climate change and biodiversity loss, while debate continues as to whether other subsystem changes, such as phosphorus and nitrogen flows, might also eventually reach a magnitude at which interconnected and cascading changes precipitate a total systemic shift (Steffen et al. 2016; Barnosky et al. 2012; Lenton and Williams 2013).

## A Planetary Turn

'Edges, Borders, Boundaries, Brinks and Limits' loom all around us, and they are now as much a part of Earth history as they are of human history. One of the messages of Arundhati Roy's *The God of Small Things* is that the small and the large cannot easily be teased apart. 'Big Things' rumble amidst the hubbub of daily life, and small things refuse to sit quietly in the shade; they gather force, resurface, irrupt into bigger things. In its own less lyrical but equally dramatic way, the study of complex systems conveys a message of how relatively minor events may not be forgotten, and how modest changes can reverberate into larger transitions, all the way up to the planetary scale. In Broecker's words: '[t]he Earth system has amplifiers and feedbacks that mushroom small impacts into large responses' (Broecker 2008). The very functioning of the Earth, it could be said, lends long shadows to short creatures.

Whether or not the International Commission on Stratigraphy bestows its imprimatur on the Anthropocene, the idea that our planet has the potential for rapid system-wide transformation is a lesson that will not easily be unlearned. Threshold changes in the Earth system, as

Bruno Latour likes to put it, have 'entered the collective' – they have been accepted into the congregation of entities and phenomena that are recognized to make up the world as we know it (Latour 2005). While the unearthing of evidence of abrupt climate change may have helped 'revolutionize' our view of Earth, we have seen that this insurgency has been some time in the making. The paradigmatic shift from gradualism to a nonlinear or 'neo-catastrophist' vision of Earth history arose out of the convergence of a number of disciplines, fields and problematics. As the collaboration between stratigraphic geologists and Earth systems scientists demonstrates, the Anthropocene hypothesis is at once a product of this confluence and a stimulus for further syncretic planetary thinking. The encounter and exchange between these once relatively distinct ways of understanding the dynamics of the Earth is still playing itself out, however, and social scientists need to be aware that there are tensions or differences in emphasis within the new alliance – and even within its constituent parts.

Earth system scientist Tim Lenton speaks for many of his colleagues when he declares that '[i]t is the thin layer of a system at the surface of the Earth – and its remarkable properties– that is the subject of my work' (Lenton 2016: 17). It is this prioritizing of the thin envelope in which life mingles with air, water and rock which validates the basic understanding that the different subcomponents of the Earth system are congruent and mutually constitutive. And, in turn, this principle of co-extensiveness and mutuality endorses the idea that 'social-ecological systems act as strongly coupled, integrated complex systems' (Folke 2004: 287). For social thinkers drawn to the Anthropocene problematic, the idea of the Earth system as a sphere in which human activities fully overlap with ecological and even inorganic processes can have tremendous appeal, if it is treated critically. For such a socio-planetary coupling – full, complete and without remainder – seems to dispense with the bothersome presence of an 'inhuman' nature beyond the measure or reach of social agency.

However, we need to be careful here. Lenton's judgement above rests upon an assessment of the amount of matter moving through the outer Earth system relative to that which wells up from the inner Earth or arrives from the cosmos. That the material fluxes within that thin layer at the Earth's surface far exceed these other flows, he proposes, is an achievement rather than a given: it is an expression of the fact that 'today's biosphere is a phenomenal recycling system' (2016: 63). Earth system scientists Will Steffen and Eric Lambin make a closely related point when they observe that 'the forcings and feedbacks *within* the Earth System are as important as the external drivers of change, such as variability in solar energy input' (2006: 113). But note that 'external drivers of change' here are far from being banished and disavowed.

Likewise, Lenton has not forgotten those aspects of the Earth system that are beneath or beyond the slender membrane of the biosphere. As he elaborates:

> What is less clear is whether and where to put an inner boundary on the Earth system ... . The longer the timescale we look over, the more we need to include in the Earth system ... material in the Earth's crust becomes part of the Earth system, and we must recognize that the crust also exchanges material with the Earth's mantle. (Lenton 2016: 16)

Lenton goes on to suggest that our planet might best be seen as being composed of two systems: 'the surface Earth system that supports life, and the great bulk of the inner Earth underneath' (Lenton 2016: 17). And if the Earth in this sense is more than a single system, then this implies that there are decouplings or disconnections in the planetary body, as well as couplings. As a current hypothesis would have it, the lithosphere – the relatively rigid outer layer of the Earth – is in fact *decoupled* from the underlying Asthenosphere – the upper layer of the Earth's mantle in which hot viscous rock slowly cycles in vast convection currents (Self and Rampino 2012).

Amidst the current feting of interconnectivity and coupling by 'surface Earth system' science and its sponsors, then, it is vital that the insights of other perspectives on the Earth and its cosmic environment are not neglected. There are lessons here for social scientists and humanities scholars. Different kinds of questions and challenges – and especially problems with radically variant timescales – bring into relief very different properties, dynamics and potentialities of Planet Earth. As we mentioned in the introduction to this book, political action often seems to unfold at a fast-paced, urgent tempo, an intuition that is expressed in the pivotal significance afforded to punctual breaks, ruptures or revolutions in much critical social thought (Barnett 2004). Post-gradualist natural scientists frequently deploy a similar language of 'thresholds', 'inflection points' and 'revolutions' for describing the most momentous transformations in the life–planet system of the Earth (see Judson 2017; Lenton et al. 2016; Lenton and Watson 2011). We need to be clear, however, that social thought and physical science rarely seem to have engaged in explicit conversation about their respective notions of temporal breaks, so we currently lack a shared platform for considering the relationship between our planet 'becoming otherwise' and the processes through which social actors seek to remake their worlds.

For the scientists exploring planetary upheavals, there are questions not only about what actually happened in the Earth's past but also about what more generally defines or constitutes a 'revolutionary' transition in the planetary context. Lenton and his colleagues identify three revolutionary transformations in the history of the life–planet system: the rise of biological life and the biogeochemical cycles this life set in motion, the origin of oxygenic photosynthesis and the resultant Great Oxidation event involving the switch to an atmosphere rich in free oxygen, and the ascendance of complex, multicellular life (Lenton et al. 2016; Lenton and Watson 2011). As Lenton explains, for all their momentous differences these revolutions share basic structural features:

> They were caused by rare evolutionary innovations. They involved step increases in energy capture and material flow through the biosphere, accompanied by increases in the complexity of biological organization and information processing. They relied on the Earth system having some instability, such that new metabolic waste products could cause catastrophic upheavals in climate and biogeochemical cycling. (Lenton 2016: 73)

There are a number of variations on the theme of epochal transformations in the life–planet system (see Judson 2017; Szathmáry and Maynard Smith 1995; Knoll and Bambach 2000). Without going into the field in detail, the point we want to stress is that this mode of inquiry involves more than just the retrospective identification of the transitions that brought our planet to its current state. It is also about asking *what our planet is capable of doing and what it might be capable of doing and becoming in the future*. Or, to put it another way, it poses the question of what enables the Earth to *do new things* (Szerszynski 2019b).

These questions at once draw us back to the 'social' and pull us as far away from human society as we can possibly imagine. They return us to social analysis and speculation, because thinking in terms of what enables the Earth to do new things raises questions not only about what influences 'we' might be having on Earth systems or geological strata, but also about whether or not humans might have the capacity to set the planet on some entirely new and unprecedented path. Already there is a body of interdisciplinary work associated with the Anthropocene that is exploring the possibility that human-created artefacts might be forming a new planetary subcomponent or sphere of their own (Haff 2014; Szerszynski 2017c). To be considered truly 'revolutionary' in terms of the evolving Earth–life system, such a sphere would need to do much more than simply exploit, unravel or rearrange the existing spheres: it must constitute an organizational leap in the capture of energy, the processing of information and the cycling of materials.

At the same time, and in ways that are not entirely dissociated from the potentiality of our species and its techno-cultural artefacts, the question of how *this planet* has revolutionized itself raises the broader issues of what other planets might be capable of doing and becoming. As evolutionary biologist Olivia Judson reflects on her energy-based schema of the major transitions of the Earth–life system: '[u]sing energy as a lens thus illuminates patterns in the entwined histories of life and Earth, and may also provide a framework for considering the potential trajectories of life–planet systems elsewhere' (Judson 2017: 1). Or as Lenton puts it, '[b]y generalizing our models of the Earth system and its development, researchers are beginning to formulate what I would christen "Exo-Earth system science" – a general science of habitable and inhabited worlds' (2016: 139).

In this way, we begin to see how the rise of a natural science oriented towards the possibility of the Earth to be otherwise – what we are terming *planetary multiplicity* – is closely tied to a vision of Planet Earth as one amongst many planets – or 'multiplanetarity'. By this logic, the issue of what the Earth has been and might yet become – its capacity for self-differentiation and transformation – makes a lot more sense as a specific case of a more generalized inquiry about how planets come into existence and change over time. To put it another way, our opening question of 'What planet are we on?' soon raises other questions: what is a planet anyway? What do planets have in common? How do they differentiate themselves? Alongside the possibilities open to Planet Earth, what might other planets become?

To a significant degree, thinking about the Earth and other planets together was tied up with the turn towards post-gradualist, nonlinear Earth and life science from the outset. The International Geophysical Year included the launch of Sputnik in 1957 and a rush of US satellite launches, its combined terrestrial and astronomical focus inaugurating a new concern with comparative planetology. 'Instead of comparing seas or continents', reflects environmental historian Stephen Pyne, 'this new phase of discovery compared whole planets' (1986: 108). The founding of the US National Aeronautics and Space Administration in 1958 was one of the offshoots of the International Geophysical Year, and in turn Lovelock's Gaia hypothesis emerged out of a NASA project aimed at devising new ways to detecting life on other planets (Lovelock 1979: 1–3).

We have come some way from the idea that humans are now influencing Earth systems and strata-forming processes. In keeping the counsel of science studies, we attest to the importance of viewing the Anthropocene within the disciplinary and social context from which it emerged, and this has drawn us into conversation with a set of multi-decadal transformations in the Earth and life sciences that for us constitute a broad-based 'planetary turn'. Before developing our own proposals for 'doing' planetary social thought – through an extended example in chapter 3, and more programmatically in chapter 4 – we will look at how the social sciences more broadly have responded to the provocation of the Anthropocene. In the process, we also consider certain strands of social and cultural thought that have themselves begun to grapple with the question of how the power, force or agency of the geophysical domains impinges upon social processes in ways that trouble any straightforward 'socialization' of the Anthropocene.

# 2

# Who Speaks *through* the Earth?

## Introduction: An Epoch of Contention

Recent developments in the Earth and life sciences, it should now be clear, do more than sound alarms about a changing climate. They also offer new ways of helping us to make sense of how the Earth comes to be capable of shifting from one operating state to another – how it self-differentiates or becomes otherwise. As we put it in chapter 1, the post-gradualist and nonlinear sciences offer a window onto what we are referring to as planetary multiplicity.

But this opens up a lot of questions. For one thing, the science itself is full of uncertainties. So complex is the Earth system that it is effectively impossible to compute exactly how or when significant shifts will occur and how they will rebound and cascade through the different components of the system. Such unthinkable complexity, and the abstractions necessary to render it visible, also raise questions about how its insights can be brought into meaningful dialogue with ordinary people and everyday life. Science studies scholar Sheila Jasanoff (2010: 238) cogently asks '[h]ow ... will scientists' impersonal knowledge of the climate be synchronized with the mundane rhythms of lived lives and the specificities of human experience?'

As the scientific idea of Earth system change and the Anthropocene concept has established itself, such questions have taken a darker turn. Many critical social thinkers have grown increasingly uncomfortable with the grander claims of the Earth and life sciences, and ever more wary about who is speaking, from where, and on behalf of whom.

Political scientist Eva Lövbrand and her colleagues caution that Earth system sciences 'run the risk of producing an empty view of humanity that tells us little about the lived experiences, fears, vulnerabilities, ideas and motivations of real people, in real places' (2015: 216). Still more dismissively, media theorist Sarah Kember denounces the idea of the Anthropocene as 'a marker of masculine disembodied knowledge practices or intellectual, Cartesian habits of mind' (2017: 350), while for historian Christophe Bonneuil, the Anthropocene is a 'naturalistic grand narrative of an undifferentiated humanity uniformly concerned by and responsible for global climate change' (2015: 20).

In this chapter we ask why it is that questions highlighted by the Anthropocene are at once drawing social scientists and humanities researchers into engagement with Earth processes as never before and also inciting vehement resistance. High amongst the concerns of critics of Anthropocene discourse is a sense that natural scientists have learned little from critical social thought about the close relationship between power and knowledge – and especially about the problems associated with speaking on behalf of others. As we will see, many critical-analytic thinkers argue that the Anthropocene needs to be socialized or politicized in ways that differ markedly from ascendant scientific accounts of 'human' geologic agency.

But we are just as interested in what responses to the Anthropocene say about ourselves as 'social' thinkers. Are we social scientists allowing the insights of Earth science to intrigue, unsettle or transform us? This is not only a question of engaging with scientists. It is also about how we converse with those amongst us who are already willing to open their thought to the forces of the Earth.

To return to an example we touched on in the introduction, combustion or 'fire' features prominently in discussions of Earth system change: both the burning of fossil hydrocarbons and the not-unrelated outbreaks of wildfire we have been seeing recently in south-eastern Australia, California, Indonesia and many other regions. This has prompted critical responses that address continued reliance on fossil fuels as well as official policies on forest management and fire prevention. But there are other ways to think about fire. For example, after a lifetime of studying how people across the planet engage with their natural worlds, anthropologist Loren Eiseley paused to wonder: '[w]hat if I am, in some way, only a sophisticated fire that has acquired the ability to regulate its rate of combustion and to hoard its fuel in order to see and walk?' (1978: 151). Writing at a time when environmental problems were irrupting all around, Eiseley was inviting us to think about how fire may have left its mark deep within us, how handling flame has helped make us who we are – and thus the extent to which the planetary predicament might also be a matter of elements, forces and powers that we too often assume to be our own. Eiseley's words make our point for us: it is not only a matter of asking who speaks *for* the Earth, but of asking of who speaks *with* and *through* the Earth – or even how the Earth speaks *through us*.

## Who Speaks for the Earth?

As we saw in chapter 1, the last fifty to sixty years have witnessed a new scientific emphasis on an Earth whose intrinsic unity makes it possible for the planet to be more-than-one. Concern that cumulative human impact is a potential agent of systemic change at the whole Earth scale has helped extend what we refer to as planetary multiplicity from being an object of thought to an object of politics. As Lövbrand and her colleagues observe, the Earth system over recent decades has come to be constructed as a 'governable domain' – a proposition that they bring into question (2009: 8).

In our own early experience of talking to natural scientists about the Anthropocene, it often felt as though they saw acknowledgement of a human contribution to Earth processes as an overture to the human sciences – as an incentive to collaboration across disciplinary divides. Subsequently most of the principal publications on the Anthropocene, to some degree, have advocated interdisciplinary research. Geoscientists, we suspect, hoped for a warmer welcome from their social and humanistic counterparts than they have often received. And there are some good reasons for a positive reception. It still rankles with social scientists and humanities scholars that we missed the opportunity for formative input into the discursive framing of the climate change problem. That the vacant niche of social analysis of the global climate challenge was partially and unsatisfyingly filled by the narrow economism of cost–benefit analyses was, for many of us, a harsh lesson in the need to mobilize decisively around emergent environmental concerns (Szerszynski and Urry 2010).

Precisely how dramas of responsiveness and hospitality will play out at the threshold is usually hard to anticipate, as we saw in the previous chapter. But if anything, the response of critical social thought to the idea of a 'geology of mankind' and an epoch named for the *anthropos* has followed a rather predictable script: a storyline dominated by militant reassertion of the authority of the social sciences to define, differentiate and diagnose the human condition

It's worth noting that other geological nominations have evaded the scrutiny that the Anthropocene has attracted. The yet-to-be-formalized 'Hadean' – an evocative term for the first 600 million years of Earth history, coined by the equally colourfully named Preston Cloud in 1972

– has not sparked great controversy amongst social thinkers. In this regard, Derrida's counsel is useful. 'No one gets angry at a mathematician or a physicist whom he or she doesn't understand, or at someone who speaks a foreign language', he reflects, 'but rather at someone who tampers with your own language' (1995: 115).

In 'Who speaks for the future of Earth?' – a paper that helped inspire our title for this chapter and section – Lövbrand et al. offer a deft summary of the concerns that have prompted critical social thinkers to enter the Anthropocene debate:

> When linking environmental change to social categories such as class, race, gender, power and capital we thus find that the challenges of the Anthropocene are far from universal. Rather, they emerge from different socio-political settings, produce different kinds of vulnerabilities and precariousness and will therefore most likely generate different kinds of political responses … [W]e suggest that a critical Anthropocene research agenda will resist unified accounts of 'the human' and instead work to situate people and social groups in the rich patterns of cultural and historical diversity 'that make us into who we are'. (2015: 214–16)

There are five main points we would draw out from Lövbrand et al.'s paper and related scholarship. The first, to be found almost everywhere in critical responses to the Anthropocene, is the charge that the scientific literature takes as its object a unitary and undifferentiated conception of the human. Interestingly, while a seminal Anthropocene paper – the single-page 'Geology of mankind' – is often targeted by social critics, very few readers have noted that author Paul Crutzen carefully qualifies the 'mankind' of the title. Speaking of fossil fuel burning and nitrogen fertilizer use, Crutzen stipulates that '[s]o far, these effects have largely been caused by only 25% of the world population' (2002). It is a basic point, and one that has been reiterated in many subsequent Anthropocene science publications. But critics are perhaps on firmer ground when they target the Great Acceleration argument – with its definitive linear graphs of exponential growth of particular social or socio-technical activities. For, in the process of aggregating global human development into a collection of simple curves, the differentiated historical responsibility for Earth system change noted by Crutzen has been lost – as has any indication of the profoundly uneven exposure to the changes in question (see Clark and Gunaratnam 2017).

This is closely related to a second point: the charge that Anthropocene scientists, in speaking 'univocally' about Earth futures, insufficiently acknowledge their own social and historical context and the partiality that accompanies this positioning. In this regard, the geosciences are accused of perpetuating the modern scientific presumption of what is variously referred in science studies as a 'god's-eye view' or 'mononaturalism' – which is to say, a worldview or ontology that arises in a particular location and yet purports to be universal or context-free. Anthropocene science, as Bonneuil bluntly puts it, offers 'a single grand narrative from nowhere, from space or from the species' (2015: 29). An associated line of critique, that likewise channels the insights of science studies, is the way that the 'objective' modes of address favoured by Anthropocene science disavow the emotional, affective and embodied aspects of doing science. To undercut the abstraction and univocality to which the natural sciences still aspire, it is argued, the voices of scientists must be construed as 'embodied', 'situated' and 'contextualised' (Lövbrand et al. 2015: 214–16).

The allegation of Anthropocene science's monocular gaze and the charge that it inadequately accounts for human difference converge on a third point: the failure of diagnoses of the planetary predicament to make room for the multiplicity of perspectives of those implicated in these changes. If Anthropocene science is to avoid setting itself up as a new master narrative, critics propose, Anthropocene discourses will need to embrace 'a plurality of narratives from many voices and many places' (Bonneuil 2015: 29). Not only must differences in class, race, gender and regional or national affiliation be taken into account, but advocates of the decolonization of knowledge are increasingly wary of the way Anthropocene science extends Western thought's self-privileging at the expense of a world of other ways of knowing and doing. In this regard, the Earth sciences are accused both of failing to reflect on their implication in the historical destruction of other ways of life and of perpetuating the West's long-standing silencing of the knowledge of Indigenous, colonized and other marginalized peoples (Whyte 2018b; Davis and Todd 2017; Yusoff 2018).

A fourth point is the failure of Anthropocene science to adequately theorize the societal dynamics that have given rise to the current planetary predicament (Lövbrand et al. 2015: 213–14). The objective of assessing human impacts in ways that are comparable to other components of the Earth system, critical commentators observe, has led scientists to prioritize such easily quantifiable variables as demographic change and technological diffusion at the expense of identifying causal processes. In particular, the exponential curves used in support of the Great Acceleration argument tell us about symptoms and effects rather than the underlying dynamics. As critics argue, any response to Earth system change that does not specify systemic social processes or target entrenched power relations is likely to reinforce rather than challenge the status quo (Malm and Hornborg 2014). Along these lines, proposals aimed at safeguarding the Earth system have been charged with bolstering 'international expert institutions, carbon pricing mechanisms, green technologies and international environmental treaties' – the very organizational forms that have presided over the worsening planetary predicament (Lövbrand et al. 2015: 214).

A fifth point of contention over the Anthropocene narrative concerns questions of urgency around proposed institutional and policy changes – for which the planetary boundaries literature is often targeted. Critics claim that expediency itself seems to be being used as a way to circumvent more searching sociopolitical deliberation in favour of the kind of technical and managerial procedures that avoid questioning the existing social order: a position often referred to as the 'post-political' (Lövbrand et al. 2015: 214–15; Swyngedouw 2010). A variant of this argument stresses how the rhetoric of impending catastrophe can itself be used to justify suspension of existing political rights and entitlements. In this regard, critical social and political thinkers have expressed their anxiety over the possible implications for due political process of a full-blown climatic or Earth system emergency – including suspicions that such a predicament might be used to legitimate large-scale technological interventions such as geoengineering, or the imposition of authoritarian social regulation (Cooper 2010: 184; Szerszynski et al. 2013; Clark 2014: 28–9).

In summary, social thinkers are making a concerted effort to break with what they see as the prevailing techno-scientific framing of Earth system change and to make sure that the Anthropocene thesis and practical responses to it are multivocal, broadly deliberated and open to contestation – to such an extent that the possibility of radical social change makes it onto the agenda (see Bonneuil and Fressoz 2016: 71). And in this way, the inherited disciplinary strengths of social thought are highlighted. As Lövbrand et al. conclude, in relation to the difficult question of how to deal with a situation in which humans are both agents of change and part of a much bigger Earth story: '[w]e believe that the social sciences are well equipped to address this tension by further socializing the Anthropocene concept' (2015: 213).

## Socializing the Anthropocene

What is at stake in the reaction of critical and interpretive social thought to the Anthropocene idea, we suggest, is the question of what makes us human and what manner of social beings we are. While the co-constitutive role of physical or material worlds is often alluded to, ultimately most social thinkers reaffirm that it is social, cultural, political, historical factors 'that make us into who we are' – and in turn it is the power that arises out of this social being that affords select human constituencies the capacity to impinge upon the Earth. What a properly socialized Anthropocene might look like it in practice, however, is not always clearly spelled out.

One example of a work of Anthropocene and climate change 'resocialization' that is detailed and well resolved is geographer Andreas Malm's *Fossil Capital* (2016). In this book, Malm argues that what brought about the rise of Earth system-changing carbon emissions was a very specific set of social relations at a particular geographical-historical juncture (2016: 263). When manufacturers in the north of England in the mid-1820s turned from water power to coal-fired steam power in their factories, he argues, it was not primarily a matter of a technological advancement or even a new level of energetic demand that could only be met by tapping the bounty of the Earth's strata. Above all, what drove this transition was capital's intent to subdue, discipline and exploit the landless and increasingly urbanized working classes. As Malm shows in detail, the momentous decision to switch from renewable hydropower to non-renewable fossil hydrocarbons was taken by a tiny minority of social actors:

> Capitalists in a small corner of the Western world invested in steam, laying the foundation stone for the fossil economy; at no moment did the species vote for it either with feet or ballots, or march in mechanical unison, or exercise any sort of shared authority over its own destiny and that of the earth system. (2016: 267)

In essence, nineteenth-century steam power for Malm is a form of social power exercised over workers in order to subordinate their unruly social and reproductive potentiality to the demands of capital accumulation. By extension, the entire global edifice of fossil-fuelled production is 'a materialisation of social relations' (2016: 19). It is the subjugation and exploitation of labour by capital that ultimately give rise to climate change and the misleadingly titled Anthropocene: a misnomer Malm mischievously accuses of 'mistaking capitalists for humans' (2016: 264).

To a significant extent, Malm exemplifies the critical approaches we précised in the last section: he depicts a deeply class-divided 'humanity', his viewpoint is emphatically historical and place-based, silenced voices and experiences of exploited people are recuperated, the dynamics of capital are ensconced at the core of the narrative, and all these points converge on the assertion that fundamental social-structural change is necessary to respond effectively to the dire current planetary predicament.

Any number of global environmental change researchers would readily affirm that climate change will cause or is already causing great human harm and misery. The point that Malm and fellow critical thinkers drive home is that this suffering was there at the beginning. Pushing working people to exhaustion and breakdown and putting unbearable strain on physical environments are not unfortunate and avoidable by-products of economic development. Rather, brutally unsustainable extraction of human bodily energy and the degradation of living worlds were and are the very foundation of the economic accumulation that propels the Great Acceleration's definitive exponential curves.

In his depiction of the industrial heartlands of 1840s England, Friedrich Engels, borrowing a term from working people themselves, referred to these conditions as 'social murder' (2009: 38). Literary theorist Rob Nixon (2011), with an eye to the global outsourcing of bodily and environmental degradation, calls it 'slow violence'. Neither 'globalization' nor 'Great Acceleration' comes anywhere close to evoking the movement that takes us from the crippling diseases of poverty, overwork and poisoned landscapes documented by Engels to the 'long dyings – the staggered and staggeringly discounted casualties, both human and ecological' that Nixon diagnoses across the contemporary world (2011: 2). The point is that, for Nixon, Malm and fellow social critics, this confrontation with suffering and degradation is not where we eventually arrive once we have traced all the systemic interconnections that global circulation models or quantifications of planetary boundaries map out for us. It is where we need to start.

This sense that the stresses and violations of embodied life are an originary complication of the current global order can be pushed further. As Engels, Emile Zola, George Orwell and many other social commentators have noted, the labouring bodies of miners at once play a crucial role in underpinning modern industrial economies and are disproportionately exposed to hazard and harm. 'The deeper down the seams went the greater the danger, the greater the heat, the greater the mechanical difficulties', broods cultural historian Lewis Mumford. 'To this day ... the mortality rate among miners from accidents is four times as high as any other occupation' (1934: 68).

Mining is more than an occupation in which value extracted and danger endured are especially intense, however. It is also historically implicated with the emergence of the social relations that Malm and others take to task for triggering the climate and Earth system change. 'More closely than any other industry', Mumford observes, 'mining was bound up with the first development of modern capitalism' (1934: 74). Historian Fernand Braudel fills in the details, recounting that it was during the Central European mining boom of the fifteenth century that the escalating financial requirements for equipment needed to access ever-deeper ores enabled absentee investors to gain control over mining. 'Capitalism', Braudel writes, 'entered upon a new and decisive stage' (1982: 321). In the process, previously independent mine workers found themselves dependent on owners of extractive capital: '[a]nd indeed this was when the word *Arbeiter*, worker, first appeared' (1982: 322). By the sixteenth century, Mumford adds, the increasing pressures of capitalism on labouring bodies saw the mine emerge as an early site for 'the use of the strike as a weapon of defense, the bitter class war, and finally the extinction of the guilds' power' (1934: 75).

It was Mumford, too, who over eighty years ago first explicitly hitched a geological time period or stratum to a social formation when he described the current order as 'carboniferous capitalism' (1934: 156–8). But Mumford's carboniferous capitalism is not quite the same thing as Malm's fossil capitalism. Fossil capitalism, we recall, is 'a materialisation of social relations', which is to say that a pre-existing set of unequal and exploitative relationships manifests itself in the turn to new energy sources and productive machineries. For Mumford, however, tapping into the hydrocarbon resources of the Carboniferous has an impetus or vitality of its own.

Just as mining and capitalism shaped each other from the outset, in Mumford's narrative, so too does access to whole new domains of subterranean energy impact upon the social relations that organize its extraction. '[T]he sudden accession of capital in the form of these vast coal fields put mankind in a fever of exploitation', he observes. 'The animus of mining affected the entire economic and social organism' (1934: 157–8). Mumford wasn't saying that access to massive coal reserves directly instigated a new phase of industrial capitalist development, and he certainly wasn't implying that the germ of capitalism was slumbering in the buried sunshine of the Carboniferous stratum. What exactly he meant is not precisely spelt out. But then, Mumford was one of the first Western thinkers to ask what the encounter with an excess of energy might mean for social life – and this is a question that still feels challenging and less than fully resolved (though see Mitchell 2011).

It's an important issue – not just for how we conceive of production powered by exhumed fossilized hydrocarbons, but also for the broader project of socializing the Anthropocene. If capitalists are not to be mistaken for humans, we suggest, this is more than a question of specifying what manner of humans they might be. It is also a matter of exploring how forces and powers that are literally 'inhuman' play a part in the figurative inhumanity that generations of radical thinkers have rightly descried at the very core of modern social relations.

## Energy and Excess

The intellectual world of Marx and Engels was one in which it is our labour and the know-how it embodies that give form to the elemental world, rather than the other way around. When Marx explains how labour transforms materials to produce value and when he shows how much of this value capital appropriates, he is demonstrating how a specific economy of people, things and values operates. In order to prove that capitalists are syphoning off value, Marx needs to know exactly where this value comes from and where it goes – as does Malm (2016) when he indicts mill owners for using steam-powered machines to ratchet up the exploitation of their workforce. But this reasoning itself has an 'economic' logic. It assumes the value of what enters and leaves the system and all the changes that take place in between can be known, that it can be captured in thought just as it can be captured in social practices.

However, in the work of Marx and those influenced by him, there is another kind of logic, a different 'economy' rumbling away in the background. For just as Marx recognized that exploiting labour is fundamental to capital accumulation, he also grasped that there is no harnessing of human beings to the production process that is not troubled by the potential of these labouring bodies to be more or other than what is demanded of them. And though they have avoided predicting exactly when, where or how it will happen, Marx and subsequent generations of Marxian thinkers imagine that sooner or later the unruly, exuberant energies of the modern worker will break out of the strictures that bind them – into revolutionary transformation.

There is nothing wrong with calculating value and attributing blame or responsibility. Most forms of justice, including climate justice, hinge upon identifying casual chains and accounting for harms or benefits that flow along them. But when Marx or subsequent critical thinkers reckon with the irruptive potential of the exploited and oppressed they are bringing another kind of reasoning into play, as indeed they are when they allow themselves to be aggrieved, angered or inspired by the suffering inflicted on others. This is a logic or economy that turns not on the valuation of what is known or predicted, but on the encounter with situations that precede, exceed or defy calculation. Marx and Engels (1975) were critics of what they called 'critical criticism' – of simply pointing out injustices in the world, and preaching the necessity of revolt. Instead they were calling for an understanding of the forces of history that were building in the background, and threatening to explode the machinery of capitalism.

What does acknowledging 'excess' in this way mean for thinking about energy – or for engaging with a dynamic Earth more generally? There were thinkers in the mid-twentieth century who began to construct entire social theories around notions of excess. Among the most notable was Georges Bataille (1988; 1993), who set out from the problem of the superfluity of solar energy received by the Earth and the question of how humans and other living things dealt with this overabundance. But well before Bataille and his successors offered us a logic and a language to talk about excess, there were many others who sensed that the energy that was being extracted in ever greater quantities from within the Earth conveyed powers that in some way overflowed the tasks for which it was intended.

Mumford was an avid reader of Upton Sinclair's bestselling novel *Oil!* (1927), which told of the social frenzy that accompanied the early exploitation of Californian oilfields. 'Their frail human nature was subjected to a strain greater than it was made for', expounded Sinclair; 'the fires of greed had been lighted in their hearts, and fanned to a white heat that melted every principle and every law'. American country and western singer Merle Travis offered similar cautions about coal in the 1946 recording 'Dark as a dungeon'.

> Come and listen you fellows, so young and so fine,
> And seek not your fortune in the dark, dreary mines.
> It will form as a habit and seep in your soul,
> 'Till the stream of your blood is as black as the coal. (1947a)

Growing up in the mining community of Rosewood, Kentucky, Travis undoubtedly intended the double meaning of coal permeating miner's bodies as well as their souls. Along with outputs from mines or wells, deaths and injuries from extractive labour have long been enumerated, as the evidence presented earlier by Mumford indicates. So too have miners' daily outputs been relentlessly, and not always fairly, tallied – the theme of another classic Travis lyric: 'You load sixteen tons, what do you get? Another day older and deeper in debt' (1947b). These sums are important, in any number of ways. But what Travis is getting at with his coal in the blood, Mumford with his 'animus' of mining, and Sinclair with his law of 'white heat' is something else: something immeasurable yet perplexing, pervasive and potent.

Bataille, as we mentioned above, liked to remind us that the Earth receives far more energy than living things require for their survival, a point gleaned from his conversations with physicist Georges Ambrosino and his readings of the early biospheric thinking of geochemist Vladimir Vernadsky. Some of that solar energy captured by photosynthesizing organisms and processed into living tissue over hundreds of millions of years was sequestered beneath the Earth's surface, where it was condensed by heat and pressure into fossilized hydrocarbons (Alley 2000: 170). As political theorist Timothy Mitchell expresses it: 'great quantities of space and time ... have been compressed into a concentrated form' (2011: 15). Rapidly exhuming and combusting all that buried sunshine, as climatologists tell us, is changing the atmospheric composition of the planet. As energy theorist Amory Lovins made clear back in the 1970s, 'we are more endangered by too much energy too soon than by too little too late (1977: 12).

There are intriguing speculations as to whether Marx and Engels attended the 1859 lectures in London when physicist John Tyndall first introduced the idea of the natural greenhouse effect (Foster and Burkett 2016: 102). We can safely say, however, that when the capitalist mill owners of Malm's narrative turned to fossil-fuelled steam power, neither they nor their contemporary social critics could have understood the long-term climatic repercussions. But the implications of accessing the geological bounty of fossilized hydrocarbons go far beyond its geophysical effects. As it is for Earth systems so it is for social systems: whatever projects or imperatives it is applied to, there is no simple way of anticipating the ultimate societal and subjective ramifications of a massive rush of energy from the geological past. Tapping into the solar-charged biomass of the Carboniferous, Permian and Triassic periods changed the very contours of social existence. 'The constantly accelerating supply of energy altered human relations in space and time', as Mitchell puts it (2011: 14).

Even with several centuries to contemplate the consequences, it's still hard to fathom the full impact of suddenly releasing all that ancient energy. And there are reasons for this. A world in which the pre-eminent event is the use of heat to drive pistons, hammers and crank arms is one in which a sprawling multitude of heat-induced metamorphoses narrows down to a small set of controllable mechanical or kinetic functions (Clark and Yusoff 2014; Prigogine and Stengers 1984: 102). By isolating cause and effect in what is effectively a closed system – with the steel-encased heat engine as its model – it becomes possible to not only establish a tight causal chain linking outputs to inputs but to *quantify* the relationship of the former to the latter. Just as this has implications for understanding both social and physical processes, so too does it come to frame how the human psyche is understood. In its prevailing formulation, philosopher-psychoanalyst Teresa Brennan proposes, the modern Western subject came to be construed as 'if it existed in a self-contained energetic system' distinct from both nature and other subjects (2000: 65). This notion of psychic closure from wider energetic flows, Brennan suggests, has helped to drive the breathtaking energetic and material profligacy of modern society, with its incessant conversion of the energies of the living world into lifeless commodities.

It hardly needs to be said that there is something odd going on here. For at the very juncture at which a flood of seemingly limitless energy enters the modernizing world, we see a generalized turn towards boundedness, reduction, containment – or as we would now say, closed-system thinking. Work becomes redefined in a singular way, as force exerted on a stationary object; the purpose of labour becomes understood narrowly as the production of a value that only labouring bodies can create; certain knowledge can only be obtained by a self-sufficient subject. And then, almost as soon as it is established, each assumption or assertion of systemic closure is confronted with its excess: mechanical work fills the cosmos with waste heat, labouring bodies cavort or revolt, rational minds obsess, fantasize and hallucinate, become the puppets of unconscious forces (see Parisi and Terranova 2000).

Unravelling this strange complicity of limit and excess, of calculation and the incalculable, is not easy. To combust and channel the powerful condensed energy of fossil hydrocarbons required a formidable container: the kind of robust chambering Max Weber riffed off when he suggested that the subject required a *stahlhartes Gehäuse* – a 'steel-hard casing' – if it were to endure the pressures of the modern world (2012: 123). There is more to it than this, however. As Mitchell explains, it is the very boundlessness of the new energetic underpinning of social life that enables the constitutive elements of the human order to be enclosed, objectified, quantified. This logic finds its consummation in the early twentieth century when the tapping of seemingly infinite oil reserves fully entrenches the principle of limitless growth. 'Its ready availability, in ever-increasing quantities, and mostly at relatively low and stable prices, meant that oil could be counted on *not to count*', Mitchell contends. 'In turn, not having to count the cost of humankind using up ... most of the earth's limited stores of fossil fuel made another kind of counting possible – new kinds of economic calculation' (2011: 234).

While the very idea of the economy as a cumulative, quantifiable and 'de-natured' domain of human achievement finally comes of age in the mid-twentieth century, as Mitchell suggests, we can also discern its precursory forms in the earlier ascent of fossil-fuelled modernity. For here too, less explicitly and more uneasily, we can already see the carving out of what Bataille referred to as a 'restricted economy' – a realm comprised of the knowable and calculable – from the 'bottomlessness and boundlessness of the universe' (1993: 168). If it is Bataille who recognizes the work done to separate out the modern order 'as an isolatable system of operations' from the cosmos as a whole (1988: 19), it is Mitchell who helps us to see how important a growing bounty of ancient energy is to inciting that enclosing and securing cut.

To sum up, in the modern West we dwell amongst a world of things whose value can be identified, measured, accumulated. This logic also applies to the way we know this world: what counts as knowledge is carefully delineated, its gaps filled, its content constantly augmented. And yet the very self-sufficiency of these systems or 'economies', we have been arguing, is made possible by the vast stock of energy at our disposal – open-ended in its magnitude, spatially and temporally boundless. We can discount this monstrous exterior – shut it out of our reasoning – precisely because we believe that we can always count on it. And in this way an entire reality is constructed that need not trouble itself with its exteriority, a world that can avoid, as Bataille put it, 'the exhausting detours of exuberance' (1988: 13).

This is not simply a delusion we can foist on capitalism, modern science or other systems of authority and control. As social scientists or humanities scholars, it is also our problem. The energetically enabled delineation of a self-sufficient domain of sociality is the conceptual foundation of the idea that labour gives form to the forces and forms of nature, but not the other way round. To put it more generally, not having to account for its own material-energetic underpinning or context is the condition of possibility of modern social thought's self-understanding as an autonomous, self-legislating sphere. And in this way, it is ultimately the informing principle behind the idea that it is possible to 'socialize the Anthropocene' without at the same time permitting social thought to be contaminated and altered by the energetic-material forces with which it is grappling.

## Geologizing the Social

As we have also been suggesting, that which powers orderly accumulation also threatens it from without and within. Waste heat billows from the boiler; the labouring classes fume against factory-floor discipline; the psyche roils in its enclosure. And what Spivak refers to as the 'risky night of non-knowledge' slips in and out of the well-modulated interior of modern knowledge systems (1994: 25). By the same logic, we argue, the fiery energy of the Carboniferous seeps unnoticed into social thought.

Contemporary climate science elucidates for us how the carbon dioxide and other greenhouse gases that are the excess or by-product of fossil fuel combustion stay in the Earth system, resulting in increased atmospheric absorption of sunlight, ocean acidification and an intensified hydrological cycle. More broadly speaking, the natural sciences have been discovering their own versions of 'excess' for over a century and a half – though they tend not to conceive of it in quite this way. This is partly a matter of the physical sciences progressively supplementing the Newtonian universe that runs on determinable laws of motion, and moving away from the idea that the most basic operations of matter and energy as studied by kinetics can explain more complicated events and processes, and towards non-reductionistic ideas such as 'emergence' (Clayton and Davies 2006).

As we saw in the previous chapter, the study of open, complex and nonlinear systems has been increasingly drawing the sciences towards an appreciation of the way that relatively small changes can trigger large transformations, and the associated idea that many real-world physical systems have the potential to shift between a range of different operating states. This is what we are referring to as planetary multiplicity – and the point we have made in the previous section is that excess is an intrinsic aspect of the way the planet and the cosmos work.

So while 'excess' may not be a term they routinely use, many natural scientists now deal with systems that are vulnerable at once to perturbations arriving from outside and to potentially transformative changes generated within the system itself. And in this way, it would seem that the more that science learns about the dynamics of life, Earth and cosmos, the more the conditions of existence of any 'being' look to involve chance and contingency rather than certainty and predictability (see DeLanda 2002: 155).

While the natural sciences bump up against the 'risky night of non-knowledge' in their own ways, modern social, cultural and philosophical thought has been more explicitly confronting the challenge of worlds of excess – though often with an eye to what is going on in the sciences. Bataille (2013: 34) spoke of the need to think about systems of value and meaning as always open to their outside, building up to his idea of 'the economy equal to the universe'. Derrida and fellow deconstructivist thinkers probed the idea of 'bottomless, endless connections and … the indefinitely articulated regress of the beginning' (Derrida 1981: 333–4), and exhorted us to look out for 'radical contamination' whenever we found apparent closure and certainty (Spivak 1994: 28). Gilles Deleuze and Félix Guattari encouraged us to be attuned to the risky, unknowable effects of joining up with and enfolding into our lives the great inhuman forces of Earth and cosmos (1987: 161, 503).

With a little poetic licence, we might see these more grandiose philosophical declarations as generalized ways of saying what miners and others familiar with large-scale extraction knew from experience: that there's no joining forces with great masses of matter-energy without getting more than you bargained for. Bringing together these insights from extractive communities, from social and philosophical theories of excess and from sciences of complexity and nonlinearity, we want to make the case that any 'socializing of the Anthropocene' should also entail a certain 'geologizing of the social' (Clark and Gunaratnam 2017). And if this is a matter of acknowledging that human society is powered, perturbed and pervaded by the forces of the Earth which it embraces, so too is it a recognition that research and reflection on social life are likewise open to 'contamination'.

As geographer Kathryn Yusoff rightly insists, when we access, capture and set to work geological powers or properties they become a part of us: their very inhumanness contributing to the kind of humans that we are – or that we are in the process of becoming. That is, we must 'begin to understand ourselves as geologic subjects, not only capable of geomorphic acts, but as beings who have something *in common* with the geologic forces that are mobilised and incorporated' (2013: 781). In this way, the Carboniferous, the Jurassic, the Triassic quite literally get in our blood, our bodies, the collectivities that we form (Yusoff 2016).

This is not an assertion of one-to-one causality, of determination or quantifiable impact. Precisely because an energy- or mineral-rich geological stratum is a condensation of forces that vastly exceed our own situated existence and anything we can get our heads around, our incorporation of the geologic will inevitably exceed the uses that we had in mind. This is not just a matter for societies reliant on mineral-energetic extraction, or humans in general, but for all biological life, as philosopher Elizabeth Grosz would have it. Underpinning and sustaining all earthly life, Grosz proposes, is what she refers to as 'geopower', the great forces of the Earth and cosmos:

> What we understand as the history of politics – the regulations, actions and movements of individuals and collectives relative to other individuals and collectives – is possible only because geopower has already elaborated an encounter between forms of life and forms of the Earth. (Grosz et al. 2017: 975)

In this regard, tapping into the energy reserves of the Carboniferous might be a relatively novel event, but in another sense it is one more variation on the theme of channelling the forces of an inorganic exteriority through which all human collectives and all living communities have forged and reshaped themselves. So just as Deleuze and Guattari ventured that all 'history is a geo-history' (1994: 95), so too can we add that all social formations are 'geosocial formations' (Clark and Yusoff 2017), and that all life is 'geologic life' (Yusoff 2013).

To acknowledge in this way the openness of sociable life – human or otherwise – to the 'bottomlessness and boundlessness of the universe' is to unsettle any idea of unbroken accumulation of wealth and value or of know-how and adaptive traits. With the potentiality for change that comes with openness comes also the possibility of being undermined or overwhelmed. The risk, as Marx and Engels (2002: 223) famously put it, that '[a]ll that is solid melts into air' or in Sinclair's version that 'white heat' melts 'every principle and every law', in this sense, is not so much the correlate of any particular social order or human lineage as the way of all earthly existence. It is the price any creature or living community pays for its dependence on and exposure to forces far beyond its measure (see Jonas 2001: 80).

Malm is right to urge that using 'the abundance of coal in the pits of northern Britain' to fuel a system of mechanized production that sapped the life out of a 'superabundance of unemployed hands' (2016: 161, 153) was only one of numerous options. It is in the nature of open systems that actualized orders and structures are only a small subset of what is possible. And this is precisely why thinking social life *with* and *through* the geologic is vital and urgent. It is equally important to stress that geologizing the social does not detract from or negate socializing the Anthropocene or any related socialization of the geologic. It is not a zero-sum game – at least not if we recognize that most real-world systems have a degree of openness, and that excess and limits are mutually implicated.

To socialize the Anthropocene, the Great Acceleration, the fossil-fuelled Industrial Revolution, is to insist that the geohistorical trajectory that was followed expressed particular social interests, that it materialized the imaginaries and imperatives of specific social groups, that it was situated in select regions of the world at unrepeatable historical junctures. But to geologize the social is to prise open the question of how certain social actors acquired previously unthinkable powers or agencies, it is to ask what else might have been or might yet be done with the geopower they sought to make their own, and it is to begin to speculate about what other earthly powers we might join forces with in the future.

## Planetary Partiality

We have been arguing that when modern Europeans began to rely heavily on the energetic resources of ancient geological epochs the outcomes were more and other than they intended. This sense that tapping into or connecting up with new forces is inherently indeterminate is not restricted to particular times, spaces or scales. Neither is it a human prerogative. As Stephen Pyne reflects on the emergence of the first fire-wielding creatures a million or so years ago, 'the Earth did not get quite what it supposed' (2001: 26). As with Eiseley's remark that we quoted earlier, this is intended provocatively. Pyne is reminding us both that there was nothing necessary about hominins learning to manipulate fire, *and* that the planetary consequences of this event could not be anticipated – neither by us nor by any other information processing system. Indeed, we might say, the Earth system is still finding out what transformations a fire-handling species can trigger.

As we saw earlier, a recurring charge against Anthropocene or Earth system science is that its planetary perspective constitutes a placeless, disembodied, decontextualized 'god's-eye' view. We need to be very careful here, however, as the claim that natural scientists aren't very good at reflecting on their own positionality or situatedness can easily slip into the idea that any inquiry at the planetary scale equates with a view from nowhere. When Pyne observes that Earth is 'a fire planet' (1994: 889), for example, this isn't so much a presumption of universality arising from an omniscient gaze as it is an attempt to identify some definitive features of *this particular planet* in relation to other astronomical bodies in our solar system. Likewise, when he turns to epochal shifts in the behaviour of terrestrial fire, Pyne is not projecting sameness across the Earth's surface so much as acknowledging the geohistorical specificity of certain patterns and dynamics of open air combustion. '[T]he fires of the Carboniferous period differ from those of the Permian', he notes; 'Miocene fires rippling over grasslands differed from Eocene fires that had no grasses to burn' (2014: 93).

With regard to the Australian continent, anthropologist and Indigenous studies scholar Marcia Langton makes a similar point about fire regimes changing over geological time – extending this to a claim about the challenges that such transitions posed to the first Australians: 'Indigenous populations lived in parts of this continent for at least 65,000 years, adapting and innovating as they witnessed an ice age, the disappearance of the megafauna, the rising of the seas, the drying-up of the continent' (2019). Present-day Aboriginal burning practices and other land management, she suggests, most probably took shape with the onset of the Holocene (1998: 49).

Indeed, for Langton, it is this geologically broad-spectrum perspective that lends weight to the idea that European colonists utterly miscon-strued the role of Aboriginal customary burning in managing the Australian landscape – with continuing fatal consequences (quoted in Nakashima 2000). Pyne too focuses in on the way that different human communities across the planet have developed burning practices that respond to the changing interplay of fire, ecology, landform and climate.

What he also shows us is that North-Western Europe has a peculiar and somewhat exceptional fire regime. Its annually well-dispersed rainfall and lack of a distinctive fire season, coupled with dense settlement and rich post-glacial soils, render this region 'an anomalously fire-free patch of Earth' (2001: 168). Consequently, the attempt by Europeans to export their own distinctive brand of fire suppression to much of the rest of the world – 'the attempt to install Europe's vestal fire as a global standard' – has been, Pyne insists, ecologically and culturally disastrous (1997a: 532–543).

From both Pyne's and Langton's work, we get a sense of what thinking about the Earth looks like when it takes seriously 'the lived experiences, fears, vulnerabilities, ideas and motivations of real people, in real places' (Lövbrand et al. 2015: 216). And we see the results – cruel and often tragic – of mistaking partial or site-specific knowledge for universal wisdom. As an influential feminist science studies scholar once put it: 'The moral is simple: only partial perspective promises objective vision' (Haraway 1988: 583).

It was over three decades ago that Donna Haraway famously insisted that we renounce the quest for the 'god-trick' of abstract, decontextualized vision and face up to the partiality or situatedness of all our knowledge claims. It was Haraway too who, observing how extraterrestrial space was being coded as 'escape from the bounded globe in an anti-ecosystem', raised the pointed question: 'Who speaks for the earth?' (1992: 318). However, it is important to recall that she did not seek to prohibit a particular scale of thinking or to disavow any category of objects – and especially not the Earth. Though resistant to readymade 'global systems', Haraway readily affirmed the necessity of 'an earthwide network of connections' (1988: 580). And in this regard, the task she set us is somewhat more demanding than a simple search-and-destroy mission against would-be omniscient observers. The onus was on those who would contest the universality of any truth claim to clearly demonstrate how identifying the partiality in question would make for a better account of 'a 'real' world' (1988: 578–9).

Langton and Pyne's fire scholarship, we are suggesting, offers excellent examples of what the route to objectivity through partiality looks like in practice, and where it takes us. They each bring us back to ordinary people, embodied and often exposed to danger, collectively accruing knowledge and skills over many generations. But it is vital to note that *their accounts of culturally embedded, site-specific practice are strengthened rather than compromised by extending this contextualization to continental spaces, geological timescales, and eventually planetary scales*. If both Pyne and Langton, in their own ways, address the question of who speaks *for* the Earth, their responses also, inseparably, draw our attention to human collectivities speaking and acting *through* the Earth. Just as it is important to attend to localized experiences and knowledge, so too does Pyne and Langton's work demonstrate how the fine-grained particularity of place-based understanding can be enriched when situatedness or contexuality is extended to larger scales – or indeed zooms in to even more microphysical analyses.

Staying in touch with lived and embodied experience, we have been arguing in this chapter, is of critical importance. But at the same time, all individuals or collective bodies bear deep traces of geohistories and planetary processes that exceed 'lived experience'. All of us, whenever or wherever we are positioned on the Earth's surface, incorporate and express physical forces that stretch far beyond our immediate context. Even as much contemporary positioning work in the social sciences and humanities teases out more-than-human entanglement, it is still relatively rare for these mappings to follow these connective threads deep into unequivocally inhuman terrain (Clark 2011: xvi–xvii). And here we would do well to heed philosopher Timothy Morton's counsel: 'contextualism tends to want to prevent the explosion of scales; it wants to restrict things to a certain scale or narrow range of scales' (2018: 110).

We need to be very careful, then, about any straightforward assertion that it is 'cultural and historical diversity that makes us into who we are'. The contemporary Earth and life sciences, we argue in this book, have much to offer, precisely because of the way they help make us aware of rhythms, temporalities and singularities that exceed localized experience. That being said, most physical scientists are not especially adept at positioning themselves and their work environments *at* the tipping points or *within* the rifts that their research brings into relief. They may have singular understandings of the precarious state of the Earth system, and valuable insights into the implication of localized processes in planetary-scaled forces; as yet, however, this rarely translates into reflection on how their own truth claims are *of* rather than *about* these moments or conjunctures.

## From Planetary Multiplicity to Earthly Multitudes

'Fire', as philosopher Gaston Bachelard once put it, 'links the small to the great, the hearth to the volcano, the life of a log to the life of a world' (1964: 16). Combustion in all its forms, we have been suggesting in this chapter, is a useful way to help us make connections between lived experience and forces or dynamics that extend far beyond the range of most people's day-to-day lives. When it comes to combusting fossil fuels, critical-analytic work like Malm's research on the turn to coal-fired heat engines plays a vital role in showing how social relations condition the uses that some human actors make of the resources of the Earth. We have also argued, however, that conceptual manoeuvres of this kind need to be opened up to moves coming from another angle – to the recognition that as the forces of the Earth work their way into social life they can exceed or overflow their initial objectives. Indeed, the experience of communities working at the geologic interface frequently gesture in this direction, Travis's words 'seep in your soul' anticipating the philosophical theme of 'radical contamination'.

Taking a deep temporal or planetary-scaled perspective on earthly powers and processes, we have argued, can be compatible with a focus on more intimate and place-based experience. But this does not resolve the troubling charge that most 'big picture' science arises from research clusters and networks that are far from representative of our species' ethnic, regional-national, class and gender differences. In other words, there are serious discrepancies between the dominant processes of theorizing planetary multiplicity, and the multiplicity or alterity of which social thinkers speak – and which speaks for itself. So as we read Bachelard's 'life of a log' linking up to 'the life of a world', the question persists of *whose* trees have been logged, *who* stoked the fire, *whose* hands are being warmed and *whose* homelands are overheating most rapidly.

Any conversation with contemporary Earth and life science needs to take very seriously Potawatomi scholar-activist Kyle Whyte's claim that catastrophic narratives of climate or Earth system change 'can erase Indigenous peoples' perspectives on the connections between climate change and colonial violence' (2018a: 225). So too do we need to consider writer Amitav Ghosh's equally provocative assertion that beyond the borders of Europe and the 'Anglosphere', other powers in the early modernizing world – such as China, Japan, Burma and India – exhibited their own potent carbon desires and ambitions (2016: 148–69). Layered into and often intersecting with the deep social-structural division of the globalized world are the issues of social class raised by Malm, and the questions of profoundly uneven exposure to the harms of economic development raised by Nixon and by a great many environmental justice scholar-activists.

The challenge, as we see it, is how to take full account of 'a plurality of narratives from many voices and many places' without at the same time closing ourselves to the incitements of contemporary Earth, life and astronomical science. Even today, the starting point for most critical framings of the encounter between Western knowledge and a world of other lifeways, knowledges and worldviews – as discussed in this chapter – is the assumption of European modernity's unitary vantage point on a similarly unitary nature. But how might this contact and exchange zone appear otherwise, we want to ask, if we take seriously, push further and elaborate upon the idea of planetary multiplicity? How might the scientific – but also more-than-scientific – idea that the Earth is self-differentiating or generative of its own alterity help us to stage different kinds of conversations about living through planetary change?

The other side of this question – picking up on our 'geologizing the social' theme – is about how to acknowledge the contribution made by the variable forces of the Earth to all human modes of being, doing and knowing. We have already briefly mentioned the concept of 'earthly multitudes' – our way of talking about collective means of engaging with the challenges and opportunities that arise out of planetary multiplicity. As we will see in chapter 4, whereas Hardt and Negri's (2004) concept of the multitude hinges upon capabilities associated with cultural and informatics industries prominent in the current global order, our interest is in the more deep-seated, diverse powers of living with and through an Earth on which 'variability abounds at ... all scales'. For social differentiation and self-organization have always been linked to the self-ordering and self-differentiating tendencies of the Earth itself.

In this regard, miners, heat engine inventors, broadcast burners – and those who use newer technologies and media to engage with the material world – are all examples of earthly multitudes. In the next chapter we look at some familiar household practices that are also – in a roundabout way – modes of engaging with the variability of the Earth. Setting out from domestic labour, we explore some forms of gendered artisanal production whose deep history helps us to see how earthly multitudes are bound up with the differential becoming of the Earth that we are referring to as planetary multiplicity.

# 3

# Planetary Social Life in the Making

## Introduction: Flat Iron, Deep Earth

If the planetary social thought we are advocating is going to run, it needs to work on just about anything. In chapter 4 we will set out more programmatically our specific proposals for how it might be done. But in this chapter we will first stress-test the very idea of planetary social thought, by taking a practice that is commonplace throughout much of the world – indeed much derided in its very mundaneness – and seeing if we can prise it open so as to explore its connections with geologic and planetary processes.

Our choice for this first extended case study (others of which you will find in chapters 6 and 7) is the application of a heated metallic surface to recently washed fabric in order to smooth out rumples and creases. The gendered nature of ironing in the Western world serves to remind us of the necessity of accounting for social divisions or distinctions that are too easily eclipsed by the description of a planetary 'human' in some versions of applied Earth systems thinking. Ironing and related practices of laundering soiled fabric also draw us more deeply into the side effects of the coal-fired Industrial Revolution discussed in the preceding chapter. As we dig into the history of the high-heat technologies of which ironing is an expression, and the equally long history of producing plant-based textiles, we encounter significant moments in the social acquisition of geological agency – with implications for the way we might think about the gendering of geopower.

The earliest evidence of blacksmiths forging purpose-built smoothing irons or 'flat irons' in Europe is from the late Middle Ages – though simple round stones believed to have been used in conjunction with smoothing boards to press fabric have been found in Viking women's graves, suggesting a much longer tradition (Gretton n.d.). Our aim in engaging with this long history is not to make a case that ironing is a taken-for-granted activity that would benefit from having its normative assumptions unmasked and disassembled. Ironing is already so thoroughly contested and de-normed that in many of its former regions of high intensity it is in steep decline.

The historically recent downturn in ironing in much of the Western world is partly a result of the prevalence of synthetic fabrics that are less prone to creasing than their organic counterparts, and may also reflect a certain relaxing or de-formalizing of sociocultural expectations about the presentation of self. Most of all, it would seem, ironing's receding from daily life has been brought about by the feminist movement's challenge to gendered practices of domestic labour – for which it has been something of an icon (see Guerts 2015). 'Don't iron while the strike is hot' was the slogan for the 1971 US Women's Strike for Equality that marked the rise of second-wave feminism – for which Tillie Olsen's short story 'I stand here ironing' (1961), with its challenging of the demands of domestic labour in patriarchal society, has often been read as a precedent. With multiple intended 'ironies' the London-based Women's Press founded in 1978 chose the iron as its logo (Edwards 2016).

Technically, the logic behind ironing is the application of heat to organic fibres in order to reorganize their structure. Plant-based fabrics such as cotton, linen and hemp are composed largely of cellulose – a polymer (a substance made of similar units bonded together) consisting of thousands of glucose molecules arranged in chains. These are bound together with relatively weak bonds, constantly subject to breaking and reforming, and only gain strength though their dense networking. The human activity of twining and spinning plant fibres greatly enhances this strengthening through providing additional interconnectedness. When fabrics are rumpled, the bonds in the fabric quickly rearrange and reform into creases – made worse when water molecules enter the process. With its combination of heat and pressure, ironing reorganizes the cellulose molecules into a parallel arrangement so that they lie flat (Lorch 2017).

In general terms, the effect of heating on fabrics is closely related to the impact of cooking on glucose polymers such as edible starches, which causes bonds to loosen, making the plant fibre easier to digest (Wrangham 2009: 60). The immediate and long-term evolutionary benefits of cooking plant fibres for human nutrition have been much discussed, but no such grandiose claims have been made for ironing fabrics. There are advantages in killing potentially pathogenic micro-organisms that have survived the washing process, and it has been argued that reordering the molecular structure extends the life of fabrics (GoIroning 2018). Most commentators, however, contend that the main purpose of ironing is to improve the appearance of fabrics – a practice that became closely linked to social respectability at certain historical junctures (Guerts 2015).

But more than simply relating the cultural history of a specific domestic practice, our focus on ironing in this chapter is a point of entry to consider the more general meeting or articulation between high heat and textiles. Attending to the long, multivalent tradition of human intensification of heat and its application in the restructuring of both organic and inorganic matter extends our analysis of the previous chapter – drawing us deeper into the social engagement with the geological strata of the Earth. At the same time, looking more closely at the use of plant fibre in the crafting of textiles foregrounds human interventions in the living envelope at the Earth's surface. In short, these are two of the most momentous sets of practices around which earthly multitudes have convened over much of the epoch that Earth scientists refer to as the Holocene – and the role of these practices in whatever will follow that periodization looks hardly less significant. How did these modes of intervention in the stuff of the world emerge, we ask, and how did they later converge? Or have the arts of high heat and textile been implicated with one another from the very beginning?

Our 'domestic' staging of an encounter between geological strata and the Earth system sets out from the mid-twentieth-century North American suburban home, uncoincidentally an originary site of second-wave feminism. From there, in successive steps we delve in increasing depth into the historical conjuncture of high heat and woven plant fibre.

## Domestic Labour's Great Acceleration

Even amongst the generalized drudgery of household labour that women faced well into the modern era, laundry has been particularly reviled, nineteenth-century Nevada diarist Rachel Haskell describing it as 'the Herculean task which women all dread' (cited in Strasser 2000: 104). Whereas Monday in much of the Euro-Atlantic world was traditionally devoted to the stoking of the fire and the gruelling cycle of boiling, scrubbing, rinsing, wringing and hanging to dry of laundry, Tuesday was ironing day.

> Three to six irons, each rubbed with beeswax and wiped before each
> use, stayed hot on a piece of sheet iron set on a hearth 'free from ash

and cinders', or late in the century on a stove … Every iron fresh from the fire had to be tried on a piece or paper or spare cloth to be sure it would not scorch the cloth,

recounts historian Susan Strasser (2000: 108), citing Catharine Beecher's intimidating manual of 1841.

But the surge of economic growth and technological change that Earth system thinkers refer to as the Great Acceleration would leave its mark on the rituals of laundering. In principle, the mechanization of domestic work in the West over the course of the twentieth century lessened the manual labour associated with laundry. The automatic washing machine and the tumble dryer took off in the USA in the 1940s, but were preceded by several decades by the electric clothes iron, which – since it did not need a hot stove, could be used anywhere and did not involve overheating the house in summer – spread almost as fast as households were connected to electricity grids (Nye 1990: 264; see also Strasser 2000: 267–8). According to a 1921 survey of 1,300 Philadelphia households with electricity, the electric iron topped the poll of most widespread electrical appliances, easily beating vacuum cleaners, washing machines and fans (Nye 1990: 268).

Coupled with the rise of 'wrinkle-resistant' synthetic fabrics, the electrification and automation of laundry shifted the dynamics of domestic labour. The overall effects, however, were more equivocal. As Strasser notes: 'it changed the laundry pile from a weekly nightmare to an unending task, increasing the size of the pile, the amount of water and fuel and laundry products most households used, and possibly even the housewife's working time, which was now spread out over the week' (2000: 268).

This temporal restructuring of laundering practices is also related to growing attention to personal appearance and changing fashion, which are in turn linked to the growing influence of advertising and visual mass media over the course of the twentieth century. Equally important are developments in the mass production and affordability of clothes and other fabric-based consumer items. A succession of synthetic fibres including nylon, olefin, acrylic and polyester entered consumer markets between the 1930s and 1950s. Composed of hydrocarbon-based polymers, they were often marketed as 'drip-dry' or 'wash and wear' – but still turned out to require ironing. At the same time, functions such as the ability to absorb dyes, stretching, waterproofing and resistance to stain and insect larval infestation, coupled with reduced cost and increasing mass production, encouraged increased acquisition of clothing – contributing to the accelerating laundry cycle.

If the myth of laundry 'at the flick of a switch' helped precipitate second-wave feminism, the infrastructure behind the switch itself and the consumer landscape to which the electric iron belongs leads us to other critical perspectives. For Marxist geographer David Harvey, the spaces in which the mechanization of domestic labour proceeds are closely related to capital's post-war expansion and its demand for new sites of investment – a dynamic spearheaded by the suburbanization of the United States. As Harvey observes:

> it entailed a radical transformation in lifestyles, bringing new products from housing to refrigerators and air conditioners, as well as two cars in the driveway and an enormous increase in the consumption of oil. It also altered the political landscape, as subsidized home-ownership for the middle classes changed the focus of community action towards the defence of property values and individualized identities. (2008: 27)

From its North American heartland, this pattern of dispersed, automobile-centred settlement, and energy- and consumer-durable-intensive daily living, radiated across the Western world and became the model to which much of the rest of the world aspired. Extending Harvey's observations, geographer Matthew Huber teases out the transformations of subjectivity that hinged upon this spreading form of life: 'the mechanized household allowed individuals to conflate the power of these machines with their own powers as entrepreneurs actively making a privatized living space' (2013: 82).

At first glance, the transitions that Harvey and Huber are talking about here resonate with the Great Acceleration concept in Anthropocene discourse. But this kind of critical thinking about post-war suburbanization and the mechanized intensification of domestic labour also complicates the way that Earth system scientists frame the mid-twentieth-century growth spurt. As we noted in chapter 1, the moment when 'the human enterprise suddenly accelerated after the end of the Second World War' was recommended – though not unanimously – by the Anthropocene Working Group as the terminal point of the Holocene (Steffen et al. 2007: 617; Zalasiewicz et al. 2015). The Great Acceleration is most often represented by a rather disparate group of exponential curves that include population growth, rising foreign direct investment and increasing fertilizer consumption – but equally important is the fact that measurable impacts on the Earth system, including rising carbon dioxide, nitrous oxide and methane levels, increasing ozone depletion and accelerating species extinction, can be described in equally dramatic curves (Steffen et al. 2015a; 2011a).

It is this lumping together of 'human enterprise' in the Great Acceleration narrative that jars with the stories that Harvey and Huber are telling, and as we noted in chapter 2, raises the ire of many other critical social thinkers. This is compounded by explanations for the surge in growth that give a rather rosy vision of opened trade and capital flows, global economic integration, a rush of new technologies and the rise of innovation-spurring collaborations between government, industry and academia (Steffen et al. 2011a: 850). Neither does it help that the question has been posed in terms of 'What finally triggered the Great Acceleration' as if the boom was somehow fated to happen (Steffen et al. 2011a).

Recent updates of the Great Acceleration concept acknowledge the criticisms from social scientists and humanities scholars about treating humanity as a whole and have taken steps to address them. More attention has been given to the economic growth in countries such as Brazil, Russia, India, China and South Africa, and to non-OECD countries more generally (Steffen et al. 2015a). But this research still speaks of a generic 'human enterprise' (Steffen et al. 2015a: 92). No reference is made to capitalism. And gender does not get a mention either.

In a reading more sympathetic than most, Jeremy Davies makes the point that it doesn't take a great deal of effort to show how the transitions shorthanded as the Great Acceleration manifest global socio-economic and geopolitical transitions that are well within the compass of critical thought. 'The wretched of the earth were not excluded from the Great Acceleration but an integral part of it', he insists, 'albeit on terms set by the economic elite' (2016: 101). But can the same be said about 'the wretched of the *hearth*' – the term used by feminist theorist Robin Morgan in 1969 to describe that half of the world's population who 'have been subjugated longer than any other people on earth' (2014: 175)?

Setting out from the mundane, all-too-situated practice of ironing, we are suggesting, opens up avenues of critique that can help us disaggregate the smooth indiscriminacy of the Great Acceleration curves and explore the causalities behind them. If for Harvey much of the acceleration of 'human enterprise' would be better explained by rapid post-war expansion of material and energy-intensive ways of life as an outlet for surplus capital, for second-wave feminist theorists like Morgan this was experienced as another turn in the long history of patriarchy – a 'development' that rescinded certain wartime freedoms and occupational diversifications achieved by women, increased both the outputs and inputs of domestic labour, and prepared the way for the selective (re)entry of women into the commercial workforce (Guerts 2015).

Unpacking the gender relations that go unrecognized in the Great Acceleration can help us to see where the burdens of change have fallen, and where the stress is likely to fall as the abject unsustainability of the suburban assemblage reveals itself. At the same time, feminist resistance to ironing and kindred forms of domestic labour also points to political resources for transitioning from carbon-intensive lifestyles that may not be given their due in narratives centred on the energy–environment nexus.

Let's take stock here. Thus far, our analysis fairly comfortably responds to the call of critical social thinkers to more zealously socialize and politicize the Anthropocene narrative. Although we have touched on the way that supply lines of relatively cheap oil and the mechanization of the household were translated into a re-entrenchment of gendered divisions of labour, we are still treating the Earth as if it was a stage – a flat and uneventful surface – upon which the 'real' action takes place. We have not yet given explicit consideration to the geological forces and powers that are being channelled through social life (though it might be noted that where Upton Sinclair (1927) depicted the surge of oil power as a 'white heat that melted every principle and every law', for suburbanized Western women the lived experience of extended energy grids was more likely to be that of a moderate heat that carefully realigned an endless chain of organic and inorganic polymers).

In the following section, we begin to develop the idea of planetary social thought by looking more closely at the organizations of matter and energy that ironing encapsulates and channels. What manner of forces and properties needed to be brought together in order that a forged chunk of iron could be heated over a chambered fire and applied to a swatch of woven fabric? Returning to the issue that was opened up in the preceding chapter about tapping subterranean energy sources, we look at the Industrial Revolution as a historical moment at which people in one part of the globe began to reorganize their relationships with the volumes or depths of the Earth. But this is also a time in which there are significant changes in the social engagement with the flows and cycles of matter-energy in and around the Earth's surface. To make sense of heat meeting fabric atop a trestle table in an industrial-era domestic space, we need to see how these surficial and volumetric transformations are brought together – in particular places and in specific activities.

## Heat and Cloth in the Carboniferous Kitchen

Some irons, still used in parts of the non-affluent world, are literally small furnaces – robust cast-iron chambers that contain burning charcoal. Like a microcosm of contemporary heat engines, later variations on this theme burned natural gas, kerosene or gasoline (Sterjova 2017). Prior to the electric iron, the more common fabric-smoothing apparatus was a flat-based triangular hunk of cast iron furnished with a handle and originally heated over the hearth fire. Industrialization saw the flat iron increasingly drawing its heat from the stovetop. As energy analyst and historian Barbara Freese depicts the thermal hub of the nineteenth- and early twentieth-century household, '[t]hese hot, black, soot-covered, carbon-smeared monsters sat at the heart of millions of homes like giant sculpted pieces of coal, endlessly demanding and hard to control, but able to radiate the energy of the Carboniferous into the kitchen' (2016: 145).

In this way, Freese reminds us that that the Industrial Revolution, however uneven and exploitative the social relations it involved, brought the societal processes taking place on the Earth's surface into a new relationship with the geological strata that compose the planet's crust. Geologists tell us that most of the coal in the early industrializing regions of England and Germany were laid down by swamp-immersed, tree-like club mosses and ferns during a relatively brief subdivision of the Carboniferous system between 313 and 304 million years ago, when the landmasses in question would have been positioned close to the equator (Cleal and Thomas 1996; Waters 2009). Along with industrial machinery from the same era, flat irons and domestic stoves would probably have been constructed using iron smelted in large quantities in blast furnaces fuelled by coal-derived coke, a process pioneered in England at the beginning of the eighteenth century. Conveniently for North-Western Europe's earlier industrializers, iron ore was often co-located with coal in the late Carboniferous sediments (Bloodworth 2014).

As we saw in chapter 2, Lewis Mumford anticipates Freese's idea of the carboniferous kitchen by evoking industrial capitalism's general dependence on the vast inheritance of condensed energy from the depths. As geographer Gavin Bridge put it more recently: 'These immensely concentrated flows represent geological subsidies to the present day, a transfer of geological space and time' (2009: 48).

There is another momentous subsidy, however – a more lateral or horizontal transfer of matter-energy – that is no less important to the Industrial Revolution. The garments and other items of woven cloth that are being subjected to the flat iron's coal-fired impress are themselves products of mechanized production. Indeed, they can be viewed as its primary and formative outputs. Where Malm conceives of 'fossil capital' (2016), feminist cultural theorist Sadie Plant sees 'cloth capitalism', which she describes as 'a runaway process which quite literally changed the world' (1997: 64). Supplies of wool, the raw material for much early industrial or 'cloth capitalist' textile production, were greatly increased by enclosures of common open field land in England and Scotland and its turning over to being 'devowered by shepe', a practice that also ensured there would be plentiful labour for the early mills (Fairlie 2009: 23). But as mechanization of spinning and weaving advanced, production was increasingly based on cotton, sourced from plantations in the American South.

Effectively, what the turn to 'King Coal' does for social relations with the volume or verticality of the Earth, the rise of 'King Cotton' does for the social incorporation of the flows and cycles that envelop the surface of the planet. In an exemplary piece of planetary thinking, philosopher-literary theorist John Protevi reads the growth of the plantation economy of US Southern states and the slave labour upon which it depended as a mobilization of complex material systems. He explains how solar-powered hydrology drains much of the North American landmass into the seaward-flowing Mississippi River, and how relations of turbulence and flow determine 'the rhythm of the river's flow and flood' and the gradual building of fertile alluvial planes through the deposition of sediment (2009: 165–6). Broadening this horizon, Protevi shows how the slave trade depends upon winds and currents, and how slave labour involves a channelling of carbon-mediated solar energy into coerced bodily exertion:

> So the sun helps explain how Africans came to the Caribbean and to Louisiana. To see the ecosocial context of this forced migration, we need to talk about yet another multiplicity in which solar energy is the key, the heat-exchange system of the planet. ... By meshing the multiplicities of the global heat-exchange system and the organically accessible solar energy system, we see the actualization we call the Atlantic slave trade. (2009: 167–9)

In no way downplaying the brutal exploitation at the plantation system's core, Protevi's point is that we cannot make sense of the system that produced cotton in unprecedented volumes (along with sugar cane and other cash crops) without a systematic understanding of the cycling of energy and matter that it cuts into and redirects to its own ends. Anthropologist Anna Lowenhaupt Tsing further elucidates this process, showing how both the monocultural 'interchangeability of planting stock' and the corresponding interchangeability of enslaved labour in the plantation economy institutes a form of standardized mass production that is itself an inspiration for later factory-based industrialization (2015: 39–40).

In this way, enfolded into the flat iron's dreary encounter with rumpled fabric is the drama of a double set of planetary renegotiations: an intensified vertical traversal of the geological layers of the Earth's crust coupled with the equally intensified interventions in the energetic-material flux of the outer Earth. The encounter of coal combustion with textiles comes with its own burden for domestic labour. With the rising challenge of keeping clothes free of the 'black and smutty Atomes' that are coal's ubiquitous remainder, the significance of cleanliness as a marker of social distinction escalated (Evelyn, cited in Freese 2016: 36). Cast our gaze further afield and there are appropriations, brutalities, displacements at every link in the chain of the vertical and horizontal reorganization of the planetary body – wrenching upheavals for human and nonhuman life alike.

The traumatic social consequences of reworking the stuff of the Earth, as we have seen, are not the strong point of Anthropocene science. When it comes to explaining the transformations associated with industrialization, however, we would argue that the problem is not that geoscience accounts are overly geological – *but that they are not geological enough*. In many ways, the mainstream Anthropocene story of an Industrial Revolution, 'with its origins in Great Britain in the 1700s', leading to a turn from agrarian reliance on the solar flux to surging fossil-fuelled mass production, is a very familiar narrative (Steffen et al. 2011a: 847). Despite the well-grounded grasp of the ramifications of combusting fossil hydrocarbons, this is still primarily a story of enterprising human agents, in a particular time and place, turning their attention to a novel fuel source. If it is a narrative that does not give nearly enough attention to the unjust social relations of class, gender and slavery, neither does it in any explicit way offer us an account of how geologic or elemental forces have acted on and through the social beings who engage with them. And this applies as much to the foregrounding of the Great Acceleration as the Holocene end event, we would argue, as it does to discussions of the Industrial Revolution.

The reason we raise this point is because Anthropocene science itself raises another possibility. As we mentioned in chapter 1, one of the most original developments to come out of the Anthropocene debate is the growing synergy between 'hard rock' geologists and Earth systems theorists. As Jan Zalasiewicz and his colleagues remind us, '[t]he former are overwhelmingly concerned with ancient, pre-human rock and time, while the latter have, as a strong central focus, the analysis and under-standing of contemporary global change' (2017: 85). More than just a novel conversation, this exchange offers new ways of thinking about how the planet's relatively solid and slow-moving lithic strata articulate with the faster flowing envelope around the Earth's surface – the sphere in which life plays such an important role (see Zalasiewicz et al. 2017; Steffen et al. 2016). As Zalasiewicz et al. conclude, '[g]eologists ... benefit from this mutual exchange with the Earth System Sciences, as it enables better process models of the stratigraphical data', while Earth system scientists profit from 'placing ongoing global change within a deep time context' (2017: 97–8).

When the two of us as social scientists think about how the volumes or depths of the Earth come into articulation with the planetary surface in new ways, as we have been doing in this section, the evolving conversation between Earth system science and stratigraphic or 'hard rock' geology is one of our main inspirations. But whereas Anthropocene scientists use this exchange between Earth systems and geological strata primarily to bring precision to their diagnosis of the moment when human activities attain a geosynchronous or planet-wide impact, we are more interested in how the coming together of the outer Earth system and lithic strata generates this human, planet-changing agency in the first place. That is: humans have become geologic agents in various ways and to differing extents by virtue of finding new means of hinging together the Earth's surface and its volumes. And at the same time, this is how the forces of strata and Earth system work *through* us, permeating and powering us in ways that are beyond our knowing.

Both the working with the geological forces of the Earth and their coursing through us are aspects of what we refer to as earthly multitudes: the collective ways in which humans articulate themselves in the structures and processes of a dynamical planet. But the fact that the examples we have addressed include slavery, exploitative factory labour and gendered drudgery anticipates a point we will make in more detail in the next chapter – that however generative they may be, there is nothing necessarily generous or virtuous about earthly multitudes.

The Industrial Revolution, or industrial capitalism, involves a significant reorganization of the way (some) humans tap into the geologic depths and the surficial fluxes of matter-energy – this being the condition of possibility of a coal-heated lump of iron encountering a piece of mass-produced cloth in a Victorian kitchen. But once our attention turns to actual processes by which embodied human agents collectively acquire their abilities to effectively cut into the flows and strata of the Earth, the singling out of a place-bound cadre of inventor-entrepreneurs – or 'capitalists in a small corner of the Western world' – loses some of its shine. This is the direction Deleuze and Guattari (1987: 406) map out, when they encourage us to think in terms of gradually evolving, technological lineages or 'machinic phyla' – another point we return to in the following chapter.

In the next section, we dig deeper into the question of how high heat has been put to work to make use of the matter of the subterranean Earth and how the textile arts intervene in the complexity of ecological systems. Thinking along these lines, we lose some of the capacity to pin the blame or the credit for key developments on individuals or narrowly defined social groups. But in the process, agency comes to be distributed much more widely – or to put it another way, our human earthly agents become multitudes. And as our understanding of what counts as agency opens up, we begin to see that what matters is not only the surfaces and volumes of the Earth, but the dynamical processes through which the planet as it appears to us is shaped, sustained and reformed.

## Domestic Geology

As an ancient Middle Eastern text reminds us, human collectives have been aware for some time of the way that their interventions in the Earth move across layers or volumes:

> Iron is taken out of the earth, and copper is smelted out of the ore. Man sets an end to darkness, and searches out, to the furthest bound, the stones of obscurity and of thick darkness. ... As for the earth, out of it comes bread; Underneath it is turned up as it were by fire. (Book of Job 28:2–5, *World English Bible*)

It is time to push this understanding further, and while we are at it, to complicate the gender relations characteristic of the Old Testament. The techniques and practices that made it possible for North-Western Europeans to put the resources of the Carboniferous stratum to work in the late eighteenth to nineteenth centuries had been a long time in the making. As historian Jack Goody reminds us, high-heat technologies have been shuttling across the Eurasian continent for centuries – and more often from East to West than the reverse. Until well into the eighteenth century, he notes, Europe lagged behind China in the development of kilns and furnaces and their use in mass production, the Chinese having been using coal for iron smelting and ceramic firing on an industrial scale for at least five centuries (Goody 2012: 305, 175, 218). Unsurprisingly, the practice of ironing in imperial China seems to have long preceded its European counterpart, with evidence that the Chinese were using metal pans filled with hot coals for smoothing fabric over a thousand years ago (Wang 1982: 207).

Far Eastern leadership in high-heat technology appears to go back to at least 1500 BCE, by which stage artisans were attaining kiln temperatures well over 1,200 °C, enabling the manufacture of both glazed stoneware and cast iron (Goody 2012: 165–6). Prior to that, the centre of metallurgy and other kiln-based technologies was the Middle East. Archaeologist Aslihan Yener (2000: 67, 126) speaks of a mid- to late-third-millennium BCE 'technical and industrial explosion' in metal production that occurred when advances made by metalworking nomads of the plateaus found novel outlets in the burgeoning lowland agricultural centres.

But the employment of intense heat to transmute minerals and ores can be seen as more than just a means of making use of stratified geologic matter. When ancient craftspeople cranked their kilns or furnaces up to 1,200–1,300 °C, metallurgical historian J. E. Rehder notes, they were reaching temperatures that contemporary volcanologists estimate to be the maximum heat of lava (Rehder 2000: 54). Effectively, as they melted and recrystallized rock, metamorphosed minerals, formed new compounds, decomposed and concentrated metallic ores in their furnaces, artisans were beginning to reproduce the very igneous and metamorphic geologic processes that forge and transform the rocky matter of the Earth's crust (Clark 2018a).

In stepping back from discrete inventions in specific places in this way, we are not letting go of the question of context or situatedness. Rather we are opening up what counts as situation or context, by acknowledging that significant developments tend to inherit whole lineages or 'phyla' of techniques that have emerged out of widely distributed bodies of skill and experimentalism. The high-heat expertise at the heart of European industrialization was underpinned by knowledge about the chambering of fire and its metamorphic potential that had been gradually accrued by artisans dispersed over several continents and a great many generations. As such, they are an example of what we are calling 'earthly multitudes': collectives, lineages, networks of know-how associated with dwelling amidst the variegation and volatility of the Earth. This resonates with political theorist Jane Bennett's reflections on the theme of metals and metalworking. As she observes: 'metal is always metallurgical, always an alloy of the endeavours of many bodies, always something worked on by geological, biological, and often human agencies. And human metalworkers are themselves emergent effects of the vital materiality they work' (2010: 60).

Like Bennett's metallurgists, our earthly multitudes do something more than just put the Earth and its resources to work. As we turn our attention to the ways that different peoples or groups articulate with specific planetary processes, what comes into relief is the way they 'become with' the dynamics of the Earth. We see how certain kinds of ecological and geological forces come to be corralled, incorporated and elaborated upon by human actors – and how these actors fashion and refashion themselves in the processes of joining forces with earthly dynamism (see Grosz 2008; 2011: 189). But working with kilns, furnaces and industrial heat engines is just one set of ways of enfolding elemental powers. The other half of our story – the manufacture of threads and textiles – draws us in to a different, but no less momentous, set of collective articulations with the Earth.

As we have suggested, textiles are every bit as central to North-Western Europe's Industrial Revolution as steam power or furnaces. Integral to accelerating production of threads and fabric is a succession of machines: the flying shuttle, the water frame, the spinning jenny, the spinning mule, the power loom and the cotton gin (Plant 1997: 64; Barber 1994: 62–3). In turn, these more conspicuously 'mechanical' developments have earlier and more widely distributed lineages. This includes the manual spinning wheel, believed to have been invented in the Middle East around the early eleventh century and adopted in China soon after (Pacey 1990: 23–4), and a much more ancient series of weighted and axled spindles (Barber 1994: 76). Braudel refers to the loom as '[t]he most complex human engine of all' (1981: 337), while Plant makes a convincing case that weaving on the loom is the primordial form of all subsequent automated machinery (1997: 60–9, 189–91).

Just as we can view the chambered fire of the furnace as a literal domestication of the rock-forming and transforming power of geology, so too can we conceive of the textile arts as a kind of capture of and elaboration upon the constitutive forces of ecological systems – and by extension Earth systems. For Barber the crafts of spinning, weaving and sewing are variations on the basic process of twisting filaments together to make string or cord – which she suggests may well be one of the most world-altering inventions of our species: an innovation 'that enabled us to move out into every econiche on the globe during the Upper Palaeolithic' (1994: 45). In important regards, as we intimated earlier in the chapter, anthropogenic twisted fibre is a variation on the theme of the dense networking of cellulose chains that gives plant tissues their strength and suppleness. Sadie Plant is our inspiration for pushing this idea further:

> When weavers interlace their threads, they jump into the middle of techniques which have already emerged among tangled lianas, inter-woven leaves, twisted stems, bacterial mats, birds' nests and spider's webs, matted fleeces, fibers, and furs .... plaiting, weaving, and the spinning they imply draw on threads which are already assembling themselves. (1997: 80–1)

Anthropologist Tim Ingold offers a similarly inspirational take on the broader ecological significance of twisted fibre, in his reflection on the way that the winding together of strands in the process of string-making and spinning creates a dynamic equilibrium between two or more spirals with contrary forces. These dynamics, Ingold observes, recur at multiple scales in the organic world: 'Bodies are wound and held together in much the same way. They are a tissue of twisted fibres at every level of resolution from the DNA of the chromosomes to the coils of the guts, and to the vocal cords and heartstrings' (Ingold 2013: 121).

It is no coincidence that ecological thinking is replete with metaphors of interlocking, entanglement, intermeshing, entwinement and networking – figurations of complexity that echo and inherit Charles Darwin's famous depiction of 'an entangled bank' at the close of *The Origin of Species* (Darwin 1859: 498). So too should we add that the idea of feedback loops – pivotal to understanding the dynamics of complex systems – resonates with the looping operation that generates the warp threads through which the weft then shuttles back and forth.

In short, the craft of weaving can be seen as an extrapolation from two basic form-building processes of the living world that recur at multiple scales: the structure-generating capacity of binding together many similar units, and the dynamism that emerges when an array of different entities is organized into a working multiplicity. If the chambering of fire has been key to the social negotiation of the Earth's strata, then weaving and the related arts of cordage-making and knot-tying, basketry and net-making, sewing and knitting play variations on the theme of the complexity of living systems in ways that greatly enhance human capacities to intervene effectively in these systems.

To conceive of spinning, weaving and high-heat technics as ways of elaborating upon earthly dynamics, we would insist, in no way implies a repudiation of the call to socialize the Anthropocene. What it does encourage us to do, however, is to push questions of social difference back, deeper, further afield. And in the process, it prompts us to consider how social differentiation emerges with and through our 'multitudinous' ways of enfolding ourselves in the becoming of the Earth. Ironing, we are trying to show, looks and feels different when we situate it at the conjunction of deep, distributed lineages of planetary involvement.

In the ancient world, materials that issued from the artisanal furnace were shaped into the building material and implements that constructed the everyday spaces of urban life. So too did the glittering output of the high-heat crafts serve as objects of desire and as 'visual displays of identity' that signalled where and when people belonged in increasingly complex social worlds (Roberts et al. 2015; Clark and Yusoff 2014). Something very similar can be said of the products of spinning and weaving. 'Cloth, like clothing, provided a fine place for social messages', observes Barber (1994: 372). In the third and fourth millennia BCE, the growing use of coloured thread and proliferating garment types expressed the symbolic significance of clothing and textiles in burgeoning urban centres (1994: 315–18). As trade became increasingly important and ever more extensive, vital synergies emerged between textile and metals: 'Luxury goods such as fancy textiles and ornate metal vessels, manufactured in the growing cities, often paid for the new raw materials with which to make more, in a never-ending cycle' (1994: 420–2).

While the products of high heat and textile arts helped define social positioning in the earliest cities, the organization of the crafts themselves was also closely tied to social and gendered identity. According to Barber (1994: 178), archaeological evidence indicates that, aside from some cases of urban specialization, spinning and weaving have been overwhelmingly women's arts. On the other hand, transhistorical and transcultural accounts of metallurgy suggest that until very recently it has been a universally male domain (Haaland 2007–8).

But thinking with and through the geological dimensions of 'work' – if we follow it through – can also complicate these otherwise rather predictably gendered divisions of labour. Archaeometallurgists conjecture that the smelting of metals was most probably an accidental derivative of ceramics, a craft that is in turn linked to the daily experience of the cooking hearth or oven (Aitchison 1960: 9) – situating it very much in the female domain. It is the hearth, so much maligned in second-wave feminist thought, that metallurgical theorists elect as the crux of an emergent explorative attitude towards the properties of minerals and ores: 'Its walls', speculates Theodore Wertime, 'were a self-registering pyrometer showing in their colors and hardness the degrees of temperature attained as well as the oxidizing or reducing atmospheres' (1973: 672).

In this way, as we dig ever deeper into the history of human appropriation and refining of biogeophysical agency, what we find happening is not the receding of questions of social identity, but their reformulation. Whereas narrower-gauge histories, critical and otherwise, tend to position women labouring in factories or households as being at the receiving end of epoch-making developments, a deep excavation of the logics of tapping into dynamical Earth and life processes brings into focus, in Barber's deft turn of phrase, 'another culture overflowing with women's courtyard arts' (1994: 229).

In fact, if we really want to understand the primordial sources of the gathering geopower that may have eventually tilted the Earth system out of Holocene conditions, it makes a lot of sense to attend to the long evolution of chambered fire and textile manufacture – both of which look to have emerged out of artisanal experimentation by women (Barber 1994: 191, 229). This is not a question of blame. As we suggested in the previous chapter, the ultimate impacts of any truly novel innovation in tapping into or joining forces with the Earth defy prediction. Moreover, we need to view the trajectories and developments that eventually came to weigh upon the Earth system as socially selected canalizations of a much broader or 'multitudinous' array of possibilities opened up by unprecedented interventions in self-ordering material processes. And this in turn means that the potentiality unlocked by the earthly multitudes in question may be far from exhausted.

## (Un)Earthing Gender

In this chapter we set out from ironing not simply in reference to its iconically troubled status in feminist critiques of domestic labour, but because of the way that the application of heated metal to organic fibres offers a good example of how human agency can hinge together the depths and surfaces of the Earth. Tracking the gradual emergence of this agency shows us at once how social capacities to impact at geophysical scales have gradually emerged out of vast, distributed platforms and how this agency incorporates different aspects of the dynamical processes that structure the planetary body.

But we are not yet done with our abyssal archaeology of the arts that make the practice and technics of ironing possible. As we have already intimated, the deepest recoverable origins of the technics of both high heat and textiles take us beyond the bounds of the sedentary, urban existence that goes by the name of 'civilization' and deep into prehistory. As we move backwards out of the Holocene and into the Pleistocene epoch, the very operations of the Earth – as geoscience narratives inform us – become increasingly erratic and changeable. We are moving into 'deep time', as it is often shorthanded.

These are also terrains in which social identities – gender identities in particular – seem to be shifting or in the making. Thus far in this chapter, for all that we have been dealing with differentially gendered contributions to the emergence of new forms of geopower, we have still been speaking of gender as if we more or less knew what the categories 'female' and 'male' stand for from the outset. What happens to our thinking about gender, then, as we venture into deep time? As archaeologists Olga Soffer, James Advasio and David Hyland remind us, 'gender differences in the past need to be demonstrated rather than assumed' (Soffer et al. 2000: 523). We need to be mindful too that the material traces from which such differences must be reconstructed are scant and enigmatic. With these provisos in mind, we turn to realms where shifting gender identities, new modes of engaging with geologic and life processes, and 'deep' planetary transformations appear tantalizingly co-present.

The oldest known purpose-built structures for containing and intensifying fire were unearthed in the 1920s at the Dolni Věstonice and Pavlov sites in what is now the Czech Republic. Dated at 28,000–24,000 BCE, these prototypical kilns would have been constructed deep within the last Pleistocene ice age. Indeed, the settlements to which they belong are likely to have been close to the edge of the great northern ice sheets. Here, as one commentator puts it, semi-nomadic peoples would have been 'scratching out a living on a semi-frozen landscape' (Whitehouse 2000). But that living is beginning to look like rather more than bare subsistence.

Dolni Věstonice–Pavlov provides the earliest evidence yet discovered of the intentional use of chambered heat to transform the structure of inorganic matter – but what is remarkable about the site is the profligacy of its productions. Archaeologists have recovered some 10,000 fired objects, including a number of 'Venus' female figurines – the oldest known ceramic human representations – as well as various animal figures and a profusion of pellets, tubules and amorphous shapes. Fashioned from glacial loess soils and baked at 500–800 °C, these primordial fired-earth works reveal considerable 'control over materials technology' (Vandiver et al. 1989: 1008). And yet there is no trace of vessels, or anything of any discernible utility. This absence of functionality has led researchers to speculate whether the superabundant trove of fired objects may have more to do with ritual or performance than any valorization of the actual product (Vandiver et al. 1989).

What we are looking at in the complex of practices disclosed here is the forging of a new kind of geopower: a capacity to conjure enduring objects out of bare earth. If this is women's work – as the gendering of the hearth would suggest – its non-utilitarian nature and sheer extravagance seem to point in very different directions from the drudgery of later domestic labour. But if we are seeking the hazy outlines of high-heat technology that would eventually lead – in one of its many trajectories – to modern mechanized household 'heat work', there are other material traces at Dolni Věstonice–Pavlov worthy of attention. In the 1990s, archaeologists working at these sites identified patterns pressed into fired and unfired clay as the impression of woven fabrics. Over seventy clay fragments have been recovered bearing traces of cordage and textiles that appear to be woven from plant fibres. As Soffer and her colleagues elaborate: 'the relatively wide range of textile gauges and weaves suggests mats, perhaps wall hangings, blankets, and bags, as well as a wide array of apparel forms including shawls, shirts, skirts, and sashes' (2000: 513). Moreover, Soffer et al. attest that the finest of the weaves preserved in clay are comparable with those of contemporary machine-woven cotton and linen-wear, which is indicative that looms rather than hand twining would have been required (2000: 524).

As well as pushing the origins of weaving back some 15,000 years beyond previous estimates, this research has helped transform understandings of Upper Palaeolithic material culture and especially the role and significance of women's work (Soffer and Adovasio 2014; Soffer 2004). Bringing together analysis of weaving and sewing with reflection on the co-present 'Venus' figurines and kindred figures from other Upper Palaeolithic sites, Soffer, Advasio and Hyland suggest that what we can witness here are the material traces of the very process of 'constructing female identities' (Soffer et al. 2000: 523). While well aware of various and contested interpretations of the famously voluptuous figurines, Soffer et al. suggest that the way some of these figures are clothed and adorned, the quality of the textile work now coming to light, and the labour-intensive efforts devoted to decoration and bodily adornment demonstrate the high value in Upper Palaeolithic collectivities of women's lives and their work. As Soffer et al. conclude: 'we are dealing with gendered technologies that assign the production of valuables to women's labor' (2000: 524).

For us, then, what the ceramic record of cloth-making from the Dolni Věstonice–Pavlov sites suggests is that high heat and textiles did not simply gravitate towards each other, over great stretches of time, and with world-altering effects. Rather, they were mutually implicated at their earliest discernible beginnings. In other words, there seems to be an originary complication between the human channelling of igneous and metamorphic geology, and human interventions in the complex entanglements of organic ecologies.

Taking inspiration from the work of Soffer and her colleagues, we would also suggest that these interventions in 'geologic life' are more than matters of early divisions of labour between women's and men's work. What we may be dealing with, in shadowy and irrecuperable ways, is the crystallization of certain kinds of gendered identity. Whatever their precise meanings, the Venus figurines (they have few, if any, discernibly male counterparts) viewed in conjunction with fabric arts are, 'a medium for active construction of social identity' (Lesure 1997: 229). As the oldest identified use of shaped and fired earth materials to represent the human body, the Dolni Věstonice–Pavlov figures represent geopower literally set to the task of fashioning gendered social selves.

In turn, we can fold this capture and extrapolation of geopotentiality into its deep time context: an epoch in which, in the words of climatologist Richard Alley, 'climate was wobbling wildly' (2000: 3). In her deep history of women's crafts, Barber presciently makes the connection with environmental volatility. Finding profuse creativity where we might logically expect to see hard-scrabble survivalism, she observes: 'forty thousand years ago, as the great ice sheets that had covered the northern continents retreated by fits and starts, humans started to invent and make new things at a tremendous rate' (1994: 87). To this we can add that the material creativity and self-construction we glimpse at Dolni Věstonice–Pavlov – in the shadow of mobile ice caps – took windblown glacial soils and fast-shifting biota as its media. If in ways that defy full recovery and calibration, what we witness here are earthly multitudes striking out on novel pathways of geological becoming from the very midst of the violent exertions of planetary multiplicity. And these lineages of collective expression, we suggest, are at once modes of human creativity voiced through the materials of the Earth and forms of planetary generativity embodied in the medium of human activity.

## Why Planetary Social Thought?

Ironing interminable piles of laundered textile is a contingent outcome of two great lineages of material-energetic technics whose trajectories, in geological terms, take us out of the proposed new geological epoch, through the eleven or so millennia of the Holocene, and into the depths of the Pleistocene. Every run of a hot iron across crumpled fabric can be seen as a small, prosaic rehearsal of a hinging together of the depths and surfaces of the planet, a convergent harnessing of the dynamic processes that compose the Earth's living envelope and its geological strata.

To conclude, we want briefly to reflect upon the value of thinking social identities, their formation and their trajectories, through the dynamic processes of the Earth – or planetary multiplicity. We offer three reasons why, faced with the current global planetary predicament, it might be timely to think about human collective life in terms of its negotiations with the Earth's surface and depths, its implication in the dynamics of the planet, and its situatedness in the deep time of the Earth.

First, if we are interested in understanding how (some) humans acquired the capacity to transform Earth systems, then it makes sense to address the long series of geohistorical developments through which our species has, step by step, turn by turn, fold by fold, accrued its geologic power. As we saw in chapter 2, this is more than a matter of identifying causal pathways and attributing blame; it should also entail looking at the various ways that we have joined forces with the powers, properties and potentialities of the Earth. We need the broad spectrum and the very *longue durée* so that, rather than seeing ourselves as social beings who at some late stage turn our attention Earthward, we can make sense of ourselves as emerging *as* social beings through our interactions with fire and minerals, plants and fibres, ecological systems and geologic strata. As we have sought to demonstrate in this chapter, identifying where the agency and innovation lie in a mundane practice like ironing looks very different when we step back from the immediate socio-material context and begin to trace the deep history through which it became possible to work confidently with high heat and to bring it to bear on fabrics derived from plant fibre. To conceive of ourselves as earthly multitudes, in this way, is to foster attention to deep-seated and wide-ranging networks of practice and knowhow. And as we suggest in the following chapter, such 'excavations' raise poignant questions about our indebtedness to those, human and otherwise, who have come before us.

Second, an extended gaze can and should unsettle the focus of much social inquiry on a modernity defined and contoured by four to five centuries of European or Euro-Atlantic global ascent. Although the examples at the core of this chapter focused mostly on gender, it is also notable that as we expanded our gaze, the narrative shifted from North America and Europe to the far east of the Eurasian continent, and then to the Middle East, and finally to the western end of the Eurasian ice age steppes. With more room to elaborate on this tale, we would have dwelled further on other centres of high-heat technology, such as the Sub-Saharan complex of iron smelting and forging. In short, a journey into the implication of social life with planetary dynamics by no means leads straight to unacknowledged universalism: if sustained and detailed, it is more likely to draw us towards provincialization – both social and physical – of whatever region we set out from. This is, however, a complex, fraught and perhaps interminable process – one to which we return in more detail in following chapters.

Third, what is at stake at the contemporary juncture is not just the question of how to derail the dominant global order from its blatantly unsustainable trajectory, or a matter of which societal forces needed to be singled out for blame – however necessary this might be. It is also a matter of imagining and beginning to construct alternative, speculative modes of 'geologic life', as Yusoff (2013) puts it. More than an issue of how to reduce our expenditure of energetic-material reserves on domestic labour that is 'never done', or a matter of lessening our dependence on fossil biomass or subterranean ores, it is a question of what planetary dynamics we might yet join or rejoin forces with. By tracking the lineage of everyday socio-material practices across continents and into distant evolutionary and geological epochs, we do not simply arrive at a moment of originary purity and plenitude. This was Donna Haraway's point when she famously concluded her Cyborg Manifesto by proclaiming 'I would rather be a cyborg than a goddess' (Haraway 1991b: 181). Significantly, she premised this by saying '[t]hough both are bound in the spiral dance'. Focusing on earthly multitudes, to put it another way, is a prompt to explore pathways that may have been sidetracked, undervalued, overwritten: a provocation to reconsider the human multiplicity that is bound up with the multiplicity inherent in planetary processes.

Weaving and high-heat technology, we contend, have been key crafts or technologies throughout the Holocene and will probably remain so in whatever future we are entering. By spiralling back through time to an emergent moment of fabric-making and high-heat artisanship – where kiln-fired votive figures gesture towards the metallic circuitry of the cyborg-to-come – our aim is not to rewind human history to a safer, fairer, more innocent juncture but to foreground an originary complication. It is to offer an example of how a near-extraordinary potentiality may lie in what seem like ordinary or mundane sites: to show how an almost inconceivable creativity arose at a time and place where we might too easily see only bare, hard-scrabble subsistence. Most of all it is to show how a generative and promising futurity is opened up rather than foreclosed when human agency is implicated in the structural richness and complex dynamics of the Earth.

To keep on spiralling back, downwards, into the depths of the Earth and out into space is to remind ourselves of the contingency of our morphological and evolutionary being. But so too is it intended as a reminder that this is a planet of multiple layerings and changeable operating states, and that however much damage some of our species have caused we still dwell amongst an excess of possibility. In the following chapter, we pick up where we left off in our exploration of the deep structure of the Earth – as one of many planets – and use this as an entry point to consider in more detail what we mean by planetary social thought.

# What is Planetary Social Thought?

## Introduction: Hard Rain

What appears before us, for the first time, is a blue pearl-like sphere surrounded by the inky blackness of space. The planet, swathed in clouds, stands out from the dark void that surrounds it, radiant, life-like, fragile.

But looks can be deceiving. The planet is not Earth but HD 189733b, discovered by astronomers on 6 October 2005 orbiting a sun some sixty-three light years away from our own solar system (Howell 2013). Its atmosphere has been extensively analysed using a combination of high- and low-resolution instruments, both from Earth and from space. Monitoring of visible light by two different techniques confirmed that the exoplanet would appear bluish to the human eye, though it's important to keep in mind that the image we see is a graphic reconstruction, not a photograph. Rather than coming from the reflection of liquid oceans, astrophysicists suggest, this cobalt blue coloration is generated by atmospheric clouds dense with silicate particles. Winds, it is estimated, spiral around the planet at over five thousand miles an hour, driving silicate shards in a howling horizontal rain. This would make a typical moment on the surface of HD 189733b akin to being caught in the midst of an exploding plate-glass window. The planet, scientists conclude, has low prospects for extraterrestrial life.

Despite a passing resemblance, aided perhaps by artistic licence, HD 189733b and Earth are very different astronomical bodies. Recent discoveries, made possible by new techniques of apprehending distant astronomical bodies from vehicles in space and from the Earth's surface, are disclosing the variety of planets and the range of solar systems (Summers and Trefil 2017). In this way, exoplanet research is beginning to liberate astronomical science from geocentric thinking. Whereas critical social thinkers have long been engrossed in the implications of viewing the Earth from space, exoplanet inquiry suggests that it is at least as important to question how we have viewed space from the parochial perspective of our own planet and solar system.

While we sympathize with the idea that in our current global environment crisis 'there is no Planet B', there are good reasons to reflect on the expanding alphabet and grammar of celestial bodies. More than just disclosing the sheer diversity of planetary types, a more inclusive vision of planetarity prompts us to think about planets in new ways: helping us to see planets as a specific kind of being, and posing questions of what a planet is and what planets are capable of doing. This in turn sets the scene for any attempt to make sense of what our own planet might be turning into at the current juncture.

In the previous chapter we ended up looking at the formative processes of the Earth, having started from an all-too-familiar pile of steaming laundry. In this chapter we set out from the screaming storms of an alien planet and work our way back to the agency of beings who are recognizably ourselves. Whichever direction we are moving in, our intent is the same: to view the contemporary human predicament in the context of our planet's capacity to self-differentiate or become other than it is.

As we approach the middle of the book, we take stock of the journey so far and explain our notion of 'planetary social thought' in more detail. After laying out some of the assumptions behind our rethinking of the human *through* a dynamic, self-differentiating planet, we disassemble planetary social thought into two component parts that have been introduced in earlier chapters. First we discuss 'planetary multiplicity': our way of describing an astronomical body with the inherent capacity to become otherwise; to reorganize its constituent parts – at multiple scales – into new arrangements. We then set out four methodological devices that we use when discussing different examples in the book. Then we turn to 'earthly multitudes': our term for how humans group themselves around specific engagements with the self-ordering matter-energy of which the Earth is comprised.

Our aim is not simply to ramp up the dangers posed by a planet-in-transition to its inhabitants, but to give a sense of the depth and diversity of the ways in which humans have accommodated themselves to the inconstancy of the Earth and to the flows and structures that are generated by planetary dynamics. As much as it is a matter of learning how to see our planet in new ways, this is also about conceiving of ourselves – of our own difference or differential becoming – in the context of a planet that is capable of becoming other to itself.

## What is a Planet?

It is notable that with all the interest in planet-sized thinking in recent years – planetary management and governance, planetary politics, planetary urbanism – there is still little explicit engagement with the question of what a planet is and what manner of planet birthed a creature such as ourselves. The burgeoning field of exoplanet studies, we have been suggesting, provides new incentives for considering planets as a category of being and as sites of becoming. Not only providing novel evidence of the different ways astronomical bodies are structured or composed, comparative planetology helps us to see planets as historical beings – entities whose states and trajectories change over time, worlds that become capable of doing things they could not do before.

For astrophysicists, a planet is a body composed of condensed, classical baryonic matter ('normal' atoms), comprising a range of chemical elements and existing typically at a thermal mid-range between the cold of space and the intense heat of stars. Beginning as a relatively undifferentiated cloud of atoms and particles around a forming star, planets coalesce into dense, approximately spherical bodies with their own gravitational fields. Planets come to dominate an orbital region around their star: as a planet forms and creates a large gravity well, it typically moves around, clearing out smaller objects in the vicinity, eventually settling down into an orbit that is relatively stable over long timescales.

According to the definition agreed by the International Astronomical Union, planets are also gravitationally collapsed and differentiated. In terms of their internal structure, as they coalescence, gravity and chemical properties determine how a planet organizes itself into differentiated strata and compartments. In the processes of gravitational collapse, diverse chemical elements find their level in the congealing planetary body and adopt different phase states (solid, liquid, gas, mineral type) according to the temperature and pressure in that part of the planet.

By such processes, mature planets may become largely closed to exchanges of matter – but they nevertheless typically remain energetically open, which is to say that they are subjected to flows of energy over long timescales from their parent star and their own interior, in the form of electromagnetic radiation and heat respectively (Szerszynski 2019c: 225). For planets that retain fluid compartments, whether these are gas giants like Jupiter with their massive atmospheres of hydrogen and helium, or smaller, rocky or 'terrestrial' planets like Earth with lower layers of hot, molten rock and upper layers of cooler ocean and atmosphere, this constant flow of energy prevents the planet from ever completing a descent to quiet equilibrium and encourages the fluid and solid compartments to come into dynamic relation with each other (Frank et al. 2017). And in a way, even on a planet without life, the different parts of such a planet thus start to 'sense' each other (Margulis 1998; Clarke and Hansen 2009).

The constant flow of energy also activates thermodynamic imperatives within the body of the planet that make it prone to revolutionary and often irreversible shifts from one state to another in a cascade of symmetry-breaking bifurcations (DeLanda 2002: 17, 20). At any stage or moment in the geohistory of a planet many possibilities remain unrealized; but when particular pathways emerge, particular patterns become established that make certain things much more likely to happen.

Some planets are nevertheless very different from the Earth, or even from our near neighbours in the solar system. We already know from studying our own solar system that planets and moons can have subsurface oceans, often under miles of ice but kept warm enough to remain fluid through tidal interactions with other bodies around them. And some planets – indeed perhaps most planets – are 'rogue' or 'orphan' planets, not linked to any star at all but travelling through interstellar space. Some of these would have formed like a star, but gathered insufficient mass to start nuclear fusion, instead becoming a huge gas giant planet, or 'brown dwarf'. Other rogue planets will have been formed within a planetary system around a new star, but then been ejected through gravitational encounters with other planets in the system. Rogue planets – and any moons around them – would not receive a constant supply of energy to their surface from a nearby star, but could nevertheless receive enough energy from residual heat, radioactive decay and tidal forces to prolong their passage to equilibrium and allow them to realize some of their own potentialities – perhaps even biological life. But such starless systems would be dark, with activity concentrated deep within the planet and/or its moons (Summers and Trefil 2017: 101–10).

For us, if the substitution of more 'situated' or 'place-based' perspectives on the Earth for god's-eye visions fail to take into consideration the specificity of our planet and its particular trajectory, then they may not be much of an improvement. The very fact that we as carbon-based life forms inhabit a planetary surface, with our feet on relatively firm ground and our world illuminated by a sun, should not be taken for granted.

Even when our focus is largely on living worlds, we should consider the possibility that organisms found on other planets may not be carbon-based, the likelihood that extraterrestrial life will be located well beneath planetary surfaces, and even that some life may have evolved on 'rogue' planets that are not circling suns. Or as Summers and Trefil put it, in the process of questioning our geocentrism we must also query our 'carbon chauvinism', 'surface chauvinism' and 'stellar chauvinism' (2017: 18–19) – for which both exoplanet science and speculative fiction can be very useful provocations.

We have been drawing attention to the fact that, while there are common dynamics in planetary formation, each planet develops along its own trajectory – and is to this extent unique. Planets, we are arguing, are multiple not just in contrast to each other but in terms of their own history. The 'multi' in planetary multiplicity, in other words, does not simply divide planets from each other but also divides them *from themselves*. Before circling back on our take on the concept of multiplicity, we will take a turn through the specific trajectory of the Earth – of which our own genus and species are one (unlikely) outcome.

## The Earth Thus Far

To pick up questions we broached in the introduction to the book: 'when' and 'where' is our planet at? With its plentiful liquid water and life-sustaining mildness, much has been made of the Earth's 'Goldilocks' positioning not too near and not too far from its star. But as the variety of exoplanets makes itself felt, it is becoming more apparent that the Earth's location, rather tautologically, is really only the optimum for it to be the kind of planet we know and love (Summers and Trefil 2017: 15–16). The new appreciation of planetary diversity similarly has implications for the question of when the Earth is at in its evolving geostory.

As we saw in chapter 1, Earth systems theorists and evolutionary biologists have depicted the Earth system passing through a series of 'revolutionary' transformations characterized by increasing complexity of biological organization and ever more efficient biogeochemical cycling. But contingent events coupled with matter's self-organizing powers had already made much of the young planet before the appearance of life. Gravitational collapse performed its sorting work on the chemical elements of the coalescing planet, giving rise to a series of alternating solid and fluid volumes in dynamic relation with each other. Like any other consolidating planet, proto-Earth swallowed many competing planetesimals, including – according to one popular hypothesis – the smaller would-be planet Theia with which it collided. As well as forming the moon, the Theia catastrophe gifted Earth with a huge boost of dense metal, cemented to its own metallic core by the pull of gravity (Hazen 2012: 42–5).

The Theia episode serves as a reminder both that there have been crucial junctures at which the Earth system has been open to its cosmic environment and that our local geostory encompasses the full volume of the planet. Though it's informed by astro-diversity, Summers and Trefil's chiding about surface chauvinism has lessons for apprehending our home planet. Around 15 per cent of the volume of the mature Earth is made up of its metallic core, and most of the rest of the planet is comprised of the mantle – a slowly churning mix of seething, viscous rock. That means that only about 1 per cent of the planetary volume comprises crustal rock – the thin, brittle excrescence of which geoscientists know a great deal more than all the other layers combined. And so, however important the Earth system might be for those of us who participate in it, from a deep planetary perspective it is, in the words of palaeontologist Richard Fortey, a 'gloss on the surface' (2005: 415).

Geoscientists believe Earth to be the only planet in the solar system where the transfer of heat and material in the mantle is dynamic enough to be constantly resculpting topographical features (Zalasiewicz 2008: 14–18). What are, at least in terms of our own solar system, exceptionally active plate tectonics are driven by the vast self-organized system of convection currents in the mantle layer – and it remains a matter of some contention whether it took hundreds of millions or several billion years for this subterranean heat engine to assemble itself. So too is it open to question what terrestrial life would be like were this interior motor less powerful. 'Earth's pattern of natural selection and evolution is driven in part by the fact that plate tectonics is constantly shifting the geography of the planet', observe Summers and Trefil. 'We can ask, however, what evolution would look like on a world without a constantly changing surface' (2017: 17).

By the close of the Hadean eon some 600 million years after the congealing of the planetary body, there are already hints of biotic life on the outermost Earth. For the next several billion years, the biosphere was dominated by prokaryotes: microscopic, mostly single-celled organisms with relatively simple cell structures (Margulis and Sagan 1995: 68–72). Evidence suggests that eukaryotes – organisms with more complex cellular structures including a membrane-enclosed nucleus and other distinct 'organelles' – emerged in marine environments around 2.3 billion years ago. The eukaryotic Earth was a biogeographically uniform planet, still largely at the mercy of externally imposed physical and chemical conditions, and characterized by low diversification, low extinction and slow evolution. With the rise of metazoa – multicellular animals with differentiated tissues – came a new form of biospheric metastability generated dynamically from high levels of biomass and energy use, extensive nutrient recycling, fast evolution, high diversification and episodic extinction events (Butterfield 2007).

Crucial to the planetary reorganization was the unprecedented capacity of mobile metazoa to move nutrients across gradients and boundaries in the Earth system. Apart from being the first of the multicellular kingdoms to emerge, and even though (on the land at least) their mass was to be swamped by that of land plants, their presence played a crucial role in developing the complex ecological nets of the current geological eon. 'Animals', it has been argued, 'figure disproportionately in the maintenance of the modern Earth System, not least because they invented it' (Butterfield 2011: 87).

One of the key contributions of animals to the Earth system is their capacity for locomotion to a predetermined point, powered by energy stored within the moving body itself – a radically new form of motion in a planetary sense. In evolving metazoa, new forms of sensory mechanism were closely linked to mobility. Animals developed proprioception – an awareness of their body in space and time (Sheets-Johnstone 1999). The search for food and sexual partners provides the pressure to move towards and engage with other organisms, favouring bilaterality (having a front and a back), and eventually cephalization – the concentration of sensory equipment towards the newly 'front' end (Szerszynski 2016a). In this regard, metazoic powered 'locomotion' and attendant sensorial transformations provide us with another case in which we need to provincialize our thinking – this time in relation to body form, mobility and sensing. Which is to say: we need to suspend any assumption that we motile animals should be the measure of all things, and so avoid presuming that anything which does not move 'under its own steam' suffers from some kind of metaphysical privation.

We are not going to dwell on the long sequence of planetary and extra-planetary events – many of them improbable – that led to the emergence of primates and ultimately the genus *Homo*. However, there are two aspects of the geostory we have been telling that seem especially pertinent. One is the way that certain lines of development of bilaterality and cephalization eventually resulted in the freeing up of the mouth and hands as organs of expression in our primate lineage. Human language and dexterity, that is, inherit a long chain of metazoic extrapolation on the theme of mobility and proprioception.

The other is the continued contribution of convection-driven crustal instability to the lifeworld of ancestral hominins. Palaeoanthropologists are now affording increasing significance to the evidence that the genus *Homo* branched into emergence in the midst of the largest, most long-lived fracture zone on the Earth's surface: a zone characterized by 'complex tectonics and intense volcanism' (King and Bailey 2015: 277). The escarpments, lava outcrops, pooling water bodies and fertile sedimentary basins of the East African Rift Valley, observe geophysicist Geoffrey King and archaeologist Geoff Bailey, offered a propitious environment for agile but otherwise defenceless primates – while the major pathways of human migration across and beyond Africa appear to have followed tectonically and volcanically active zones (2015: 276–9).

Most social thinkers would agree that there are many possible ways to tell the human story. Sooner or later the question arises as to the human capacity for complex story-telling that involves reflection upon the world – or as Martin Heidegger put it, how we came to be especially 'rich in world'. As literary theorist Claire Colebrook elaborates, '[t]o be rich in world is not only to have a sense of the here and now but to have a sense of other possible worlds' (2019: 178). The version of this narrative that we have been relating so far is one that eschews preconceived notions of human 'richness in world' in favour of implicating the accomplishments of our genus and species within the Earth's own capacity to move between possible worlds – or what we are calling planetary multiplicity.

The other-worldliness of the Earth itself – its capacity for self-differentiation – has made for a long, complex and fraught journey. One way to conceive of the trajectory across thresholds and through critical junctures is in terms of the planet itself working out solutions to certain challenges or problems: to view new forms of self-organization as a response to shifting forces and pressures both within and from beyond. The evolution of convection currents in the mantle is a response to heat rising from the interior, the interaction between mantle convection and the Earth system operates as 'a gigantic machine for producing strata' (Zalasiewicz 2008: 17, 14–15), while the circulation of surface fluids of atmosphere and hydrosphere serves as a giant engine for redistributing the solar flux (Kleidon 2016). Carbon-based life itself can be seen as a way to speed up the exchange of electrons between hydrogen and carbon dioxide (Summers and Trefil 2017: 163–4).

We will be returning to the theme of how the self-ordering capacities of a planet – and of matter more generally – are able to generate solutions to problems. At this stage, however, we want to make the point that there is more going on than the 'technicality' of problem-solving, and to caution against any sense that there is a closed set of options or an inevitable progression of planetary stages. Here it's worth recalling Deleuze and Guattari's counsel to 'be on our guard against any kind of ridiculous cosmic evolutionism' (1987: 49). Their point was not to deny that some things need to happen to make other things possible, but to remind us both that any complex developmental process contains more possibilities than can ever be actualized and that there will always be events that cut across and mix up orderly sequencing (see Protevi 2013; 47).

So too should we be wary of modes of story-telling – disapprovingly branded 'epic science' by physicist-turned-philosopher Martin Eger (1993) – in which the narratives of the social science and humanities are reduced to a slender addendum to multi-million-year sweeps of geophysical or cosmic development. What a planet does next is partially conditioned by what it has done before. But as Summers and Trefil make clear, our very capacity to generalize about planetary trajectories – especially where life is concerned – remain profoundly constrained by our over-reliance on a solitary case study (see also Waltham 2014), and indeed on a reliance on the empirical sciences to the exclusion of more speculative methods. What we do want to stress, however, is that it makes little sense to examine, weigh up and ruminate upon the end-of-Holocene event without locating it amidst the wrenching changes in the particular planetary body that brought us to the current juncture, just as it can be profoundly misleading to dissociate the history of our own astronomical body from the contextual richness of planets-in-plural. And this in turn means that the human difference and alterity so celebrated by social thinkers need to be situated within capacities to be otherwise that stretch far beyond the conventional range of the social science and humanities.

## Towards Planetary Social Thought

What resources are there within social thought that we can draw on to respond seriously to such a challenge – that can help us incorporate topics of thought that hitherto have been confined to the natural sciences? In this section we summarize some of the social and humanities thinking that we have found useful in this endeavour. But first of all we need to address a potential charge that is often levelled against social or philosophical thinkers who embrace insights from the natural sciences: of falling into 'scientism', taking scientific findings at face value, as given or beyond dispute.

Haraway, Latour and other science studies scholars are right to insist that scientific knowledge must pass through trials if it is to contribute to a judicious remaking of our collective realities. As we discussed in chapter 2, if scientific truth claims are to help us speak though the Earth, we must examine their contexts, interests and partialities – less in order to undermine or relativize them than to consider how they might be improved. Even then, it makes sense to keep our ontological fidelities provisional (see White 2000). For assessments will inevitably be made under conditions of incomplete information, or what Derrida (1992a) refers to as 'undecidability', all the more so when we are working outside our own spheres of expertise. So too should we be mindful of philosopher Reza Negarestani's insistence that to be 'rigorously inhuman' we must practise as well as profess ontological commitments to the content of the human, subjecting all our ideas of what it is to be human to incessant revision and elaboration (2014).

Our approach to planetary social thought is resolutely interdisciplinary; but this is not simply using social sciences and humanities modes of inquiry to add human creativity and invention. We would insist upon the creativity and invention inherent in physical worlds themselves – at every scale from the microscopic to the cosmic. In this regard, our angle on interdisciplinarity also draws on the suggestion by Derrida that natural science itself can be deconstructive, in the sense that the findings of the science themselves have in some cases begun to unsettle fundamental assumptions about the relationship of truth claims and reality, about who or what is a subject and who or what is an object (Kirby 2011: 5–7).

We have already noted the significance of Georges Bataille for our own project. One of the inspirations for Bataille's planetary or cosmological thinking, as we mentioned in chapter 2, was the early twentieth-century geochemist Vladimir Vernadsky – a physical scientist whose inquiries began to destabilize basic Western ideas about the distinction between matter and life. Rather than thinking about inorganic matter in terms of its lack of vital qualities, Vernadsky spoke of organisms as 'living matter', viewing the dynamism of life as a new kind of mobilization of the mineral realm that brought the Earth's crust into 'uninterrupted movement' (1998: 60–1). Or as Lynn Margulis and Dorion Sagan gloss Vernadsky: '[w]e are walking, talking minerals' (1995: 45). We can also catch glimpses of this way of deprioritizing the human or the living in recent Anthropocene science, for example when Zalasiewicz reflects that 'skyscrapers and coral reefs are basically large masses of biologically constructed rock' (2008: 171–2), or when he and his colleagues observe that 'we live in and drive on Anthropocene rock constructions that we call houses and roads' (2010: 2230).

But just as we can look at human and other life as a particular variation on the theme of organized matter or minerality, so too can we chip away at foundational dualities from the other direction. While he may not be the first theorist to come to mind when it comes to thinking through the planet, Jacques Derrida's notion that there is a play of differences or differential forces that far exceeds human writing and communication has been picked up and extended in interesting ways. In a searching reading of Derrida's notion of a generalized textuality, feminist social theorist Vicki Kirby asks whether we might see the Earth's self-differentiating tendencies as 'investigations of itself' – as evidence of a materiality or elementality that is 'as actively literate, numerate and inventive as anything we might include within Culture' (2011: 34, 66). Here too we can find anticipations of this kind of 'deconstructive' gesture in some scientific writings. While many Earth system or Gaian thinkers toy with the notion of humans imbuing the Earth's biosphere with novel capacities for self-sensing or self-knowing, Margulis has no hesitation in attributing to our planet itself the very cognitive capabilities conventionally taken as definitive of 'higher' organisms. '[T]he global nervous system certainly did not begin with the origin of people', she contends. 'Gaia, the physiologically regulated Earth, enjoyed proprioceptive global communication long before people evolved' (Margulis 1998: 142).

Another core component of our planetary social thought, as we also noted in chapter 2, is the 'geophilosophy' of Gilles Deleuze and Félix Guattari (1994). Taking issue with currents of twentieth-century philosophy that still considered the Earth to be the stable platform upon which human thought grounds its reflection on the world, their co-authored work sets out from assumptions of planetary instability (see Gasché 2014). Through their recognition that 'the earth constantly carries out a movement of deterritorialization on the spot', and by way of their sustained attention to the way that the Earth's relatively stable strata interact with more mobile flows of matter-energy, Deleuze and Guattari anticipate key concerns of contemporary Earth systems–geology collaborations (1994: 85). Moreover, in thematizing the frictions between the Earth's own deterritorializing impulses and the unrelenting investment of state powers in territorial boundedness, these authors divine what is perhaps the most pressing political-ethical quandary of the current global order.

While Deleuze and Guattari – as we will shortly see – are a crucial reference point for our concepts of planetary multiplicity and earthly multitudes, our concern with the suffering and loss that accompany planetary transition prompts us to take further ethico-political bearings from feminist, postcolonial and Derridean discourses. For as we turn in more detail to matters of self-organization, emergence and the generation of novelty, it is crucial to keep in mind that there is no 'newness' that is not also a loss of what previously existed, no potential for change that is not at the same time a kind of vulnerability and exposure. These are themes to which we will return in depth in chapters 5 and 7, focusing in particular on human communities and groups who have endured events so wrenching that they have been experienced as the ending of worlds.

## On Planetary Multiplicity

While the brief cosmic excursions opening this chapter began to flesh out the concept of planetary multiplicity introduced in chapter 1, here we lay out and make some advance on our conceptual debts. As a philosophical theme, multiplicity is born of searching interdisciplinary encounters around the issue of how change occurs or novelty emerges, across the full scope of settings or situations. In this way, it is couched as an alternative to long-standing predilections for identity thinking – a logic in which all that exists is viewed in terms of its derivation or deviation from some kind of original form.

While Bernhard Riemanns's mathematical concept of 'multiplicities' that are qualitative rather than numerical or quantitative is one tributary, thinking about multiplicity takes a more biological direction in the work of Henri Bergson. Bergson's take on evolutionary theory, as Deleuze would have it, is that 'life is production, creation of differences' (1988a: 98, 39). It is Deleuze who explicitly makes the concept of multiplicity central to his oeuvre, deploying it as a way to break with the old dyad of the one and the many and its echoes in dialectical reasoning (1988a: 44–6). More of a process than a state of being, Deleuzian multiplicity refers to the immanent generation of difference or novelty – especially through enfolding, as the derivation from the Latin *plicare* or fold indicates.

For Deleuze, as philosopher Jonathan Rajchman (2000: 60) explains: 'multiplicity is not what has many parts; it is what is "complicated", or folded many times over and in many ways so that there is no completely unfolded state, but only further bifurcations'. ('Bifurcation' derives from the Latin *furca* – a two-pronged fork.) Deleuze himself suggest that this applies not only to living systems but to matter-energy in general, extending 'finally [to] the Whole of the universe' (1988a: 77). Philosopher Gilbert Simondon develops a closely related theme of self-differentiating becoming 'a capacity beings possess of falling out of step with themselves ... of resolving themselves by the very act of falling out of step' (1992: 300–1)

More than a matter of the plurality and diversity of celestial bodies, our sense of planetary multiplicity refers to the capacity of planets to re-enfold or reorganize their constituent elements, to fall out of step with themselves – even turn into another planet entirely. As we explained in chapter 1, this is not just a characteristic of Anthropocene thinking, and thus uniquely tied to the effects of human society on the planet, but a common thread emerging from post-gradualist or neo-catastrophist science over the past fifty to sixty years.

Deleuze makes it clear that while it has no preordained direction or teleology, there is nevertheless a logic to multiplicity. Complications, implications, new structure-forming hinges and folds emerge 'around problematic points', as Rajchman puts it (2000: 60). Matter is at its most creative when it is pushed far from equilibrium, when there are stresses or pressures that are seeking out some kind of resolution. As philosopher Manuel DeLanda riffs off Deleuze, '[m]atter spontaneously generates a machine-like solution when confronted with a problem in terms of a balance of forces' (1992: 135).

The term that Deleuze and Guattari give to the entire field or reservoir of such machine-like solutions – in whatever physical systems they arise – is the 'machinic phylum' (1987: 335; see also DeLanda 1992: 135–6). Machinic solutions to tensions that arise from converging or concatenating forces are not rare: rather they are the ultimate source of many of the structures we observe around us – both enduring and transitory. Whirlpools, flames, rivers, bubbles, geological strata, astronomical bodies, living beings, gadgets and engines are all expressions of the generalized machinic phylum. As we suggested above, planets work out their own machine-like solutions to the interplay of forces they contain or which impinge upon them – as expressed in their layering and compartmentalization, their circulations and convection currents, and their occasional 'revolutionary' reorganizations. As DeLanda spells out, different physical systems often generate common machinic solutions when the problems or play of forces they confront are similar. However, the machinic phylum is only ever partly predictable, especially when far from equilibrium. DeLanda is quick to remind us that 'the system in question has a "choice" between several destinies' (1992: 139).

In this way we can think of any complex physical system exploring a space of possibilities before settling on a new permutation or configuration. As DeLanda interprets Deleuze and Guattari: 'the Earth [has] its own "probe heads", its own built-in device for exploration' (1992: 161). But Deleuze and Guattari are not our only guides to this terrain, for this brings us back to Vicki Kirby's notion of an Earth that is self-sensing or self-investigative. In the course of its complex enfolding and self-differentiation, Kirby asks, might we not also countenance that the Earth partakes in its own version of 'geo-logical' inquiry? '[I]f the world itself provides the intention to measure, the object to be measured, and the apparatus through which that calculation will be determined', she ponders, 'why is this not a geology, an earthly science?' (2011: 40). And so, in ways that are not incompatible with Deleuze and Guattari's notion of metallic probe heads (of which more shortly), Kirby points us in the direction of a planetary indeterminacy that is as much a matter of informational or sensory probing as it is about force or kinesis.

One of the main reasons why physical systems exhibit play or indeterminacy is that they tend to be heterogeneous and inconsistent in their composition. The seventeenth-century Dutch philosopher Baruch Spinoza famously captured such openness when he proclaimed that 'no one has yet determined what the body can do' (1994: 155) – an exemplary and prescient commitment to the question of the human that has been taken up by Deleuze amongst others. To this Latour has added that 'no one knows what an environment can do' (2004: 80, 156) – and this chapter's strapline could well be 'no one knows what a planet can do'. Planets, we have been proposing, can be seen as sizeable manifestations of the way matter 'can "express" itself in complex and creative ways' (DeLanda 1992: 133); while their options are partially constrained by their earlier transformations, as long as there are still shifting, unbalanced plays of forces – and of information – at work in their constitution, they remain capable of further radical innovations.

Here we need to be mindful that until very recently modern Western science struggled to capture the spontaneous material expressivity we are referring to as multiplicity. Only with the coming of powerful computational machines, DeLanda explains, has it become possible to model the self-organization of matter and energy (1992: 134–6). Materials scientist and historian Cyril Stanley Smith makes a related point about the struggle of the physical sciences to come to grips with 'aggregates and assemblies' – which is to say all the complexities attendant on the impurity, inconsistency and irregularity of real-world materiality (1981: 54, 325). Shunning the complex, nonlinear and self-organizing behaviour they were unable to represent, DeLanda recounts, the physical sciences forged themselves around the closed, linear and conservative processes that submitted more easily to their modelling (1992: 134).

Modern Western science, in short, has only relatively recently learned to 'see' a great many of the phenomenal world's most important form-building and structure-generating processes – and the post-gradualist geosciences at the core of our account are an important subplot in this bigger story. But as we shall see later, this also raises profound questions about how other knowledge systems – and pathways not taken by Western science – have or could have provided alternative frameworks for engaging with multiplicity.

## How to Think through the Planet

As we will shortly explain, our other organizing concept of 'earthly multitudes' helps us to see how planetary multiplicity plays through, animates and impacts upon everyday human life. But first, referring mainly to examples given in the previous chapter, we will set out the main moves that we use when doing analyses of any phenomenon – be it human, inhuman or more-than-human – in terms of planetary multiplicity. In this way, we offer a sketch of planetary multiplicity not only as a concept but as a method.

The first move is that of *geohistorical analysis*, which involves contextualizing an entity, assemblage or event within the deep time of the Earth. We saw earlier in this chapter how planetary conditions – a combination of material closure, energetic openness, far from equilibrium states and long timescales – mean that planets go along unique historical pathways, generally involving processes of division and recombination, folding and refolding. A crucial feature of this is that all planetary entities and phenomena in their arising and conditioning depend on what has gone before. Planets may explore the possibility space that is open to them, and come up with surprising moves within that space. But as we saw in our brief guide to the Earth 'thus far' earlier in the chapter, every move that a planet makes conditions what can come next.

Such ideas are familiar from social science ideas of lock-in and path-dependence (e.g. David 1985), and what biologists call 'phylogenetic inertia' or 'constraint' – the way that previous evolutionary adaptations, such as the four-limbed animal body plan shared by most vertebrates, place limitations on future evolutionary pathways (see Blomberg and Garland 2002). Our notion of geohistoricity takes this kind of idea and extends it as a general condition of planetary development. In terms of social analysis, it means that what humans are and how they can act are conditioned by planetary 'positivities' (Foucault 2002) and ancient 'geotraumas' (Land 2012) of inhuman origin that constitute and condition what it is to be human.

Second, cutting across this idea of lineages, historicities and originary trauma are *metapatterns*, an idea first developed by anthropologist Gregory Bateson (1979), and developed by biologist Tyler Volk (1995) and others. Volk el al. (2007) define metapatterns as 'large-ranging, overarching patterns exhibited by systems' on a range of scales and in a range of domains. The major metapatterns that Volk originally identified were mainly *geometric and topological*, how the Earth divides itself into different volumes with shapes and properties: spheres, tubes and sheets (including the threads and chambers we discussed in the previous chapter); centres, borders and pores; and gradients and breaks. Other metapatterns are more about processes of *combination* – Volk et al. (2007) talk about layers, binaries, clonons (the accrual of copies) and clusters; we can now add the weaving together of separate strands or spirals in organic forms and human artefacts to create structures with new properties. We also extend the concept of metapatterns to kinds of *process*, whether of transformation or translation, such as the effects of heat on fibres in fabrics and polymers in foodstuffs discussed in the previous chapter, or the forms of motion that, as we shall see in chapter 6, have arisen again and again in the history of the Earth. The idea of metapatterns is closely related to Deleuze and Guattari's notion of the 'machinic phylum' discussed above – the idea that there are general solutions to problems that are available to entities and assemblages in the Earth, evidenced in the recurrence of mathematically congruent 'universality classes' of fractals and power laws that can be found across phyla and kingdoms, living and nonliving (Buchanan 2000).

So whereas geohistorical analysis involves looking at the way that a phenomenon is conditioned by the lineage (broadly conceived) to which it belongs, a metapattern analysis looks at forms and behaviours that arise *across* lineages. As we would put it, the planet *itself* reproduces conditions that enable the same solutions repeatedly to arise. This is a generalization beyond the realm of living things of ideas such as behavioural transmission (Jablonka and Lamb 2005) and niche construction (Odling-Smee et al. 2003). This operates like a planetary 'anamnesis': entities and phenomena arise within the Earth having 'forgotten' these solutions because of the nature of their arising (Szerszynski 2019b), but are 'reminded' of them by the very conditions maintained by the Earth.

The third move or method we employ, *stratal analysis*, involves inquiring into how a phenomenon or entity sits in the wider Earth system with its cycles of matter and cascades of energy. It involves asking which 'compartment', 'reservoir' or 'sphere' of the Earth it sits in, such as the atmosphere or biosphere, and which stratum within that – but also asking how it moves or connects between them. Crucial here is the way that a phenomenon or entity is situated in the wider Earth system with its cycles of matter and cascades of energy. As we saw in chapter 3, this can help us see that the way that humans might be achieving geological agency is part of a wider pattern of what happens when connections are made between strata.

Useful here is the way that Deleuze and Guattari talk about assemblages as hinges or articulations between what were previously distinct organizations of matter. As they put it, '[t]he assemblage is between two layers, between two strata', and it is precisely because an assemblage 'between two strata' is a unique, undetermined, unpremeditated event that it has the potential to transform the reality in which it emerges (1987: 40). It is this event of meshing the components of disparate strata that makes an assemblage novel or inventive. However, by the same token, any new and untried combination of fundamentally different kinds of materials is also inherently risky: it inevitably comes with the possibility of unintended consequences – even potential catastrophe

(Deleuze and Guattari 1987: 161, 503). As we will see in chapter 7, the connecting of strata plays a key role in the process whereby once-local practices are leveraged up to global significance, a dynamic which will become more important as we start to discuss 'earthly multitudes' in greater detail.

Finally, and in a sense framing the three previous moves, we advocate a *comparative and speculative planetology*, that involves looking at the Earth as one amongst many planets. We suggest that the issue of what the Earth has been and might yet become – its capacity for self-differentiation and transformation – can be addressed more comprehensively if we regard it as a specific case in a more generalized inquiry about how planets come into existence and change over time. What is a planet? What do planets have in common? How do they differentiate themselves? Alongside the possibilities open to Planet Earth, what might other planets become? Here we draw on solar-system astronomy, but also exoplanet research, which is helping to free astronomical science from the geocentric assumptions that the Earth is a model for astronomical bodies in general and our local sun–planet arrangement a proxy for all solar systems. But we also use speculative methods, grounded in philosophy and literature, to try to expand the imagined possibility space of planets.

## Engaging with Earthly Multitudes

The idea of planetary multiplicity suggests that the Earth is not simply a static stage for the human drama, or a passive lump of raw material that can be bent to the human will. Instead, it gives us a picture of our home planet as an assemblage that, at many different scales, is constantly working out its own solutions to problems posed by the disequilibrium of the forces, flows and forms of which it is composed. And this requires us to develop a corresponding idea of human existence and activity, one that enables us to conceive of social change and differentiation in the context of the transformation and differentiation of the Earth. This is the task we set our concept of earthly multitudes.

Once again, Deleuze and Guattari are an inspiration. For Deleuze and Guattari, human agents explore their potentiality primarily by learning to tap into and work with the machinic solutions that physical reality works out for itself (1987: 409). To effectively inhabit a variable physical environment, to work with available materials, they suggest, one must gradually come to an understanding of the dynamics through which matter flows and transforms itself. Only by engaging practically with specific elements and terrains, through trial and error – often over many generations – do human actors learn how and when to intervene effectively in the becoming of the world, in what Grosz describes as 'the fluctuating, self-differentiating structure of the universe itself' (2008: 19). Or, in Kirby's terms, we might say that our cultures or technics arise as a particular variation on the theme of the Earth's own inquiry or self-investigation (2011: 34).

As Deleuze and Guattari (1987: 408–12) make clear, modern science is not the first, the only or necessarily the best place to look to find evidence of human collectives engaging productively with the machinic phylum. Directing our attention to artisans and miners, to pastoralists and other nomadic peoples, they seek to illuminate much older and more widely distributed traditions of negotiating with 'matters in movement' (1987: 410). However, before we go any further, it must be stressed, that such ways of living and knowing may be no more in need of Western philosophical recognition than they are of Western scientific counsel.

Deleuze and Guattari's favoured example of astute tracking of the machine phylum is metallurgy. Long before they had an understanding of the precise thermochemical reactions they were inducing, metallurgists learned how to use heat to coax metallic ores through a series of complex transmutations (1987: 410; Clark 2015). Like other forms of artisanship, metallurgy for Deleuze and Guattari involves procedures that are 'anexact and yet rigorous' (1987: 407). Metallurgy cannot be an exact science because artisans are working not with pure elements but with heterogeneous aggregates of materials, using nonstandardized fuels, under shifting ambient conditions, and only through sustained experimentation do metallurgists learn to identify the pathways along which metallic elements pass in the course of heat-induced metamorphosis (Deleuze and Guattari 1987: 410–11; Forbes 1950: 201).

As we saw in chapter 3, the metallurgical arts themselves inherit a great deal from earlier artisanal experimentation. More than this, the development of modern science itself was deeply dependent on the skills, discoveries and know-how of technicians and craftspeople. '[T]hrough most of history', observes Smith, 'science has arisen from problems posed for intellectual solution by the technician's more intimate experience of the behavior of matter and mechanisms' (1981: 325). Generally collective rather than individualised, artisanal knowledge contributed not only knowledge of the properties of materials and the ability to make and use instruments, but what science historian Clifford Conner refers to as 'the habit of experimentalism'. 'Artisans', he concludes, 'contributed not only the mass of empirical knowledge that furnished the raw material of the Scientific Revolution but the empirical method itself' (2005: 17, author's italics).

But craft or artisanship is just one tributary of the wider human propensity to engage with physico-material multiplicity. While attesting that metallurgy is especially reliant on operating 'astride the thresholds' of matter, Deleuze and Guattari also gesture towards skilled interventions in the open field – to engagement with 'flows of grass, water, herds which form so many phyla or matters in movement' (1987: 410). However, had they not been so focused on the arts that have been central to 'civilization' (and the intensive archaeo-anthropological investigations these crafts have received), Deleuze and Guattari might have given more attention to the no-less anexact and rigorous outdoor or broadcast deployment of fire. For here too, as we touched upon in chapter 2, generation upon generation of practitioners have gradually acquired the skills to respond to complex variable 'aggregates and assemblies' of matter-energy. And no less than the metallurgist, they have put their bodies on the line in the course of working with inherently volatile admixtures (see Clark 2011: ch. 7).

Once we open our inquiries to the wider world of adroit interventions in dynamic material environments, there is no stopping. Philosopher Michel Serres's favourite examples are peasants and sailors, two great classes of skilled operators whose working lives attune them to the constant rhythms of the weather and the larger-scale tempos of climate (1995: 28–9). But just as farmers or navigators must adapt to the periodicities and singularities of their environment, so too must those whose lifeways revolve round foraging and hunting in all their many variations. No reflection of the content of the human – however future-oriented – can afford to forget that we have been gatherers and hunters for more than 99 per cent of the span of the genus *Homo*.

If not always for the right reasons, there is growing appreciation of the 'encyclopaedic' biotic knowledge of hunter-gatherers. Our telling of the story of the Earth would also stress that those who hunt or harvest game must not only be able to identify the marks that other animals make and understand their migratory habits, but be able to manoeuvre through an environment as if they shared the proprioceptive capacities and mobilities of their quarry. Tracking, claims anthropologist Louis Liebenberg (1990: 45–6), is a form of hypothetico-deductive reasoning, and as such is a good candidate for 'the origin of science'.

Concepts like traditional ecological knowledge seem to struggle to do justice to the vibrancy and dynamism of what might be better termed sciences in their own right. As Kyle Whyte explains, drawing attention to the need for a systematic understanding of eco-physical variability:

Indigenous knowledges, in the simplest terms, refer to systems of monitoring, recording, communicating, and learning about the relationships among humans, nonhuman plants and animals, and ecosystems that are required for any society to survive and flourish in particular ecosystems *which are subject to perturbations of various kinds*. (Whyte 2017: 157, our italics)

And as we will see in more detail in chapter 7, Indigenous people are hardly in need of lessons that living with the dynamism of their physical worlds is as much a matter of reading meanings and significations as it is of registering forces and energies.

In the term 'earthly multitudes' we are trying to pull together all such modes of being by which human collectives attune themselves to the self-differentiating dynamics or multiplicities of the Earth. 'Multitude', unsurprisingly, has a close conceptual kinship with 'multiplicity': both gesture back to Spinoza's affirmation of the positive, embodied power of the 'multitude' (see Goddard 2011), while political philosophers Michael Hardt and Antonio Negri's use of Spinoza's concept explicitly converses with Deleuze and Guattari's thinking of multiplicity. Developed over the course of their 'Empire' trilogy (2000; 2004; 2009), Hardt and Negri's notion of the multitude refers to the self-organizing capacity of those otherwise marginalized and oppressed by the global capitalist order. For them, the force of the multitude is a power in common that derives both from the physical cooperation of bodies and from the innovative intellectual collaboration that contemporary culture industries demand of their workforce (Goddard 2011).

For all our enthusiasm about the idea of widely distributed intellectual 'commons' of creative and communicative faculties, our own preference for 'multitudes' (plural) over 'the multitude' (singular) reflects misgivings about Hardt and Negri's quest for a new subject of history. Moreover, our notion of earthly multitudes resonates more closely with Deleuze and Guattari's more earthy and physical thematizing of multiplicity than with Hardt and Negri's focus on pre-eminently cultural-communicative capacities. So while we are intrigued by the potentiality of ever more globally networked intellectual powers, our preference is to dig far and deep into collective histories of material-semiotic tussling with multiplicities that are proper to the Earth itself. Thus what constitutes an earthly multitude for us is a shared mode of responding to planetary multiplicity at any scale or in any field – which includes all the different ways that collectives make use of the flows, reservoirs and structures that are engendered by the self-organization of the Earth.

As we saw in the examples of spinners, weavers and high-heat artisans in the previous chapter, earthly multitudes tend to be spatio-temporally distributed. Knowledge and techniques are acquired through practice and tend to diffuse along networks and relays that connect up those with similar material concerns. An earthly multitude is not a constituency that can be clearly identified or enumerated. It may or may not involve self-conscious group formation, though practitioners are generally quick to recognize others who possess similar skills and aptitudes. In keeping with the repeated enfolding and self-differentiation characteristic of planetary multiplicity, earthly multitudes are generally composite and plural – in most cases their constitutive practices are so complexly inter-sected and interwoven that they defy teasing apart. All of us partake in earthly multitudes: we would not be here if we did not.

There is nothing inherently virtuous or progressive about earthly multitudes. Our multitudes may need to be experimental, at times playful, in their probing of physico-material possibilities; however, as we will see in the next chapter, there is nothing to stop the configurations or ensembles that emerge from being brutal, exploitative and unjust to fellow humans or other beings. And while earthly multitudes may not be immediately or constitutively political, they have a tendency to sooner or later be politicized – as they are asked to give an account of themselves, their practices are called into question, or they are played off against each other. Or as is too often the case, they find themselves defending their mode of being against other, encroaching and aggressive earthly multitudes.

On a planet replete with variability at every scale and rifted by episodic transitions, it is to be expected that collective adaptive strat-egies or coping capacities will sooner or later be exceeded. It is quite conceivable that even a well-tested ensemble or set of practices can over-react to stimuli, fall short or cease to be appropriate as condi-tions change. Deleuze and Guattari offer warnings against hasty or over-ambitious material interventions – cautioning against 'too-sudden destratification' (1987: 503). They also recognize that novel machinic processes do not just establish new productive relations but inaugurate 'relations of dependence' (1994: 157). Even more emphatically, we want to stress that alongside coaxing new forms and structures into existence, dealing with loss, pain and damage is a constitutive task of earthly multitudes.

To put it more bluntly, on an Earth that will never cease to surprise us, enduring suffering and knowing how to die are vital aspects of knowing how to live. Writing in the midst of the COVID-19 pandemic, journalist Steven Thrasher points to what we could learn about confronting viral death from those who have lived with and died of HIV/AIDS, and what might be learned about political action without physical presence from disability activists, before adding that '[o]ne thing we have to grieve is the myth that our way of life is coming back' (2020). With similar candour, geographer Lesley Head confronts the event of the Anthropocene from the premise that 'grief will be our companion' (2016: ch. 2). Whether the trigger is a pandemic or the bushfires that Head speaks of, similar questions arise about dealing with pain and debilitation, mourning our losses and responding to the contraction of hope or belief in the future (see also Scranton 2015).

To approach these questions by way of earthly multitudes, we would suggest, is to attune ourselves to the way that different groups or collectives engage with the loss and hurt that are inseparable from whatever a changeable Earth affords. Just as ongoing planetary self-organization prompts the interminable trial and error of creative responses, so too does it call forth improvisation, experimentation and ritual around suffering and dying. And so one response when overwhelming events are visited upon us, as they surely will be, is to ask who has already lived and died through some variant of these befallings, who may already be practised in confronting their consequences, and what we might learn from them. With the proviso, of course, that their and our idea of how to apprehend and respond to the unthinkable may well be unaligned.

No less ardently, we affirm the pleasure in exploring new terrains and novel pathways of material transformation: the 'creative participatory joy', in Smith's words, that characterizes the sensual experience of working or playing with expressive matter (1981: 355). For us, thinking with and through earthly multitudes – whether the practices in question are gratifying, arduous or dangerous – is nothing if not a reckoning with a vast inheritance (see Derrida 1994: 16, 54). 'Life on Earth retains a memory of its past', pronounces Margulis. 'Living bodies store in their complex chemistry memories of past environmental limitations they overcame' (2001: 18). Although our prime concern in this book is with how *human* collectives constitute themselves in the context of planetary multiplicity – which for now is enough of a handful – it makes sense to see every living creature as a complex, composite repository of machinic solutions to the provocation of terrestrial existence, either passed down through lineages of descent or made available by the wider conditions sustained by the planet as a whole. Likewise it behoves us to acknowledge how much our own species has learned from other forms of life and how often our worldly accomplishments have hinged upon joining forces with our fellow creatures.

Thus far in the book we have been taking Anthropocene science as an incitement to do some thinking about the way that all human collectives or social formations are to some degree shaped by their engagement with a restless, unfinished planet. By taking a very lengthy run-up, spanning at least as long as humans have been around, we've tried to make it clear that planetary social thought is about more than just how we ought to respond to the current global environmental predicament. The following chapter continues with the theme of acknowledging the importance of the current conjuncture while also 'de-exceptionalizing' the social experience of a shifting, disruptive Earth.

Here, we ask what the classic social science theme of modernity might look like if we recognized that a sense of planetary multiplicity was always already at work in the world we came to call 'modern'. This takes us into the brutal history of European encounters with other peoples and other ways of inhabiting the Earth. Our discussion hinges on the role played by anxiety over the newly discovered volatility of the Earth in the complex, shifting and fraught relationship between the West and its 'others'. In the process, we layer in some new dimensions to the notion of *speculative planetology*, while at the same time driving home the point that earthly multitudes are by no means wholly generative and beneficent.

# 5

# Inhuman Modernity,
# Earthly Violence

## Introduction: Living on Broken Earth

> Well, some worlds are built on a faultline of pain, held up by night-
> mares. Don't lament when those worlds fall. Rage that they were built
> doomed in the first place. (Jemisin 2017: 7)

In the last two chapters we have offered some examples of how human
collectives have learned to live with and through the changing of the
Earth. *The Stone Sky*, the third volume of N. K. Jemisin's *Broken Earth*
trilogy, opens with harsh words of warning about how *not* to construct
liveable communities on a dynamic planet. Jemison's multi-Hugo award-
winning science fiction-fantasy series offers a creative masterclass in
what we are terming *geohistorical analysis*, *stratal analysis* and *speculative planetology*. The story is set on a planet that is recognizably our
own, yet volcanically and seismically hyperactive. The inhabitants of
this world have long lived with recurring 'seasons' – geologic upheavals
serious enough to transform ecology, topography and climate – the
landscape around them being littered with the rubble of civilizations that
failed to respond adequately. Then comes a season so monstrous that it
will know no end ...

But the 'speculative' dimension of thinking with and through planetary
alterity is by no means restricted to fiction, and neither is it an invention
of recent physical science. Author Samuel R. Delany once described
science fiction as 'significant distortions of the present' (2012: 26). If this
is a fitting description of Jemisin's *Broken Earth* series, however, it seems

no less applicable to most Western social thought. Over the last two centuries, successive social theorists have constructed richly plausible worlds based on the premise of an astronomical body much like our own – save for one 'significant distortion': the planet in question is stable, inert, unchangeable (Clark and Yusoff 2017).

While the premise of planetary quiescence eventually became taken for granted, at the outset it needed to be spelled out. In a memorable passage from the 1817 *Jena Encyclopedia*, G. W. F. Hegel took it upon himself to make explicit the idea that Earth processes are fundamentally inconsequential for the task of imaginative and practical world-building:

> One can have interesting thoughts about the long intervals between such revolutions, about the profounder revolutions caused by alterations of the earth's axis, and also those caused by the sea. They are, however, hypotheses in the historical field, and this point of view of a mere succession in time has no philosophical significance whatever. (1970: 283)

If we read 'no philosophical significance' as no 'social or political significance' (as Hegel surely intended), then we have a reasonable summation of the role ascribed to geophysical processes in mainstream social thought from then on. When today's critical thinkers speedily reduce the question of living on a volatile Earth to a matter of uneven social responsibility, we would suggest, they are still basically adhering to the Hegelian edict that modern social existence ought to be self-grounded and thus immune to the rumblings of its home planet.

But there's something odd going on here with Hegel. As the reference to 'revolutions' intimates, his problem is not ignorance of what the Earth can do – it's that he knows too much. Hegel was in fact a keen follower of early geological inquiry, an avid mineral collector and the assessor of the Jena Mineralogical Society (Kolb 2008; Rudwick 2005: 26–7). What he has been coming up against is the gathering evidence not only that the Earth has an unimaginably long history, but that this history has been rocked by 'tremendous revolutions'. In short, over two centuries ago, Hegel is already beginning to think in terms of what we refer to as planetary multiplicity – an Earth with the inherent capacity for self-transformation. And he is desperately keen to do something about it.

In the philosophical system he will spend his life constructing, Hegel goes to great lengths to show that human agents must logically leave the tilting and heaving of the Earth behind them. Human self-determination or 'freedom', he will argue, develops potentials that are present but arrested in the natural world, and, once that possibility for freedom has been realized, the blind exertions of nature are consigned to developmental prehistory. So what Hegel confers upon the social and philosophical thinkers who follow him is not so much ignorance about the workings of the Earth, but a deliberate and sophisticated strategy for ensuring that geological upheaval will not, cannot, ever get in the way of the collectively self-making and world-building human subject. In our terms, it is a kind of staving off of geohistorical and stratal analysis, a prohibition on seeing human self-organized development as 'earthly'.

In this chapter, we explore the idea that, relatively early in its course, Western modernity stumbled across the evidence of planetary multiplicity. Modernity, we might say, was constitutively 'planetary' or 'inhuman' from early on, but then actively went to work on humanizing – or 'deplanetizing' – itself. But this recoiling from the volatility of the Earth did not just shape the way modern Europeans thought about nature; it also impacted upon the way they conceived of a world of other human beings. In the process of dissociating itself from potentially annihilating Earth processes, we argue, the modernizing West shifted vulnerability and exposure to nature onto 'others' whom it imagined did not share the ability to transcend the natural order.

The question of what the European disavowal of planetary multiplicity came to mean for worlds beyond Europe brings us back to Jemisin and the simultaneously more-than-human and less-than-human relations that are the roiling core of the *Broken Earth* series. Fantasy or not, Jemisin is clearly writing for the current conjuncture of climatic or geophysical uncertainty. Hers is a tale told for audiences who are beginning to grasp that they dwell on an Earth that can change – and change fast. But there is a lot more going on than that. Jemisin is also asking an important question: on a planet that is constantly rumbling and periodically lurching into full-blown cataclysm, which bodies find themselves on the front line, most exposed to the blows of a battering Earth?

The *Broken Earth* trilogy revolves around a minority of people, referred to as 'orogenes', who have the ability to both trigger and quell geological activity. Disparaged as subhuman for this capacity, orogenes are ruthlessly enchained to the task of absorbing geologic shocks and convulsions by those who hold political power, so that others may be cushioned from the worst that the planet has to offer. Jemisin's description of a key character leaves us in little doubt as to the social history that is her reference point: 'he reaches forth with all the fine control that the world has brainwashed and backstabbed and brutalized out of him, and all the sensitivity that his masters have bred into him through generations of rape and coercion and highly unnatural selection' (2016a: 6).

Jemisin began writing the series at the height of the targeted police violence in the US that sparked the Black Lives Matter movement. As she recounts of the development of the storyline and of her main character:

I spent three months learning everything I could about seismology. I went to Hawaii and visited four volcanoes. Then I started thinking about the woman herself and what would make her so angry. That was the summer when, just about every other minute, there was the unjustified killing of a black person at the hands of police. Ferguson was happening, and I was angry myself. I wanted to throw a mountain myself. So a lot of that went into the world-building and the story. (2016b)

But it's vital to note that for Jemisin geological turmoil is not simply a metaphor for social upheaval and injustice. Rather, what she seems to be suggesting is that uneven exposure to the turbulent forces of the Earth is itself a core aspect of oppression and social violence. Exploitation, Jemisin proposes, is more than a matter of extracting value from the disempowered and the marginalized; it is also about positioning these 'others' in such a way that their bodies will form a barrier or force-field between the threatening Earth and those social orders who have set themselves up to be fully, properly 'human'. Perhaps even more provocatively from the point of view of the conventions of critical race and anticolonial theory is that Jemisin imaginatively probes the possibility that those pressured to live at the sharp edge of formidable Earth processes might actually possess certain geologic or earthly powers that others both fear and wish to utilize. Her 'orogenes', in this regard, offer a highly specialized and hyperbolized rendering of what we are describing as earthly multitudes. Indeed, they are one of our inspirations.

We begin by surveying Europe's inadvertent but formative encounter with planetary multiplicity, before turning to the implication of the disavowal of a revolutionary Earth for the racialized violence and injustice inherent in the global colonial project. But rather than simply circling back to a global vision of full and inclusive humanity, we draw on Jemisin's *Broken Earth* and cognate work in Afro-diasporic literature and Black and Indigenous studies to consider the possibility that those most violently subjected to 'dehumanization' might actually be the bearers of other ways of becoming human with and through the inhuman forces of the Earth.

## Vertical Modernity

The protagonists of the *Broken Earth* trilogy journey across the surface of the planet by road and sea, along the way encountering ethnically and racially differentiated others. Rare in the fantasy genre, Jemisin's is a world of profuse racial difference and intermixture. But it is a world in which the decisive action is as much vertical as horizontal, where social stratification reflects abilities to traverse and work with geological strata. This too is relatively uncommon in classic science fiction, which often concerns journeys across or between worlds – with the action moving between the flight decks of far-from-home spaceships and contact zones with perplexing aliens.

Science fiction's privileging of horizontal mobility in the opening up of new realms of encounter and opportunity, in this way, resonates with modern Western social and philosophical thought. 'The true terrain of experience in the Modern Age was the ship's deck', proclaims philosopher Peter Sloterdijk. As maritime reason would have it, he continues, 'only those who navigate on the surface can operate successfully' (2013: 88). Rather than starting from a homegrown or autochthonous sense of self that is then projected outwards, contemporary scholars of globality contend that European identity is constructed out of these predominantly transoceanic cultural encounters – though reminders are sometimes needed that many 'encountered' cultures had for a long time been doing their own work of traversing and unifying sea space.

Movement across the Earth's surface, however, was not the only mode of economic or onto-existential adventure at the threshold of European modernity. 'While Vasco da Gama, Columbus, and other explorers were finding new sea routes', notes historian John Nef, 'the Western peoples were again on the lookout for minerals' (1964: 70). Between 1460 and 1530 the annual output of Central European silver mines increased five-fold (1964: 125), and it has been estimated that German mining in the fifteenth and sixteenth centuries could earn in a decade what more conventional 'surface' trade took a century to accrue (Mumford 1934: 75).

Whereas Sloterdijk reminds us that motley crews of navigators, slavers, pirates and traders did much of the empirical work of assembling the new global spatial order (2013: 10, 112–15), we should heed too geological historian Martin Rudwick's account, focused on the eighteenth century, of the practical contributions to the reconceptualization of the subsurface Earth:

> Mining provided ... not only ... empirical data on the dimension of depth in the earth's crust, but also – far more importantly – a distinctive way of thinking and even of seeing. Anyone involved in the mining industry, from ordinary miners right up the social scale to those who managed and administered mines, worked in a three-dimensional world of rock structures. (2005: 84)

Gradually, a sense emerged amongst Europe's earth-working practitioners and *philosophes* that the body of the Earth was composed of a hierarchy of layers in which depth equated with age. Though the basics of stratigraphic 'superposition' had been surmised in the seventeenth century, it required new ways of conceiving of the Earth as having a history of its own to make the shift from seeing rock strata as an invariant structural order to viewing them as expressions of a dynamic temporal sequencing (2005: 97).

Tied up with this idea of 'geohistory' – a precursor of our own geohistorical analysis – was an unhinging of constraints on the lifetime of the planet. In little more than a human lifetime, estimates of the Earth's age rocketed from a biblically sanctioned few millennia to hundreds of millions of years (Rudwick 2005: 124–6). German philosopher Immanuel Kant was on the cusp of this temporal unbounding. 'By 1750 men could contemplate a future lasting many thousands of years', expound philosopher Stephen Toulmin and historian June Goodfield, 'but no one before Kant had talked so publicly and seriously of a past comprising "millions of years and centuries"' (1967: 133; see also Rossi 1984: ix).

Much has been made of the Euro-Atlantic world's embrace of the idea of deep time, which is generally seen to have been 'discovered' in the latter eighteenth century and popularized in the following century. But the sheer extent of the Earth's history was perhaps not the most pressing issue, nor even was the troubling idea of a great stretch of time 'before Adam' and thus devoid of a creature in God's image to populate and render meaningful the works of creation. What came to intrigue and perturb late eighteenth- and early nineteenth-century thinkers was the question of why the Earth in its three dimensions seemed clearly differentiated and what manner of events had resulted in these distinct layers.

One of geology's basic ideas is that the upper Earth is composed of bands of rocky material, with more recently formed strata superimposed on older ones. As Zalasiewicz explains: 'These layers can be subsequently tilted, crumpled, dislocated, even turned upside down, but their relative original order forms the proxy for time' (2008: 29). It was in the late eighteenth century – the moment Michel Foucault (2002) influentially identified as marking the transition from classical to modern epistemes – that geologists underwent a shift from classifying rocks as 'natural kinds' to categorizing them on account of the processes of historical formation they shared. German geologist Abraham Gottlob Werner proposed that what mattered most was 'mode and time of formation', a distinction for which he introduced the term *Gebirgsformation* – 'rock formation' (Laudan 1987: 94–5).

What made the idea of distinct rock formations both fraught and fascinating was the enigmatic presence of objects that came to be identified as the stony bodies of once living creatures. In the 'classical' view – that envisaged the stuff of the world as forming a permanent continuous array – fossils provided a convenient bridge between rocks and living things. But as the idea of petrified life took shape, and gathering evidence from around the globe made it increasingly clear that many fossilized remains belonged to creatures that were no longer extant – anywhere on Earth (Kolb 2008: 4) – gradually, the idea took shape that each 'rock formation' came with its own complement of once thriving but now departed living things. And in this way, the question began to emerge as to what kind of an event could both bring a new layer of rock into being and take a whole world of creatures out of existence.

Like nautical voyages, expeditions beneath the surface of the Earth, with all their attendant risks, were undertaken in expectation of profit: a downward journey, the labour of extraction, a trip back to the surface and a return on investment. However, while the long-range horizontal negotiation of the globe progressively turned formerly strange and monstrous regions into more knowable dominions, deeper 'vertical' excursions turned up ever more diverse and perturbing monsters. Trans-global operations – as Sloterdijk and many others insist – unified diverse worlds into a single global space, but what the penetration of the subsurface seemed to be bringing to light were the traces of multiple worlds, alien, intriguing and shocking. Whereas horizontal traversal of the globe provided Europeans with vexing encounters with lands and peoples unlike themselves, vertical mobilization opened up vistas of Earth history *devoid of any human presence whatsoever*. The mineral-hungry explorers of Europe set out to open the subsurface to industrious and accumulative activity. In the process – beneath their own feet – they stumbled into an abyss, the mineral archive of an Earth that been broken and reassembled many times.

## Revolutions of the Earth

When Kant reflected in his *Universal Natural History* that 'millions of centuries will pass within which ever new worlds and world-orders will form and attain completion one after another' (2012: 266), he was already catching sight not only of a profoundly ancient Earth but of a fundamentally discontinuous planet. What distinct rock formations and punctuated fossil records pointed towards were events of such magnitude that they were capable of annihilating whole cohorts of living creatures right across the planet. The term that Cuvier, Kant, Hegel and many of their contemporaries would alight upon to evoke the events that divided epochs and their respective formations was 'revolutions of the Earth'.

As Rudwick reminds us, 'revolution' in its application to geohistory 'was used to denote *any* major change, whether slow or rapid, smooth or violent' (2005: 102). Both gradual and abrupt models of change, however, represented a significant shift from the Newtonian vision of celestial bodies tracing perfectly predicable orbits to an acknowledgement – as evidenced by ever-more intensive earth-working, and the work of early 'palaeontologists' such as Georges Cuvier – that our own planetary body periodically undergoes total and irreversible catastrophic transformation (Laudan 1987: 155; Grant 2006: 123).

The European mid-eighteenth century was not just a time of deepening practical and conceptual engagement with an eventful Earth history. It also witnessed an actual geological disaster of monstrous proportions. On the morning of 1 November 1755, the Portuguese capital of Lisbon was rocked by three huge tremors that destroyed most of the city's buildings, shortly followed by a series of tsunamis – with devastating loss of life (Ray 2004; Clark 2011: 86–90). As its implications sunk in, the Lisbon earthquake came to be a benchmark for the possibility of sudden geological change. With half a century's retrospect, Scottish geologist James Hall described in his 1814 'Revolutions of the Earth's surface' upheavals capable of moving great rocks around: 'the events of Lisbon and of Collao [the Peruvian earthquake of 1746], though on a scale comparatively diminutive, help to lead the imagination to the conception of this colossal disaster' (cited in Rudwick 2005: 578). Hall went on to wonder if a disaster on this scale might leave no human survivor to tell the tale.

The Lisbon disaster, it has often been observed, was particularly troubling for many 'thinking' Europeans because it came at a time of waning faith in a world orchestrated by a divine being. The youthful Kant rushed out a treatise on earthquakes in the year after Lisbon, but the event may have stayed with him for a lifetime. While his 'mature' notion of the sublime seems to flip trepidation about unruly natural forces into subjective surety and self-possession, not all commentators are convinced. Literary theorist Gene Ray (2004: 10), for one, believes that 'persistent psychological anxiety' over the Lisbon disaster haunted the philosopher life-long. There are clues in Kant's final work, unpublished in his own lifetime, to the concerns that seem to have been gnawing away at him. Part way through the *Opus Postumum* he ponders the globe being in the past 'dissolved into chaos, but now being organized and regenerating' and the way this involves the disappearance of a whole world of life and its replacement by new forms (1993: 66–7). But as Kant goes on to ask:

How many such revolutions (including, certainly, many ancient organic beings no longer alive on the surface of the earth) preceded the existence of man, and how many ... are still in prospect, is hidden from our enquiring gaze, for ... not a single example of a human being is to be found in the depth of the earth. (1993: 67)

As philosopher Iain Grant (2000) suggests, Kant's confrontation with an ancient Earth devoid of human traces presages a post-cataclysmic planet on which man too has been reduced to a lifeless, fossil remnant. What the annihilation of humankind would mean for Kant, Grant argues, is the loss of thought itself, the sudden termination of the very capacity of the cosmos to make sense of itself (2000: 48–9). For as Kant nervously announces towards the end of the *Critique of Judgment*: 'Without men the whole creation would be a mere waste, in vain, and without final purpose' (2005: 219).

'None of the questions that tormented Europeans reflecting on Lisbon was ever directly answered or even directly rejected', concludes moral philosopher Susan Neiman of the events of the mid-eighteenth century. 'Modern thought proceeded as if questions were settled [that] were simply left hanging' (2002: 250). The same could be said of the half century of escalating concern with geocatastrophe that followed. This state of suspension remains important, for it is the condition of possibility of what became, in the nineteenth century, the social sciences and humanities. As Foucault reminds us, 'the human sciences' are premised upon the reordering of thought and things at the close of the eighteenth century; a new organization that permits Europeans for the first time to fully conceive of 'a being who owes his finitude only to himself' (2002: 386).

But Foucault doesn't devote as much attention as he could to the decisive stilling of the Earth in Western thought that enabled it to be imagined that human finitude – together with the whole system of 'positivities' that shaped it – was firmly centred in the domain of the human (Szerszynski 2017a). And this brings us back to Hegel's disavowal of the philosophical-social significance of geologic 'revolution'. As we saw earlier, Hegel wanted to declare the Earth safe for the further ascent of the self-conscious and collective subject not out of any ignorance of what the planet is capable of doing, but out of a clear-sighted awareness of its frightening instability.

Like Kant before him, Hegel is looking planetary multiplicity in the eye; indeed, writing in the early nineteenth century, he has even more evidence of the Earth's radical discontinuity at his disposal. Furthermore, Hegel has had more time to ponder the mixed fate of the Euro-Atlantic *social* revolutions of the eighteenth century. He knows full well that the pursuit of human freedom is exacting, gruelling and perilous. Just as Kant recoiled from the prospect of a universe deprived of its only thinking being, for Hegel the possibility that a passing shudder of the

Earth could obliterate everything that lifetimes of collective struggle had achieved appeared near unthinkable. Or rather, he set out to render it inconceivable.

In Hegel's estimation, Kant's settlement left the human subject dangerously exposed to an Earth whose mute, unthinking exertions remained forever alien to our own powers of comprehension. Hegel's response is to reimagine thought itself as a fundamental property shared by the natural world and humankind: with 'mind' in nature remaining rudimentary, whereas humans manifest the capacity to fully recognize and activate the freedom that slumbers and stalls in the physical domains (Stone 2005). It is because our own accomplishment of self-determination realizes an ideal potentiality inhering in nature that Hegel is able to argue that the human actualization of thought permanently rises above the merely formative throes of the natural world, which therefore belong to a bygone era.

To be sure, the directions taken by nineteenth-century science were not exactly kind to Hegel's empirical claims about an ascending, inter-linked mind and nature. But in another sense, his championing of a broad, directional, 'geohistorical' movement that encompasses human and nonhuman life is remarkably prescient of the main current of the modern order that consolidates itself as the nineteenth century rolls on. And in this regard, Hegel's quelling of the threat of geological catas-trophe, for all the difference in detail, turns out to have a fortuitous affinity with further developments in the Earth and life sciences.

Whereas the rapid unfurling of 'deep geological time' may have been experienced as fearsome and disorienting in the European eighteenth century, by the mid-nineteenth century vastly extended timescales have been marshalled into a much more constructive – and consoling – role. In the consolidating of the modern episteme, as Foucault has shown, life itself takes on a new and unprecedented 'positivity' – as a drive, a power, an 'inexhaustible force' (2002: 303). An order in which life was simply one among many kinds of difference has been displaced by one in which life itself has been fully historicized – and has indeed come to be seen as the pre-eminent medium through which change takes place. And time, in this sense, is not simply the sequential chronology of an older 'natural history', but the encompassing directionality of a living world in which the very mode of being is that of incessant mutability and transformation. The rise of modern biological thought, combined with a new uniformitarianism in geology emphasizing constant, incremental processes, encourages the idea that an inherently dynamic and adaptive life can work *with* rather than against geology.

Along these lines, deep geological time shifts, subtly but momen-tously, from being the locus of successive devastations to a medium of continuous development. In keeping with his explorations of anatomical and structural transformations within organismic lineages, Cuvier would observe that 'Nature has made a fin out of an arm' (quoted in Foucault 2002: 291). And in this way, even extinction begins to appear as more of a stage-gate than a terminus, a process of transformation rather than an event of annihilation (Coleman 1973: 349).

We do not need to delve deeply into Darwin – and the crucial role that Lyell's geological gradualism plays in the *Origin of Species* – to get a feeling for the way that a potentially catastrophic geology was progressively subdued in the modern episteme into a positive and productive force. Kant and Hegel do the metaphysical groundwork of domesticating a potentially annihilating geology into a co-dependent partner in the ascent of the sovereign subject. The empirical Earth and life sciences follow through by levelling out 'terrible revolutions' of the Earth into the generative liaison of living beings and the planet's glacially evolving surface.

Just as 'inexhaustible life' has every chance of out-adapting the Earth's own mobilizations, so too does the being that had come to be seen as the pinnacle of evolution have every opportunity to out-speed, out-smart, out-accumulate whatever a slow-rumbling planet might pitch its way. As the 'most industrious' members of this species accelerated into ever more rapid, self-reinforcing growth and development, it would increasingly appear that the threat of geocataclysm had been overcome, that the stratified rock formations of the Earth could be treated more as a resource than as an omen – and that geologic instability indeed had 'no philosophical significance whatever'. Consequently, the emergent human sciences would be free to get on with the pursuit and the probing of collective self-determination – the exacting task to which they were congenitally disposed and best suited.

## Geological Time and the Other

It is all very well to entrust ourselves to an episteme in which earthly convulsion has been smoothed into a gracefully ascending arc of improvement and progression. But this uniquely and definitively 'modern' settlement left a big problem – and we did not have to wait for the Anthropocene for it to raise its head. Neither science nor philosophy, physics nor metaphysics could actually halt the dynamics of the Earth. Flesh and blood beings, sooner or later, would find themselves in the path of volatile processes – and of this there would be no shortage of reminders. In a world that was more than ever conjoined by economic exchange, extensive power relations and new modes of communication, extreme events in one part of the globe were ever more visible elsewhere (Johns 1999: xii).

As we noted earlier in this chapter, the discoveries that so awed and alarmed the earlier geoscientists built on the skills and knowledge of subsurface labourers. But this role in helping to 'verticalize' modern experience did not necessarily help miners themselves. With the growing economic importance of the subterranean resources, those doing the work of extraction came to be viewed as a kind of human subspecies: coal-blackened, benighted, degenerate. As Barbara Freese observes: 'The miners and their families, commonly referred to as a separate race of humans, were increasingly ostracized by society' (2016: 45; see also Tyfield 2014a: 66). This enhanced stratification associated with mining helping to legitimate – or at least obscure – horrific death rates, crippling health problems and all the indignities Mumford gathers under the term 'brutalization' (1934: 73).

The increasingly pronounced verticality of social structuration, however, was more than an ideological prop for a profoundly unequal world. While the task of extractive labour was to safely channel the power of the subterranean planet into socially useful forms, so too was this living, toiling, tunnelling layer of bodies put in the position of physically absorbing those forces of the Earth that could never be made safe. As our method of stratal analysis would have us stress, what we mean here is that miners are *literally* positioned in a profoundly unstable interzone between the mobile, fluid envelope of the Earth's surface and the slower-moving subsurface of rocky strata. Positioned as a kind of hinge or articulation between these fundamentally different compartments of the Earth, extractive bodies are continuously exposed to the volatile events that occur as these layers are brought into contact: the cave-ins, rock-bursts, flash floods, fires, explosions, toxic dust and gases that were and still are the hazards of working underground.

But this of course was a modernity that was as vigorously horizontal or globe-girdling as it was vertical or strata-traversing. And if globalization opened Western eyes to unfamiliar and perturbing manifestations of earthly volatility, so too did it open up vast new realms of opportunity for dealing with or processing geophysical anxieties. If a stratum of European extractive labourers and their communities could be consigned to 'a separate race of humans', how much more possibility lay in the racially ascribable bodies of entire continents?

It is widely accepted amongst critical scholars that colonialism was less an offshoot of Western modernity than a central, constitutive element of what it meant to be modern and to be European (Mignolo 2011: 348). So too is the argument now familiar that in the latter eighteenth and early nineteenth centuries, questions of difference between Europeans and a world of other peoples intensified into a temporal narrative that cast non-Europeans as developmentally anterior (Fabian 1983; Mbembe 2017: 54). Where earlier centuries had characterized Europe's others in terms of their ungodly beliefs, or by way of the differential impact of climatic and topographical factors, these later Euro-Atlantic classificatory schemas divided the world's people vertically. In the words of philosopher Achille Mbembe: 'Entire populations were categorized as species, kinds, or races, classified along vertical lines' (2017: 16; see also Ferreira da Silva 2014).

Race, it hardly needs to be said, was the key concept in marking out 'degrees of subrationality, and of not-quite-humanness' (Wynter 2003: 301). With the tilting of the difference arrayed across the Earth's surface into temporalized developmental schemes, human categorization essentially followed the geological model of *Gebirgsformation* – stratified rock formation. Those human groups – or races – furthest from the heights ascended by Europeans came to be seen as cases of arrested or petrified development – as 'the savage Other, the fossil Other' (Wynter 2003: 266–7), as '*monsters* and *fossils*' (Mbembe 2017: 17). Epidermal or phenotypic blackness, above all, emerged as the master signifier of failure to achieve full human status: 'The period represented the Black Man as the prototype of a prehuman figure incapable of emancipating itself from its bestiality, of reproducing itself, or of raising itself up to the level of its god' (Mbembe 2017: 17). Such categorizations, critical race and decolonizing theorists argue, played a central role not just in the way Europeans saw themselves vis-à-vis others, but in how they came to define and imagine what it meant to be human: what Black studies scholar and poet Fred Moten describes as 'antiblackness as the structuring force of the modern world' (Moten 2018: 25; see also Karera 2019: 46).

But why this verticalizing or geologizing of racialized difference? Why this conversion of blackness, in particular, into a transnational subhuman stratum? Unsurprisingly, most accounts note the correspondence between the hardening of racial schemas and the imperatives of Europe's surge of 'unlimited expansion' from the late eighteenth century (Mbembe 2017: 54; Anderson 2007: 25). The demands of accelerating capital accumulation required the scouring of the globe for ever new sources of cheap labour and raw materials (Moore 2015: 16–18, 221–5), and as we saw in chapter 3, 'cloth capitalism' depended directly upon the products of slave labour. In this regard, racialized dehumanization justified the expropriation of lands and legitimated the intensification of slave labour – which, as critical race theorists insist, should be seen less as a hangover of some feudal or despotic mode of production than as a formative site of capital–labour relations (see Woods 1998: 7, 46). At the same time, massive subsidies of energy and nutrients from the 'colonial outfield' helped to lift the threat of famine from Europe (Pyne 1997b: 23).

Our notion of 'geological othering' builds on and complements these critical accounts, layering in the idea that capitalist accumulation at once – inadvertently – brings to light the evidence of an unstable Earth and – equally inadvertently – exacerbates this instability. In this context, there is a brutal logic to coupling exploitation with the positioning of the expropriated and the exploited so that they bear the brunt of planetary volatility. It is no coincidence, we would hazard, that some of the principal architects of verticalized racial ontologies were also deeply concerned with revolutions of the Earth. In the work of Kant the connection is still formative, but it is clear that for him the capacity to deploy reason to rise above the threatening sublimity of nature is severely restricted in the case of the 'Negroes of Africa' and other non-European peoples (Gilroy 2000: 58–60; Spivak 1999: 24–9). Cuvier identified ancient catastrophes as a reason for racial isolation and hence for invariant physical and intellectual differences between races – positioning 'the Negro race ... visibly close to the apes' (cited in Anderson 2007: 103–4). It is in the work of Hegel, however, that the issue of racialized developmental backwardness and the question of the ascent of 'spirit' beyond the reach of potentially world-effacing Earth are most fully and complexly imbricated.

Hegel's philosophical system, as we have seen, sets out to convince us that threats posed by upheavals of the Earth, because they have been transcended by the self-conscious human making of history, have 'no philosophical significance whatever'. This resonates with his verdict on slavery, which equates with his general appraisal of 'the African race': 'it is the essential principle of slavery, that man has not yet attained a consciousness of his freedom, and consequently sinks down to a mere Thing – an object of no value' (2001: 113; see also Ferreira da Silva 2011: 90). Here Hegel is even prepared to suspend his axiomatic of 'Universality' in order to permanently consign 'the Negro ... in his completely wild and untamed state' to the arrested development of nature (2001: 110–11; see also Gilroy 2000: 64–5). Like the revolutions of the Earth that are relegated to 'a mere succession in time' and are thus forgettable, so too, after a brief dismissal, 'we leave Africa, not to mention it again. For it is no historical part of the World' (Hegel 2001: 117).

Aside from legitimating European global dominance, we need to ask, what other work is performed by the effective fossilization or geologizing of a large proportion of the planet's human population? In this regard, we need to keep in mind that, whatever Hegel's system would have us believe, global communication and destabilization wrought by colonialism itself combine to make catastrophes more visible during his lifetime than at any previous point in human history. Racial ontologies composed 'along vertical lines', we propose, take the logic that is played out on a much smaller scale with Europe's own extractive labour force and inflate it to the planetary scale. Under conditions of a deep, rumbling and repressed anxiety over the abyssal ungrounding of the Earth, Western thought reimagines human difference in such a way that Europe's others will not only serve as the economic foundations of Earth-transcending accumulation; they will comprise a physical substrate that supervenes between 'full' humanity and a dangerous planet.

Henceforth, black and brown bodies will form a load-bearing structure, a subtending layer, a geophysical shock absorber – as the *Broken Earth* trilogy's fictional rendition helps us to see. Before Jemisin came earlier intuitions of subtending blackness. Poet and political thinker Aimé Césaire, writing in the 1930s, referred to Afro-diasporic peoples as 'those without whom the earth would not be the earth' (1995: 113), while novelist-activist James Baldwin observed in the early 1960s that 'the black man has functioned in the white man's world as a fixed star, as an immovable pillar' (1963: 3). More recently, Kathryn Yusoff speaks explicitly of 'imaginaries that organise Blackness as a stratum or seismic barrier to the costs of extraction, across the coal face, the alluvial plains, and the sugar cane fields' (2018: xiii).

The questions that tormented Europeans reflecting on Lisbon and on the Earth's catastrophic geohistory more generally, we propose, were not so much unanswered as they were offloaded onto other worlds, other bodies. As Claire Colebrook puts it: 'The liberal, universally-oriented and rights-blessed humanity of the eighteenth century gained its ease, security and stability by outsourcing risk and volatility' (2017a). Which is to say, modernizing Europeans temporarily papered over the discontinuities of the Earth they had chanced upon beneath their own feet by permanently ploughing great rifts through the worlds of others.

## Empires of Exposure

Modern Europeans, Spivak is quick to remind us, are far from the first imperialists (1999: 37, 89). But no previous colonial or imperial adventures had been so global in reach, and hence no previous colonists found themselves exposed to such a range of unfamiliar – and destabilized – ecological, geological and climatic processes.

Faced with danger, the first recourse of European colonists was almost always the very racialized others they were so quick to disparage. Confronted with wildfire – or their own escaped blazes – Australian settlers called for their Aboriginal neighbours. '"Send for the blacks!"', recalls New South Wales essayist Mary Gilmore, 'was the first cry on every settlement when a fire started' (1986: 152). Enslaved people of African descent in the island plantations of the Caribbean both took the brunt of hurricane exposure and did the work of reconstruction (Smith 2012). Slave labour, and later black convict labour, carved out the 'alluvial empires' of the Southern states, building the levees that temporarily held rivers in place and repairing them when floods struck. In the words of Black studies scholar Clyde Woods:

> those men and women who drained the swamps, and who worked on the prison farms and in the levee and sawmill camps, faced death from working too hard and death for not working hard enough. African Americans continued to die building and shoring up the Lower Mississippi River levee system. The brutality used in levee construction was unsurpassed. (1998: 94)

Few of the world's foragers, pastoralists or cultivators willingly took to production geared to inconceivably distant markets: alongside slavery and indentured labour, punitive taxes and other coercive mechanisms created 'labour' where there had been subsistence or self-sufficiency. Lacking basic rights, enslaved or otherwise bonded labour could always be called upon to do life-threatening work under hazardous circumstances. Setting out from the premise of a volatile planet, however, Jemisin turns the logic around. '[B]ecause you are essential', intones one of the master caste to an orogene under their supervision, 'you cannot be permitted to have a choice in the matter' (2017: 178).

Most of the risky, arduous and exacting work of rendering landscapes liveable had of course been done by local or Indigenous people long before invasive forces arrived on the scene. Despite centuries or millennia of groundwork by First Peoples, many regions remained climatically, ecologically and pathogenically dangerous to naïve European bodies. Designation of certain sites as white men's graves was not an exaggeration, with settler mortality often exceeding 50 per cent per annum in some tropical zones (Öberg and Rönnbäck 2016). As literary studies scholar Monique Allewaert (2013) attests, fears of somatic and psychic disintegration were endemic amongst European colonists, especially in tropical latitudes – and not without justification. 'Many colonials disappeared into the tropics', notes Allewaert (2013: 31). In this context, racial ideologies needed to be potent and versatile enough to both legitimate the genocidal annihilation of Indigenous peoples and account for why, in some cases, 'natives', 'slaves' and other derogated peoples exhibited survival and adaptive capacities that far surpassed those of 'civilised' races (2013: 43).

Even when the world-making work of Indigenous peoples was acknowledged, the vertical positioning of racialized others as a stratum between the Earth and the 'civilized races' proved flexible enough to legitimate the total appropriation of their lands. Writing in 1848, emigration advocate Joseph Byrne was as willing to acknowledge the contribution of Australian Aboriginal people to transforming the continent as he was to justify its usurpation:

> the fires of the dark child of the forest have cleared the soil, the hills and the valleys of the superabundant scrub and timber that covered the country and presented a bar to its occupation. Now, prepared by the hands of the lowest race in the scale of humanity ... the soil of these extensive regions is ready to receive the virgin impressions of civilised man. (quoted in Hallam 1975: 76)

The tragedy of the European drive to annex and over-code the majority of the Earth's surface is not just the immediate impact on local inhabitants, but the fact that the vertical lines it gouged through the human condition devastated worlds that were configured by their own, very different, verticality or deep temporality. For the peoples who were denigrated as temporally or developmentally backward tended to be those who had developed ways of life over durations long enough to have accommodated to the flows, patterns and singularities of a changeable planet. As Kyle Whyte argues, 'settler colonialism commits environmental injustice through the violent disruption of human relationships to the environment' (2018b: 125). And what were and are being disrupted, Whyte and others insist, are modes of being deeply attuned to the essential changeability of biogeophysical systems: forms of human–nonhuman co-existence that revolve around 'transformation, cyclical time (in the sense of spiraling time), and shape-shifting' (2018b: 130; see also Davis and Todd 2017).

Behind the shockwave of introduced pathogens and the unrestrained violence of early contact came the heightened intensities of colonial exploitation and its administrative corollaries: land confiscation, confinement or relocation of populations, forest clearance and decimation of valued animal species, prohibitions on tradition land management practices, and, not least, destruction of languages and knowledge systems (Whyte 2018a; 2018b). Surveying the cascading repercussion of conjoined environmental and sociocultural devastation, it was not difficult for European observers to confirm their preconceptions that 'primitive' peoples indeed remained naked in the face of natural extremity from which Euro-Atlantic 'civilizations' had – in the broadest sense – successfully extricated themselves (Clark and Gunaratnam 2013).

It was not only the deep-seated adaptations to earthly variability of Indigenous worlds that were attenuated, unravelled and undermined by European colonization. As we touched upon in the previous chapter, agrarian social formations – if they are to endure – must also forge themselves around the syncopated and shifting rhythms of climate. Mike Davis (2001) offers a damning indictment of the impact of nineteenth-century colonial rule of tropical peasantries in the Indian subcontinent and elsewhere in the monsoonal belt. Davis demonstrates how forcible incorporation in global markets exposed peasant farmers to the full force of El Niño-related climatic extremes from which traditional practices had formerly afforded them a reasonable measure of insulation. Historian David Arnold offers a related case regarding the Bengal famine of 1770, pointing to the impact that mediated reports of the catastrophe had on the very colonial powers who had helped engender it:

> the magnitude of the crisis, in which as many as ten million people may have perished, helped propagate an image of India as a land still subject to the capricious sway of nature (at a time when Europe grew yearly more confident of its mastery) and as a society too feeble and fatalistic to fend for itself. (Arnold 1999: 81–2)

What Arnold's account brings into focus is the way that the vulnerability of colonized peoples to the variability of Earth processes – even or especially when that exposure had been greatly exacerbated by colonizing powers – could be used to support the idea of innate racial inferiority. Our only qualification is that beneath this façade of European confidence we conceive of deep disquiet: an anxiety that extends beyond 'the puzzle of human difference on earth' to take in the quandary of an Earth with its powers of self-differentiation (Anderson 2007; cf. Bhabha 1998).

Again, for all the power of metaphorical or ideological stratification and its brutal social manifestations, what we are proposing here is a stratal analysis that literally positions racialized bodies at a series of unstable planetary interzones: at the deadly juncture between surface and subsurface, in the turbulent contact zone between continental landmasses, on the threshold of collapsing or upheaving ecological systems. Through the offshoring of susceptibility to entire regions or latitudes of racialized others, Europeans not only physically acquired significant new levels of material cushioning from earthly inconstancy, they also gained the onto-existential consolation of seeing how far their own ascent from the mire of nature advanced from the global baseline. In short, evidence that nature still had a 'philosophical significance' to underdeveloped others offered proof that modern Europe was indeed well on the way to safely consigning the revolutionary Earth to a historical past.

## Earthly Multitudes in Rifted Worlds

Whatever ethico-political indictment it deserves, positioning others so as to take the burden or intercept the blows of an unruly Earth is a tactic open to earthly multitudes – and this is one reason why we do not conceive of earthly multitudes as inherently virtuous or progressive. In the longer term, however, the export and displacement of vulnerability to and onto Europe's others was a strategy destined to reproduce the threat of earthly upheaval on still larger scales. Decolonizing theorists have not been slow in proposing that the climate change crisis and the shock of the Anthropocene represent the coming home to the West of the 'ends of the world' that it has so often visited upon others (Davis and Todd 2017: 774; see also Whyte 2018a: 226, 236).

Such claims resonate with the earlier idea put forward by philosopher Hannah Arendt (1951), psychiatrist-political philosopher Frantz Fanon (1965) and others that the atrocities of World War II can be seen as a domestic rebounding of the racism and oppression that defined European colonialism. In the words of Aimé Césaire, writing in 1955, '[c]olonization … dehumanizes even the most civilized man' (2001: 41). But as Césaire himself intimated, the literal and figurative positioning of multitudes of racialized bodies in proximity to a forceful Earth rebounds in other ways: dehumanization also raises the possibility of other ways of being human.

To get a sense of what this might mean, it's worth returning to Jemisin's *Broken Earth* trilogy, to see what happens next with the world-weary, brutalized and very angry orogene we left in the introduction:

> So he reaches deep and takes hold of the humming tapping bustling reverberating rippling vastness of the city, and the quieter bedrock beneath it, and the roiling churn of heat and pressure beneath that. Then he reaches wide, taking hold of the great sliding-puzzle piece of earthshell on which the continent sits.
> Lastly he reaches up. For power.
> He takes all that, the strata and the magma and the people and the power, in his imaginary hands. Everything. He holds it. He is not alone. The earth is with him.
> Then he *breaks it*. (Jemisin 2016a: 7)

A revenge fantasy, no doubt. But given that this is the beginning of the trilogy, not the end, there is a lot more going on than that. The orogene in question can break the world because he has been holding it together, supporting it. To function as a substrate, a load-bearing structure, a subtending force – even if under conditions of abject coercion – Jemisin seems to be saying, is also to hold a certain power. This resonates with the line we cited from James Baldwin earlier, which is also worth completing: 'the black man has functioned in the white man's world as a fixed star, as an immovable pillar: and as he moves out of his place, heaven and earth are shaken to their foundations' (1963: 3).

For all the continuity between Baldwin and Jemisin here, something has also shifted. Whatever we might say about Anthropocene science's presumption to speak for all of us, it has provided a grammar or framework with which to think in terms of diverse modalities of human agency as *literally* shaking Earth and sky. While the genre may be fantasy-SF, Jemisin has given us what may be the most fully resolved account yet of enslavement as a geomorphic force, as a process physically implicated in the shifting of the Earth system and the shaping of geological strata. Or, as we would say, she provides a comprehensive, if fictionalized, stratal analysis of slavery.

There are at least two sides to this worth teasing out. One is that transcontinental slavery, together with the oppression and genocide of Indigenous peoples, left its lasting mark not only in social worlds but also in the texture of the Earth. Here we might see Jemisin as inheriting fellow writer Toni Morrison's earlier testimony that '[s]lavery broke the world in half. It broke it in every way' (quoted in Gilroy 1993: 178). Trans-Atlantic chattel slavery disrupted ways of life and the dynamics of population across much of the continent of Africa, trafficked tens of millions of people across tectonic plate junctures, and set them to the task of geomorphically making over the worlds to which they were trafficked.

The other side of this story is the idea that the very rifting of worlds and what Kathryn Yusoff (2018: 19) refers to as 'forced alliances with the inhuman' can ultimately be sources of new forms of bio- or geopower. Under extreme duress, kidnapped Africans brought a wealth of useful knowledge to the Americas – the cultivation of rice and numerous other crops, blacksmithing and smallpox inoculation to name a few (Conner 2005: 89–93, 102–4; Goucher 1993). To this they added prolific adaptions to novel ecologies and social landscapes: their own garden plots, 'tended by moonlight and exhaustion', as agricultural scientist George Washington Carver put it (cited in Ruffin 2010: 79), the life-or-death socio-ecological improvisation of fugitive maroon communities, exchange and cohabitation with Indigenous peoples (see Ruffin 2010: 10; McKittrick 2013: 58). Tapping a more lyrical vein, geographer Angela Last points us to the work of Guadeloupean novelist and poet Daniel Maximin, who writes of the way enslaved Africans relocated in the Caribbean had to deal with 'unknown soil, hostile sea, indifferent sun, forbidden forest' (cited in Last 2015: 60). Resonating with a lengthier tradition of African-Caribbean 'geopoetics', Maximin's work recalls Césaire's earlier evocation of inhuman becoming with and through the fearsome physical forces of new worlds: 'the enormous lung of the cyclones breathes and the hoarded fire of volcanoes and the gigantic seismic pulse new beats the measure of a body alive in my firm blazing' (1995: 125).

In the work of novelist-philosopher-critic Sylvia Wynter (1995; 2003), the experience of Afro-diasporic peoples in the Americas is crafted into an alternative notion of what it means to be human – in counterpoint to the unearthed, secularized 'monohumanist' visions of Western Europe. In the influential but unpublished *Black Metamorphosis*, Wynter takes the radical translocation of enslaved Africans between continents, and the continuous rebellion and reinvention that followed, as the incitement to a new mode of being human: what Black studies scholar and geographer Katherine McKittrick describes as 'black rebirth and cultural self-recreation in *an entirely new geographic context*' (2016: 85, our italics). Or as Black studies scholar and queer theorist Rinaldo Walcott (2009: 89) asserts, with a similarly planetary twist on the redefinition of humanness: 'the exhaustion and the limits of European modernity's categories of the human ... is not cause for defeat but is instead a new opening up and opening out of the category of the human, meant to recuperate a different kind of planetary life' (see also McKittrick 2015: 150).

We see such moves as a gesturing between stratal analysis and speculative planetology: pointing towards an understanding of the way that the particular experiences of a radical rifting and repositioning on the geobody of the Earth can become a platform for considering very different organizations of planetary and even extra-planetary existence (see Gilroy 2000: 339–49). But such thinking, we have been suggesting, can also help us to see the no-less-speculative planetary imagination that lies behind European modernity's categorization of the human: the early, fearful apprehension of planetary multiplicity and the deadly defences it helped precipitate. The damage wrought by European powers in the course of shoring up their own world has visited the end of the world on other peoples across the planet – sometimes numerous times (Whyte 2018a: 236). In this way, Euro-modernity, in its recoiling from the self-differentiating forces of the Earth, came itself to act as a devastating force of planetary multiplicity – a revolution of the Earth in its own right. Without this sense that the impacts lately branded as the Anthropocene have at their core a much earlier – and brutally repercussive – encounter with the changeability of the Earth, the concept itself is a pale shadow of what it could be.

Earthly multitudes, as we conceive of them, may be constituted out of mutual respect and conviviality. But so too can they be 'built on a faultline of pain, held up by nightmares'. Many of the racialized bodies and nonelective communities caught up in the monstrous act of world breakage that was European colonialism were able to reorganize. In the face of relentless shockwaves, they succeeded in carving out what Fred Moten refers to as 'more + less than singular refuge' (2018: 12). Most often covertly, they managed to regroup, to improvise and experiment, just as those exposed to earlier 'seasons' of planetary upheaval and transformation had done. From the very experience of being reduced to a less-than-human substratum, those who have been marginalized, enslaved, dispossessed came back with what Moten (2018: 30) calls a 'subterranean knowledge of the Earth'.

## Postscript: Hegel on a Broken Earth

We began this chapter by counter-posing N. K. Jemisin's fictional plea for the social significance of earthly volatility with Hegel's at least as fantastical assertion that the ascent of human freedom had cut itself loose from the paroxysms of the Earth. In Jemisin's world, inherited knowledge counsels about what to expect during upheavals: '[a]ll things change during a Season' (2017: 151). But if we look back to when Hegel made his own equally imperious declaration, the timing would send shivers of fear through any volcanologist. While the *Jena Encylopedia* is a compendium of lectures, making its contents difficult to accurately date, the 1817 publication date lands the work in the midst of what is now considered the worst geological disaster in recorded human history. Though he had no way of knowing it, Hegel was living through a volcanic winter so devastating that it would not be out of place in the chronology of killer seasons that Jemisin appends to the *Broken Earth* books.

The year 1816 was known in Europe and North America as the 'year without a summer'. But the spell of sudden, geosynchronous climate change in fact spanned three gruelling years. It began on 10 April 1815 when the vent of the Indonesian volcano Tambora collapsed. In the most powerful eruption in recorded history, Tambora ejected some 100 cubic kilometres of effluvia into the atmosphere. On the flanks of the mountain, literary studies scholar Gillen D'Arcy Wood recounts, massive ash flows entombed a kingdom, obliterating an ethnic group and extinguishing an entire language (2014: 23). Aloft in the stratosphere, ejected sulphate particles temporarily shifted the dynamics of the planet's atmosphere, resulting in sustained temperature drops of as much as 5–6 °F (2014: 49).

Across much of the planet, harvests failed and famine descended, followed by epidemics of hunger-related illness – with fatalities most probably running to tens of millions (Wood 2014: 49, 233). In Europe, hunger amongst the urban poor sparked mass demonstrations while the worst-hit peasantry took to the road. Faced with the spectre of political radicalism and the presence of multitudes of starving refugees, European governments turned sharply in authoritarian directions – while various forms of extremism or fanaticism burgeoned (2014: 60–4; Behringer 2017).

Hegel did not link the crisis he lived through to a volcanic event. Indeed, it was not until the 1970s that historian John Dexter Post fully teased out the link between Tambora and the European subsistence crisis of 1815–18 (Behringer 2017: 26). And yet, as is often the case, Hegel's contribution to modern Western thought is more complex, more ambiguous than it first appears. Amidst the rise of fanaticism and authoritarianism during the Tambora crisis, as accusatory fingers pointed towards marginalized social groups, Hegel was amongst those who defended the due process of political institutions and the values that underpinned them – which included taking anti-Semitic philosophers to task in his writings (Behringer 2017: 21).

For all his wilful stilling of the Earth, then, we might also credit Hegel with a kind of precursory defence against the 'state of exception'. His disavowal of the geologic, in this sense, might be regarded not simply as the denial of social significance of geological agency, but as a normative claim: an assertion that we should not – under any circumstance – let the contingent rumblings of the Earth undermine hard-earned political rights and entitlements. In the current staging and scripting of responsibility at the threshold of Earth system change, this too seems worthy of note – all the more so as it emerges from the eye of a stupendous volcanic 'season'.

In the following chapter, we bring together our thinking on planetary multiplicity and earthly multitudes in an extended case study that takes an increasingly core concept of social thought – mobility – and shows how it can be analysed through the lens of planetary social thought. Whereas the current chapter has probed the fatal consequences of modern social and philosophical thought's repression of the encounter with a volatile Earth, chapter 6 demonstrates some of the advantages that arise from positioning key socio-technical processes within the wider transformations of the planet. Activating our methods of geohistorical analysis, metapattern recognition, stratal analysis and comparative and speculative planetology, we show how an understanding of the forms of mobility manifested by the Earth itself can help us to think how we might lessen our reliance on fossil-fuelled engines and start learning to 'move otherwise'.

# 6

# *Terra Mobilis*

## Introduction: Herding in Motion

Fifty million years ago, what we now call Europe and Asia were divided by the shallow Turgai Sea, which stretched from the Arctic Ocean in the north to the Tethys Ocean that at that time separated Europe from Africa. One of the last parts of the Turgai Sea to dry out, millions of years later, was the southernmost portion – indeed, the Black, Caspian and Aral Seas remain watery to this day. On this area of new land emerged the Pontic-Caspian Steppe, now consisting of nearly a million square kilometres of temperate grassland and shrubland that stretches 1,000 km east and north-east from the north-western shore of the Black Sea. Today it forms part of southern Ukraine and Russia, but between around 3,300 and 2,500 BCE on this vast steppe lived people now known as the Yamnaya. As tribal peoples, it is likely that they didn't have a name for themselves as a whole. Contemporary names given to them and the wider groupings they belonged to, such as the 'Yamnaya' or the 'Pit Grave Culture' or the 'Kurgan' culture, derive from their burial practices involving pit chambers and mounds or 'tumuli' (*yama* is Russian for pit, *kurgan* for tumulus). But alongside these material traces, they left another set of remains – linguistic ones.

For the Yamnaya spoke Proto-Indo-European, the language from which most European languages and many in Central and Southern Asia descended. Proto-Indo-European has been painstakingly reconstructed using comparative linguistics and analysis of the underlying rules governing sound change in this family of languages. Many, perhaps most, words in the modern languages that are descended from Proto-Indo-European are made out of recombinations of the roots or 'morphemes' that formed part or all of individual words. The Yamnaya are thought by many to be the strongest candidate for the people whose version of Proto-Indo-European was to spread across Eurasia, budding the Italic, Celtic, Hellenic, Slavic, Indic, Persian and Germanic languages spoken by later cultures and civilizations. And the words that they spoke reveal much about their lives.

Archaeologically, the Yamnaya are not seen as a single ethnic unit but as a diverse set of local peoples and tribes united in a single 'horizon': a shared linguistic and material culture. From the words of theirs that survived and spread we know that the people within the Yamnaya horizon not only buried each other in pit chambers, but were also stockbreeders, herders and farmers. They seem to have had no words for city, but many for tribal relations. As anthropologist David Anthony explains, they 'cultivated grain, herded cattle and sheep, collected honey from honeybees, ... made wool or felt textiles, plowed fields at least occasionally or knew people who did, sacrificed sheep, cattle, and horses to a troublesome array of sky gods, and fully expected the gods to reciprocate the favor' (2007: 98).

But what made the Yamnaya people interesting compared to other nomads and pastoralists of the time was the way that they *moved*. First of all, they domesticated the horse, and may have been the first people to do so systematically. But second, they also moved on wheels – using carts, wagons and later chariots. The way that their vocabulary about wheels and wheeled motion spread and evolved over time as it passed into other languages enables archaeologists to trace with some confidence the use of wheeled vehicles back to them. Among this vocabulary were at least two words for wheel – *$k^wek^wlos$, originally meaning 'the thing that turns' (which survives in words such as the English 'circle'), and *rot-eh* (which crops up in 'rotate', but also in wheel-words in Welsh, German and Lithuanian). There was also *$ak^*s$-, for axle, *ei-/*oi-, for the pole or shaft that was used to attach the animals pulling a wagon (which gave us the Slovenian *oje* and English 'oar'), and *wégheti*, a verb meaning 'to transport, convey or go in a vehicle' (Anthony 2007: 33–6). It was from this last verb that the noun 'wagon' emerged, to name the thing with which you convey things. Indeed, off the back of *wégheti* tumbled a whole family of modern English words that we use to describe things that move in the Earth – 'wagon' and 'vehicle'; 'viaduct' and 'convoy'; 'way' and 'weigh'; 'voyage' and 'vector'; 'convection' and 'advection'.

Wheels had been used before, but not so much for transporting things; the utility of the machinic solution of the rotating wheel had been more apparent in crafts such as pottery and spinning that we discussed in chapter 3. Archaeologists are not sure when the wagon first became used as a practical device rather than a child's toy, but it seems to have been about 3,500 BCE. For the Yamnaya, what made the wagon so significant was that it enabled them to make their homes mobile. After 3,500, on the Pontic steppes, the spread of the Yamnaya horizon saw herders of various tribes adopting a new lifestyle around three kinds of mobility, involving human legs, horse riding and cattle-drawn wagons respectively. Like other cultures, they walked for the short distances involved in the tasks of daily existence. They also rode on horses for longer and faster trips – to scout for new pastures, to trade or raid, or to herd over larger territories. And they used their wagons to make less frequent, slower but longer journeys, carrying bulky items like tents, food and water, so that they could move their settlements around following the seasons, and could live far into the deep steppes, away from river valleys (Anthony 2007: 133, 302). Wagons acted like a solvent, dissolving the herding communities that had been concentrated in the forested river valleys and allowing the herding families to disperse across the wider steppe. The wagon would later repeat this solvent effect, when it was adopted by European farmers, reducing the need for village-based, cooperative labour and making the small family farm viable (2007: 72–3).

What do the Yamnaya tell us? How can we put them in the story of the Earth? In many ways they are not special, are only one among many late bronze-age cultures of Eurasia. But their morphemes (the smallest meaningful unit of linguistic meaning) provided the units of meaning for what would become planetary cultures, not least through patterns of European colonization. But if the Yamnaya set off a linguistic phenomenon that became planetary in scale, the Yamnaya people are also planetary in a more material way – and this is not unrelated to the power of their morphemes to travel and bind people into mutual communication. This was the way this earthly multitude moved, not just originating horseback riding and wheeled vehicles, but binding human body, horse and wagon – and the flora and fauna of the steppe – into a powerful assemblage that reorganized space and time. Well before the rise of the powerful city states in Mesopotamia to the south, the Yamnaya material and linguistic horizon was 'to transform Eurasia from a series of unconnected cultures into a single interacting system' (Anthony 2007: 459).

We are not suggesting that the Yamnaya and their culture were the necessary or sufficient condition for the later emergence of the Anthropocene. Nor should we underplay the differences between the cattle-drawn wagons of the Yamnaya horizon and the fossil fuel-guzzling vehicles of today. Our concept of 'planetary partiality' is intended to capture the idea that planetary social thought can be done in a way that is not only sensitive to important sociocultural differences, but can also help us understand such differences better. But, with care, we might suggest that the Yamnaya with their horses and wagons were indeed an Earth event – or are at least an important piece in the slow unfolding of one – and this is why we have chosen them as a situated starting-off point for an extended case study on mobility. Most of the Yamnaya's words may not have been special (though some were, as we saw); but what was certainly special was their mode of living, which bound together the sedentary and the mobile in ways that set off a positive feedback that would spread both this mode of living and its tools and words across Europe and Asia. The way they moved, we argue, contained distinctive characteristics that helped to set the conditions for an even greater mobility revolution. But at the same time, as the chapter demonstrates, the mobility of the Yamnaya recapitulated ways that many other things move under planetary conditions.

## Mobility and the Anthropocene

If an important component of planetary social thought involves the understanding of mobility, in many ways it has a lot of existing social-scientific resources to draw on. Mobility has been a growing theme in the social sciences at least since the 1990s. In an important essay published in 1990, anthropologist Arjun Appadurai examined the movement of people, money, machines and ideas in the contemporary global economy, arguing that the conditions under which global flows occur are shaped by 'the growing disjunctures between ethnoscapes, technoscapes, finanscapes, mediascapes and ideoscapes' (1990: 301). In a broadly compatible way, sociologist Manuel Castells (2000) described contemporary society as a 'network society' in which there is a clash between two spatial logics: the subordinated *space of place*, of histori-cally rooted human experiences, and the dominant *space of flows*, a space made suitable for and constituted by the mobility of people, things and information. Sociologist John Urry and others brought such thoughts together in the proposal for a wider 'mobilities turn' in the social sciences, a reaction against the latter's sedentarist and territorial assumptions (2007).

The mobilities turn was clearly given a boost by the end of the Cold War and the (contested) idea that the world was cohering as a single, interacting economic and cultural system. More generally the turn was prompted by growing awareness of the increasing mobilization of resources, goods, people and ideas in the globally organized capitalism of the late twentieth century, and the limited capacity of a social science focused on place and nation to study and understand it. It is right that the social sciences responded to these changes, developing new concepts and methods that could help make the Earth itself a global object of thought. And the focus of the mobilities turn on the extension and acceleration of motion on the surface of the Earth can be seen as a useful prefiguration of the idea of the Great Acceleration (Steffen et al. 2015a), which resituates these changes as an event in Earth history.

The Anthropocene is, after all, largely the taking of sessile things and making them motile, or the rechannelling of existing flows. Many of the canonical metrics of Anthropocene epochal change – the increasingly anthropogenic movement of minerals and fixing of atmospheric nitrogen, and the alteration of the movement of rivers, for example – are about mobility. Even the static parts of the human-made technosphere – the massive infrastructure of buildings and roads that surrounds and enables modern social life – are in large part created in order to effect these flows (Zalasiewicz et al. 2016).

But we suggest that the study of mobilities itself needs a planetary turn, one that situates the phenomenon of mobility in the story of the self-organization of the planet over multiple time scales (Szerszynski 2016b; 2019c). This requires a deeper engagement with the physics of motion and with Earth system understandings of how different forms of motion arise – and the role that they play in the Earth.

How might we rethink the movements induced by human society, such as those of the Yamnaya and their descendants, in the wider context of the motion of entities within a planet? We titled this chapter in counterpoint to the notion of *Terra firma* – 'solid Earth'. *Terra mobilis*, or 'moving Earth', is the title of a 1980s computer program designed by and for geologists to model continental drift (Scotese and Denham 1988). It's also a formulation subsequently used to great effect by the novelist Anne Michaels in the book *Fugitive Pieces* (1997). Here, Michaels reminds us that beneath the lively and sometimes traumatic movements of our own species across the surface of the Earth lie the deeper, vaster mobilizations of the planet itself. As the novel's young protagonist Jakob recalls his tutelage by the geologist Athos: '[h]e heaped before my imagination the great heaving terra mobilis: "Imagine solid rock bubbling like stew; a whole mountain bursting into flame or slowly being eaten by rain"' (1997: 21). What is it that moves in *Terra mobilis*, we ask, and how are the powers of motion of different moving things enabled by the self-organization of the planet, in its continuous revolutions? And how are different patterns of stillness and motion bound together?

## 'It Moves'

After his official recantation of the idea that the Earth moves, rather than being stationary at the centre of the universe as was the official teaching of the Catholic Church at the time, Galileo Galilei is said to have muttered in Italian, *'eppur si muove'* ('and yet it moves'). Galileo of course was talking about the whole Earth moving as one body, in motion around its own axis and in orbit around the sun. And in an astrophysical sense, as a consolidated planet rather than a cloud of planetesimals, the Earth could indeed be said to move as a whole, retaining the conformation of its parts; to use the mathematical term, it 'translates'. 'And yet ...', we might want to mutter. Because the parts of the Earth also move in relation to each other, on different timescales, and it is this motion that makes the Earth what it is. So let us now focus on the 'naming of parts' of the mobile Earth, through looking at the size of different kinds of motion within its extended body.

We can draw here on the work of geologist Peter Haff and his metric of 'mass action' for measuring the mobility of the different parts of the Earth. Size and speed of motion are not the only things that are important in understanding the importance of different kinds of motion in the Earth, but they give us a useful starting point. As Haff (2010) defines it, mass action is calculated as mass times speed times path length. Thus things that are more massive, and/or move faster, and/or move for longer distances before stopping or drastically changing direction, will have a higher mass action. Haff uses a logarithmic scale for talking about the mass action of parts of the Earth. The SI units for this are $kg \cdot m^2/s$, and the range of numbers so huge that it is best to use not standard but scientific notation, in terms of powers of 10 (also known as orders of magnitude). So for example if we compare $10^{17}$ to $10^{18}$, the first as a standard number is 1 followed by 17 zeros, and the second is 1 followed by 18 zeros. The second number is 10 times bigger than the first, or one order of magnitude bigger. And $10^{19}$ would be two orders of magnitude bigger than $10^{17}$ – but this means it is not 10 + 10 = 20 times bigger, but $10 \times 10 = 100$ times bigger. And going up three orders of magnitude makes something 1,000 times bigger, and so on. So measuring motion logarithmically, by orders of magnitude or powers of ten, enables us to cover a wide range of motion from the very small and slow to the very big and fast.

The largest movements in the Earth as measured by mass action are still 'advective' flows in the fluid parts of the Earth, where bodies of liquid and gas move as a whole – advective being that form of fluid motion where a volume of fluid moves en masse, carrying properties with it such as heat or chemical load. We say 'still', because these movements will have been amongst the first to start in the Earth, soon after its formation, but also remain by far the largest, even under Anthropocene conditions. This is perhaps not surprising, since fluids (at least normal, 'Newtonian' ones) *have* to move, if there are gradients of gravity, density or pressure. One of these vast planetary motions is the convective flow of the Earth's mantle: the huge layer of silicate rock between the top of the Earth's outer core and the bottom of the crust. Most of the mantle is classed as solid but, given the temperature and pressure, behaves like a viscous fluid on geological timescales. Although this movement is very slow indeed, it involves a huge mass of matter participating in circulatory flows over a huge vertical range. Above the Earth's crust, there are a number of fluid motions of lower mass but much greater speed, each of which has a comparable mass action, including the wind belts and jet streams that girdle the planet, the great oceanic gyres, and the thermohaline circulation or 'ocean conveyor belt'.

The movement of solids in the Earth is more difficult. In terms of our machinic phylum of solutions to problems, solid movement is a problem for the Earth, one that has only with difficulty called forth solutions. The Earth has been very good at sorting and differentiating itself through gravity, hydrological flow and processes of erosion, solution, drift and sedimentation into concentrations of elements and minerals, mountains and plains, heat and cold – gradients and differentials of all kinds. The challenge for the planet, then, is how to access the potential of these sorted and differentiated parts, and bring them into active relation. The very feature of solids that enables them to carry conformational information (information in the form of enduring arrangement in space) makes it harder for them to move – all atoms have to 'translate' together, requiring huge concerted forces. Solids are also on the whole much denser, so heavier per unit volume. Furthermore, on the terrestrial surface, the Earth's gravity produces friction between object and ground, which tends to keep solids in place.

Solid movement is thus much smaller than fluid motion in the Earth: according to Haff's way of measuring earthly motion described above, even the largest systems of solid movement in the Earth have mass action that is four or five orders of magnitude smaller than the largest ones involving fluids. For solid motion, the largest mass action occurs in cases where large and heavy solid entities are moving very slowly due to an applied force, such as continental drift, sea-floor spreading or Antarctic glacial flow. After that, solids move more easily when they are 'discretized' – broken up into smaller pieces. When broken up into small enough particles, for example as river sediment, or as windborn, aeolian dust, solids can use the enveloping fluid to reduce friction, and also hitch a ride in the advective flow of fluids.

What about the movement of living things and machines? Nonhuman living things are also a kind of mobile solid. According to Haff's calculations, the nonhuman living systems with the largest mass action are migrating animals in low-resistance environments – whales, fish, birds and caribou. But Haff estimates the combined mass action of maritime shipping to now be even greater. The accelerating movement of people, artefacts and materials in the Anthropocene can be seen as an example of this discretization. Indeed, from a planetary perspective, motile animals including human beings, and the machines that humans use to transport themselves and other things, can be regarded as a special case of discretized solids – parts of the Earth's surface that have broken away, and are thus capable of moving independently. But as we will see, the energetics and mechanics of their motion are different from river sediment – differences that become clearer and take on a new significance when we start to think about how forms and powers of motion fit into deep time – and the revolutions of the Earth.

## Mobility Revolutions of the Earth

So the Earth as a planet involves a lot of motion – and a lot of different types of motion. But let us look at that picture again, this time as a story of planetary evolution over deep time. As we argued in chapter 4, in the longer history of the self-organization of the planet, new entities with new powers are brought into being, which thus enable the Earth to do new things. Just as the Anthropocene is a window onto the wider capacity of the Earth to pass thresholds, the capacity of humans to become a geological force is a window onto the way that powers emerge from new organizations of the Earth. As the Earth self-organized over deep time, new kinds of entity and assemblage developed, with new and newly distributed powers, and new forms of motion.

Part of this innovation in mobility involved tapping the free energy that flows through the Earth system from its two ultimate sources: incoming electromagnetic energy from the sun, and the interior heat left over from the Earth's formation (Lineweaver and Egan 2008; Hermann 2006: 1689). Initially, all motion within the extended body of the Earth involved taking this energy entering the Earth system and turning it into fluid motion – first mantle convection; then, when gases were emitted and built up, atmospheric circulation; and finally, after the oceans formed from cometary collision, hydrological circulation (itself largely driven by atmospheric circulation). Then, as the Earth cooled, and different minerals reached their freezing point, solids were formed.

When did solids start to move? For the first four billion years of the Earth's history, pretty much all solid motion on the Earth (apart from that caused by the occasional bolide impact) piggybacked directly or indirectly on the fluid flows just mentioned, as discretized solids such as aeolian dust, river sediment, avalanches, continental plates and other forms of drift (Haff 2010; Szerszynski 2019a). The Earth shares this kind of inner motion with all other planets and moons that, like Venus and Mars, have retained fluid compartments and are kept away from thermal equilibrium (Frank et al. 2017).

But on the Earth at least, life quite early on found a means of bypassing atmospheric motion as a way to access incoming solar energy, instead accessing it directly through photosynthesis. Through this process the biosphere now captures a small but significant amount of the energy falling on the Earth's surface (Hermann 2006). However, photosynthesizing autotrophs ('self-nourishers') such as cyanobacteria, algae and plants used the captured solar energy largely for growth and reproduction rather than for motion. In the early Earth, living things that altered their occupation of space generally *extended* (by expanding, or making further copies of themselves, or adding units to their body or colony) or *drifted* (using ambient energy gradients to move themselves or their spores in an undirected way).

It was the arrival of animals that fundamentally changed all this. Single-celled organisms had already developed the capacity for powered motion, moving their tiny bodies towards or away from chemical concentrations, light or oxygen (Nealson 2011: 48, 51). The scales and speeds involved, however, were tiny. But then came much larger, heterotrophic organisms – animals evolved to capture the photosynthetically derived energy in plants or algae, and able to store it within themselves in the form of fats and sugars. This captured fuel, stored as 'flesh', could then be used to move – not least, in order to capture more energy (Judson 2017). We will talk more about this below, because, of course, human bodily motion derives from this animal energy revolution.

But the animal-based mobility revolution entailed more than just capturing and storing energy; it also required the use of the properties of solid–fluid and solid–solid interaction to propel the animal's body forward. Haff (2010) points out that this basically involved the use of rotational motion, whether limb motion or undulation, and that it thus could be said to be in the same part of the machinic phylum as the wheel. Note that the English word 'walk' (and also derivatives such as 'vagrant') derives, via German, from the Proto-Indo-European *walg-, *walk-, 'to twist, turn, move'. Using rotational or reciprocal motion, animal limbs turned friction (or drag and lift forces for swimming and flying creatures) from a problem to an asset. Terrestrial limb motion itself uses low energy, thanks to the low mass of limbs and the use of pendulum motion and elastic tension to store unused energy in each swing and reuse it in the next. For creatures moving on land, limbs basically serve three functions – reducing friction, controlling the direction of travel, and propelling the animal's body forward – a point which will be significant when we circle back to the wheel.

## Human Mobility Innovations

The innovation of animal motion, especially when combined with the sheer size of multicellular animal bodies, was hugely consequential for the Earth – not least because of the way it introduced a new kind of relation between Earth entities, that between predator and prey, producing a huge acceleration in the evolutionary 'arms race' (Szerszynski 2016a). Human locomotion in itself is just another example of this mobility revolution; but the way that the human being evolved to move helped to set the species apart, as the top endurance runner. The human body evolved to run, for scavenging and hunting: unlike prey animals with their fixed gaits, the human animal's long legs give no optimal, most energy-efficient speed, making it much easier to tire out different prey species. The ability to sweat also gave humans a huge advantage in endurance running over other animals (Liebenberg 2006). Furthermore, unlike many other species, humans don't have specialist navigational senses for dead reckoning or piloting, so wayfaring techniques are passed on culturally, and can change quickly (Levinson 2003: 223). As we saw in chapter 4, the ability to track animals in complex environments, and to form an understanding of their habits and likely further actions, would have been facilitated by – and may have further enabled – the development of higher cognitive functions, resulting in new patterns of motion across the landscape (Liebenberg 1990).

How does human motion relate to settlement? We might want to contrast nomadic and sedentary cultures, but the reality is more complex: there was no clear moment of transition in which formerly nomadic hunter-gatherers adopted a sedentary agricultural way of life. For a start, there are mobile agriculturalists and miners like the Yamnaya, and nomadic peoples today are nearly all in interaction with sedentary cultures anyway (Scott 2017). Even within foraging, hunting and gathering cultures, the pattern of remaining and moving, and of short and long movements, is more complex than can be accommodated by a simple contrast between nomadism and settlement. Archaeologist Lewis Binford identifies a complex range of strategies involving individual foraging and camp movements amongst hunter-gatherers, along a spectrum at one end of which foragers move people to resources, and at the other, collectors move resources to people (1980; Kelly 2013: 78–9).

To unpack the relation between staying and moving we can draw on some language used in physics for different kinds of fluid motion (see Haff 2010). *Laminar* motion occurs when a volume or 'parcel' of fluid moves as a whole, in parallel. It is called 'laminar' because different layers of fluid tend to slide past each other in an orderly way, as if in lanes on a motorway, with little mixing or turbulence. Laminar motion in the Earth is generally longer distance. Such movement predominates in the large-scale advective flows of the Earth discussed earlier – especially in the middle regions of fluid compartments, far from solid surfaces, where little resistance is encountered to produce friction and eddies. In *diffusive* motion, by contrast, each particle moves independently, and in a way that involves frequent changes of direction. In human society, this contrast can to some extent be mapped onto social power; ruling and occupying state powers have tended to use roads, travelling in vehicles and convoys or marching in a laminar fashion, while the patterns of motion of everyday inhabitation tend to be more diffusive, with lots of short paths and changes of direction, reacting to local conditions. As anthropologists Tim Ingold and Jo Vergunst put it, '[w]hereas occupants march along roads, inhabitants more usually step across them' (2008: 13; see also Widlok 2008: 59).

But to understand how people like the Yamnaya move we need another concept – that of *superdiffusion*. Superdiffusion is a label used to describe patterns of mobility where each entity is moving independently, but in such a way that over time they explore a larger area of the range available to them. A particular form of superdiffusion is the *Lévy flight* – a combination of frequent short movements and occasional longer movements, in a fractal pattern that has no natural scale. This seems to be part of the machinic phylum of the Earth – a solution discovered independently by many entities and processes. Lévy flights occur in turbulent fluids, where random, short-range Brownian jiggling is inter-rupted by sudden long movements. It is also found in many biological processes, especially those involving feeding and mating: predators such as sharks seem to use it as an optimal strategy for searching for food in dynamic environments like oceans (Viswanathan et al. 2008). And as we have recently had a sharp reminder, it is how viruses move, especially when their passage is aided by long-range human mobility.

But cognitively more complex humans also draw on the Lévy flight strategy – foragers, hunter-gatherers, farmers and fishers for a start (Raichlen et al. 2014). Humans move in this way for different reasons – for example in the alternation between taking advantage of trails for ease of movement, and moving off them opportunistically (Reynolds et al. 2018), or in the seasonal 'upping of sticks'. The anthropologist Lewis Binford quotes an elderly Inuit summing up his life as involving alternating times of willow smoke and dogs' tails: 'when we camp it's all willow smoke, and when we move all you see is dogs' tails wagging in front of you' (1980: 4). Archaeologist and anthropologist Robert Kelly's discussion of foraging cultures divides their mobility into three interrelated modes: 'individual foraging …, residential movements, and long-term territorial shifts' – but each of those three is likely to manifest fractal patterns (2013: 104). The Yamnaya, engaging in motion by foot, horse and wagon, show a similar pattern.

So if the advent of the animal body was a mobility revolution for the Earth, it was one that nevertheless participated in a wider 'metapattern' of movement that it shared with other entities. Was the wheeled vehicle the next major mobility revolution after the animal body? Well, yes and no. In some ways the wagon and cart were just a minor variation on the animal form. In effect, the wheels mimicked one of the three roles of animal limbs – reducing friction with the ground. By the use of wooden wheels that either rotated around a fixed, rounded and greased axle, or were fixed to an axle that rotated in bearings, the high friction between wheel and road was mechanically traded for the low friction around the axle, in order to ease the motion of the cart or wagon with its load. With a front axle that could pivot on a vertical axis, users of wagons could also do some steering – but this limb-related function was done largely by the draught animals and their leader, with the wagon following. And energetically the wagon was no major innovation either: it simply exploited animal (including human) energy.

While the wagon had long-term effects on human cultures – and the wheel and axle by their very nature tend to spread quickly and spread other things with them (Anthony 2007: 74) – animal-powered wheeled transport had limited use in the day-to-day lives of human societies (Basalla 1988: 7–11). For those cultures with wheeled transport, it tended to play a constrained role, as in the case of the Yamnaya's occasional shift of homestead. When adopted by farmers it was used mainly for hauling heavy goods – grain, manure, lumber and clay; chariots were developed about 2,100 BCE, and were used primarily to intimidate (Anthony 2007: 72, 462). Much later, coaches evolved in Europe, and were arguably used mainly for the purposes of social distinction (Piggott 1992). Through all this time, most human journeys across land were on foot, or maybe on horse, while movement across water used human muscle or wind power. For more than four millennia, the wheel played a marginal role in human mobility. But tapping into fossil fuel strata changed all that.

## From Combustion to Motion

> In all those busy and inventive millennia of baking and boiling, melting
> and smelting, it probably didn't occur to [our ancestors] that their fires
> held another power, too – the power of motion. For them, the grueling
> work of moving matter from point A to point B could be done only
> by muscle, water, or wind ... This reality placed a tight limit on the
> material work a society could accomplish. (Freese 2016: 43)

As Barbara Freese points out, using fire not to *transform* but to *move*
things was not an obvious step. For all our talk of combustion in
chapter 3, you may recall, there was very little mention of mobility.
It was the arrival in Europe of gunpowder from China, and its application in propelling rockets, bullets and cannonballs, that seem to have
lit the fuse. Writing in the 1930s, Lewis Mumford observed that 'the
gun was the starting point of a new type of machine: it was, mechanically speaking, a one cylinder internal combustion engine' (1934: 88).
In seventeenth-century Europe, various people including the German
natural philosopher Gottfried Leibniz embarked on a quest to repurpose
the explosive force of gunpowder to the less destructive task of gener-
ating motive force. It was a French medical doctor, Denis Papin, who,
after a series of unsuccessful attempts to develop a gunpowder-powered
*moteur à explosion*, and in correspondence with Leibniz, recognized
that steam power offered a 'less violent' route to driving a piston.
Papin subsequently designed a viable steam engine in 1690 and finally
constructed a fully functional steamboat in 1708 (Valenti 1979: 34;
Clark 2018b).

   From the beginning of their endeavour, Leibniz and Papin were
motivated by a practical goal: to increase the power of humans over their
environment by converting what Leibniz called the '*vis viva*' or 'living
force' of combustion into useful work, such as pumping water out of
the ground, milling grain or moving vehicles. Papin wrote to Leibniz
in 1705: 'I can assure you that, the more I go forward, the more I find
reason to think highly of this invention which, in theory, may augment
the powers of Man to infinity' (Valenti 1979: 38). But viewed geohistorically, they played a part in an event which was to have not only human
but also planetary significance – and a key role in this was played by
powered transport. How can the framework that we introduced in
chapter 4 help illuminate this?

   In terms of stratal analysis, powered transport typically moves on the
boundary between compartments of the Earth – on land or water. Like
animals, vehicles do so by taking advantage of the different properties

of the two media between which they move. For example, terrestrial animals and internal combustion vehicles exploit the combination of high friction between their body and the 'ground' (broadly conceived), and the low viscosity and high oxygen content of the air. But powered vehicles are interstratal in another way – in *how* they are powered. In a metaphorical sense, all motion is 'downhill', in that it involves the exploitation of an energy gradient from high to low free energy. Energetically, powered vehicles connect the human world with the fossil fuel deposits far beneath our feet. In its motion, whether it is topographically going uphill or downhill, a powered vehicle is using – and doing its part to use up – the chemical gradient between the oil fields and the Earth's surface.

There are geohistorical dimensions to powered transport too. The form of the typical powered vehicle, with its articulated structure, its on-board storage of fuel in tank or battery, its 'limbs' of motion and its front–back asymmetry, echoes those of megafauna (Szerszynski forthcoming) – and this is neither an accident nor simply a rediscovery of a metapattern. Many of the innovations of the animal body 'jumped' to the abiotic world of artefacts, through human making, so that technological artefacts were able to inherit and recombine the innovations of the animal lineage that gave birth to them (Szerszynski 2017c). And in the case of terrestrial vehicles it was the powering of the vehicle – the wedding between chambered fire and the wagon – that actualized a hitherto unrealized potential of the wheel.

Up until now, in an assemblage with the axle, the wagon bed and the shaft or 'thill' that connected wagon and draught animals, the wheel had been used to carry weight, to reduce friction and occasionally to select direction. Now it also started to apply *force*: the wheel was fixed to the axle and the axle turned with a motive force, relying on the friction between wheel and ground (now maximized by widening the wheel) to push the vehicle forward. It is impossible to overstate the difference this tiny change made for how things moved.

In his comment to Leibniz about 'augmenting the powers of Man to infinity', Papin seems mainly to have been thinking of the sheer muscle power of steam engines, and overcoming the 'tight limit' on the work that society could achieve. But it was not just their mechanical innovations, and the huge amount of chemical energy stored in fossil fuel deposits, that meant that the innovations of Leibniz and Papin could trigger a different kind of explosion. What was crucial was the way that turning combustion into motive power enabled greater extraction. In the Cambrian era, animals had perfected the 'moving-to-eat, eating-to-move' positive feedback loop. Motorized vehicles did this trick with bells – and horns – on, as vehicular motion was both enabled by and enabled the extraction and distribution of fossil fuels with their high energy density. Once powered, the vehicle went from being a marginal mobile entity in human society to one that became central to modern, 'commercial' society. The diversity of vehicles expanded, in an 'Anthropocene radiation' of vehicle types to rival that of the Cambrian, filling the possibility space with diverse forms, as carts, wagons and carriages evolved into mechanized land vehicles such as trains, automobiles and trucks. On water too, boats and ships began to be propelled by paddles and propellers powered by coal or oil, while powered flight made possible directed air travel, and specialized vehicles were developed for use in industrial environments.

Slowly at first, but with an accelerating dynamic, the surface of the Earth was filled with transport corridors and vehicles – and the atmosphere with carbon dioxide and particulates. Today, as well as capturing an estimated 24 per cent of the net primary production of the terrestrial biosphere (Haberl et al. 2007), or about 16 terawatts (TW) of energy, human society currently obtains around 5.1 TW from burning oil, 3.6 TW from coal and 3.2 TW from gas (Hermann 2006: 1692). More than half of that energy goes into moving things and people around – and half of that for passenger transport (Jarvis et al. 2015: 691). And here we encounter another metapattern, one that is crucial for understanding the powered transport vehicle as a geohistorical event: the vehicle doesn't just move itself but carries a cargo or payload within the hollow of its body.

## Cargo

Historically speaking, most of the material that has been moved around on vehicles by human society has been biomass – fuel, food, livestock and people – with some geomass, especially for use as building materials. We saw in the case of the Yamnaya – and the farmers who adopted the use of their wagons and carts – that their main payload was large bulk items such as manure, lumber and water. But in order for this kind of mobility to happen, non-motile entities and substances that are embedded in local contexts need to be converted into abstract, bulk 'materials'. This is what philosopher Andrew Feenberg calls 'primary instrumentalisation': the decontextualisation of 'raw materials' out of their naturalistic context (trees or other plants in a forest, water in a river, minerals in the ground) and their reduction to primary (and often quantifiable) qualities such as chemical composition, brittleness, homogeneity, strength, nutritional value or exchange value (1999: 203–5).

In modern society, with its powered transport, the primary instrumentalization of materials has been intensified and proliferated to the point where it is arguably a planetary geological process as important as precipitation or erosion. As Mumford put it, in the modern period 'the methods and ideals of mining became the chief pattern for industrial effort throughout the Western world. Mine : blast : dump : crush : extract : exhaust' (1934: 74), as things are broken off and broken down, stripped of their embeddedness in context and made able to move. The rise of abstract money as a medium of exchange that can be hoarded for future use and exchanged for almost anything has clearly played an important role in this acceleration: it created a selective pressure for ways of dealing with matter that favoured abstract exchangeability and flow.

Even when pre-existing wholes such as humans, other animals and artefacts are pulled into mass advection – what in fluid dynamics is called 'entrainment' – they must first be detached from their wider, territorial, ecological or social wholes and become 'timber', 'livestock', 'passengers' or 'labour' (or, in the next chapter, 'fertilizer'). In the Global North, the moving of biomass has in recent decades been overtaken in scale by the flow of minerals and metals, as advanced (and emergent) economies move towards building and maintaining a growing infrastructure of buildings, roads and durable goods – much of this with the principal function of enabling the movement of other things. Global mining and quarrying alone are now estimated to move more than 57 billion tons per year – more mass than is moved by either glaciers or water erosion (Bridge 2009).

The original act of 'motilization' – the turning of local geological, ecological or economic resources, whether sessile or diffusive, into materials capable of being entrained in laminar advection in global currents of flow – is often violent, and not just in the physical sense. It can involve cultural violence, especially to the highly territorialized forms of life of traditional or Indigenous peoples, in a clash between Appadurai's (1990) space of place and space of flows. It is also frequently accompanied by political violence (Tavares 2013). As we saw in the previous chapter, the widespread practice of enslavement during the period of European colonial expansion involved the uprooting – or kidnap – of peoples from their homelands and their forcible setting to work in distant regions: a process that has been observed to have parallels, and often direct linkages, with the extraction of mineral resources (Yusoff 2018).

We have already seen how the alternation between many small, localized journeys and occasional long-range migrations, as practised by pastoral peoples like the Yamnaya, can be viewed as an example of the metapattern of superdiffusion. This also applies to the dynamics of moving cargo. In order to move their settlement, the Yamnaya would have moved their motilized cargo along the short, multi-directional path lengths available to human bodies, moving around a local landscape with pitchforks, shovels and buckets as they loaded up their wagons. Then the wagons would have performed a long movement to a new seasonal site – or, less frequently, to a new territory further into the steppe – before the cargo was unloaded, and then carried around, dispersed and incorporated into the social metabolism of the new setting.

The same pattern occurs in cargo today, which is entrained into circulatory flows of traffic, like sediment picked up by a stream that later departs from the flow and diffuses out to local contexts. Distribution of individual entities thus tends to make a Lévy flight – diffusion locally, then a big leap in large containers on even larger ships, then diffusion on trucks and white vans, and finally micro-diffusion in everyday life. So when Mumford described the logic of modernity as 'mine : blast : dump : crush : extract' he could have added: 'load up : transport : unload : distribute : recombine' to include the way that materials get diffused into new contexts and undergo further transformation – what Feenberg (1999: 205–7) calls *secondary* instrumentalization – as they are incorporated into localized forms of life.

## Moving Otherwise

In this chapter we have situated the contemporary mobility of resources, people and commodities in the *longue durée* of planetary self-differentiation – to show how our movements are part of a broader story of all the ways that the planet has made its internal parts come to move. In thinking about modern, powered transport we have employed stratal analysis, locating powered transport in the flows of energy through the different parts of the Earth system. We have put contemporary powered transport in the context of geohistorical energy revolutions, and positioned it as a technological offspring of the biological lineage of megafauna to which we as a species belong. We have also looked at the way that modern transport exhibits metapatterns – solutions made available to various entities in different contexts by the conformation of the Earth itself. So what about planetary comparison and speculation? Can we use the existing diversity of motion in the Earth to imagine how things might move otherwise – in the manner of Deleuze and Guattari's calling forth of a 'New Earth' (1987; 1994)?

In order to do this we need to attend to 'the virtual', to latent possibilities that are still contained within the Earth's machinic phylum and inherited forms – but also to forms of motion that are being enacted all around us as 'minor' traditions. Like the wheel–axle combination, there are doubtless other ways of tapping into the Earth's internal difference to produce motion, and other latent earthly multitudes ready to explore them.

Here we will briefly explore a wider 'possibility space' for the movement of things and people. There are three stages to our speculative scenario, and as we go through them, we will gradually shift away from simply trying to replicate the existing structures and functions of society with different ways of moving, towards the more ambitious task of exploring how the repertoire of earthly motion might suggest very different ways of organizing society itself.

First, we explore the possibilities of *motion that does not rely on stored chemical energy*. This relates to the question of fossil fuels, but takes us into a broader possibility space. We have seen that animals perfected the ability to find and ingest organic matter, to store their energy internally in fats and sugars, and to draw on it in order to move their bodies. Vehicles generally copy this model, storing energy in fuel or batteries and using this to power motion. In many ways, the search for forms of mobility that are not dependent on burning fossil fuels is already exploring this space. But such searches typically stay with the animal body as a template. They assume the model of carrying fuel and then using it to power motion, but simply seek to replace hydrocarbons with power from other sources that can be stored in batteries, or as hydrogen. Instead, we could learn from how things moved before the advent of the animal body. But what are the alternatives to onboard, stored chemical energy? Energy can be stored dynamically – for example in spinning flywheels or coiled springs, or in the sheer momentum of the whole moving body. Another option is to provide power for directed motion from outside the entity, as happens with electric trains, or with capsules propelled along vacuum tubes. But another possibility, which we will focus on here, is to drift.

To drift is to rewind to the pre-Cambrian, when things basically floated in response to winds and currents, or rolled and slid down slopes. Animals at this time typically had radially symmetric bodies that reflected this kind of motion, without the front–back asymmetry and limbs of motion of modern, motile animals. From the point of view of locomoting animals like ourselves, drift has two distinctive aspects: (i) for power it only uses ambient gradients (for example the variations of pressure and speed of the surrounding fluid, or gravitational potential on slopes), and (ii) it results in undirected motion. The latter aspect of drift is important in itself: we saw earlier in this chapter how the Earth was formed, shaped and structured through processes of drift, and we will return to it at the end of the chapter. But here we want to focus on the first aspect. For many moving entities employ ambient energy to engage in 'driftwork' – putting drift to use in achieving a goal (Szerszynski 2019a). If they have limbs in any sense, in terms of the three roles of limbs discussed above – reducing friction, steering and powering – they only engage in the first two. For example gliding birds move their wings to direct but not power their motion in the moving air.

We could imagine a drift-based mobility system – one powered only by slopes, wind, water and other environmental flows – in which we used the powers of drift to 'green' structures of society. Nineteenth-century drinking water and sewage systems used gravity alone; funiculars, aerial tramways and even some trains capture the energy of going downhill to power going back up again. We can use balloons to move in new ways that, rather than using stored energy to drive through the air, use the motion of the atmosphere to propel motion. For example, as part of his Aerocene project, artist Tomás Saraceno worked with the Massachusetts Institute of Technology to produce a flight-predictor that would allow one to choose when and where to launch one of his solar balloons to maximize the chances of arriving at a chosen destination (CAST 2018).

To make a real 'drift economy' built on such driftwork we would need to develop a far deeper understanding of the world around us, and of the processes of drift that abound in it. We would need to learn from those earthly multitudes who have the know-how involved in drifting well, such as sailors, ballooners, downhill skiers and surfers. We might also include here migrants, hitchhikers and even commuters, who have the practical knowledge needed to hitch a ride on the para-flows of traffic that circulate around the surface of the Earth.

The second stage of our exploration relates to the first, and involves the dynamic connecting of strata. Combustion and the fossil fuel revolution did this explosively – actualizing the chemical gradient between coal, oil and gas deposits and the subaerial surface of the Earth. But the story of the Earth shows this to be just one of a number of mobility innovations that have involved connecting strata. We saw above that when living organisms developed photosynthesis, by directly accessing the light entering the Earth's atmosphere they in effect connected the subaerial surface – first of the sea, later of the land – with the top of the atmosphere, thereby leapfrogging the inefficiencies involved in converting solar energy to fluid motion (Kleidon 2010: 1312). This connection was then turned into motion by the animals whose collective bodies formed trophic layers of consumers taking advantage of this vegetal trick.

But there are mobile entities that are interstratal in other ways. As we saw above, many moving things – abiotic, biotic and technological – reside and move on the boundary between media. Operating at the juncture of water and atmosphere, or land and atmosphere, they exploit the different properties of the respective media. Such entities connect the media directly with their bodies, at every moment; their bodies in a sense *are* that connection. Other things move in ways that tap more intimately into the flows of the media that they connect. Sailors connect the sea and the air, stick a sail up into the air and a keel into the water, and use the resulting force to propel the boat, even upwind. *Velella velella*, jellyfish with a little sail, do the same, not just being pushed by the wind but angling their sails to it to generate lift force, thus moving at an angle to the wind (Francis 1991). Kite-boarders and kite-powered boats join moving strata that are even further apart, with tethered kites that can reach up into faster wind layers.

Other entities cannot bridge the strata with their bodies, but have to reciprocally move between them. Birds can spot when to enter and leave particular air currents that allow them to save energy by soaring – gaining lift from rising air produced by thermals, weather fronts or slopes. They can also engage in dynamic soaring in a looping trajectory to extract power from differences in wind speed at different heights (Vogel 1994: 259–61). Perhaps human society can learn to move differently by exploring more thoroughly the myriad ways to connect the strata of the Earth.

Third, and finally, we can use our analysis of planetary mobilities to ask a very different kind of question: how would we have to redesign society if all things drifted? Of all forms of motion, drift surely reminds us most clearly that our powers and our luck are not ours alone. Drift is what 'happens', in the Old Norse sense of 'hap' as luck or fortune. Before the interiorization of European experience in the seventeenth century, 'happiness' referred not to an interior subjective state but to the outer condition of those for whom the best outcome has 'happened' (Barfield 1954: 170–1). What acts of solidarity should drift draw from us? How would we want the world to be organized if the movement of people and goods took the form of dissemination by drift? Echoing the social model of disability, we can ask not how drift can be eradicated, but how the world can be made safe, hospitable, just, for drifting things, ideas and beings.

## Welcoming Lives Adrift

The linguistic remains left by the Yamnaya can help us with the question of how to live with and through mobility. The English words 'guest' and 'host' derive from same Proto-Indo-European word spoken by the itinerant Yamnaya, to refer to general norms of hospitality between strangers:

> The late Proto-Indo-European guest-host relationship required that 'hospitality' ... should be extended by hosts to guests (both *\*ghos-ti-*), in the knowledge that the receiver and giver of 'hospitality'

could later reverse roles. The social meaning of these words was then more demanding than modern customs would suggest. ... The guest-host institution might have been among the critical identity-defining innovations that spread with the Yamnaya horizon. (Anthony 2007: 303)

The Yamnaya may have unwittingly laid the foundations for contemporary fossil-fuelled hypermobility; but perhaps around the same time they also spread an antidote, in their word *\*ghos-ti-* and its descendants. Such words remind us of the possibility of treating 'guest' and 'host' not as fixed and opposed categories, but as a single symmetrical bond of hospitality. Anthony speculates that this is an after-echo of the great event of mobilization that the Yamnaya effected with their superdiffusive motion using their own bodies, horses and ox-drawn wagons: once populations become more mobile, norms about how strangers should treat each other become necessary. Similarly, if in an age of accelerating climate change we all find ourselves to some degree migrants and potential guests, we will need to discover that we are also all obliged to host and be hospitable, as geographers Andrew Baldwin and Giovanni Bettini remind us in the aptly titled collection *Life Adrift* (2017). And this will also mean learning from other cultures and other kinds of practitioners – from those earthly multitudes who have not forgotten the arts of hosting and being a guest (see Clark 2011: 193–219; 2012).

Perhaps the most radical gesture regarding mobility and the Anthropocene, then, would be not simply to replace the power source of our vehicles with renewables, or even to reduce the mass action of things that move by moving fewer things, using less energy per mile and over shorter distances. It would be to problematize the very logic that so many of us use today to talk about, comprehend and organize motion, with its notions such as 'origin' and 'destination', 'expectation' and 'delivery'; to reconsider the relationship between moving and being still; to rethink why we move and what mobility is for.

Understanding that all our possibilities for movement ultimately draw their potential from the way that the different components of the Earth encounter and articulate with each other serves as to remind us that we live on *Terra mobilis*. And a planet that is constitutively in motion, as many of the more mobile earthly multitudes well know, is one that obliges its inhabitants to move, from time to time and at a range of spatial scales. In important respects, as we discussed in chapter 4, superabundant fossil fuel has enabled some of us – at least – to smooth out the gradients, perturbations and rifts that inhere in planetary multiplicity. It has facilitated investments in stasis and in holding ground, and encouraged the deployment of certain kinds of mobility to secure and augment this occupied space. But the science of the Anthropocene and all its Great Accelerations can be read as a reminder of just how exceptional this moment has been. To dwell fully on *Terra mobilis*, then, may be to acknowledge that the logics of mobility and stasis that have increasingly prevailed over recent centuries cannot be sustained: that they are, in the words of Claire Colebrook, 'violent interruptions of a life that is migratory and in constant search of refuge' (2017b: 116).

By thinking mobility through the planet, we have been proposing, we may become more open to the greater 'mobility commons' of lineages and metapatterns that the Earth has built up around us, and learn to attune ourselves to the still latent possibilities lurking in the multiplicity and disequilibrium of our planet. Like the soil built up on a forest floor, where each square inch is ready to receive a seed if chance were to deliver one there, a society that treated drift as the primary mode of motion would be organized through what might be called (adapting Bataille's language) a 'general' rather than a 'restricted' mode of expectation: one that was prepared for surprise as to who and what might arrive on one's doorstep. Echoing Marcel Mauss's (1954) study of Melanesian 'gift economies' in which goods are given without guarantee of return, a 'drift economy' would be one that blurred the distinction between guest and host. The logic would be to direct economic surplus and excess not into private hands, or into the growth of the technosphere, but into universal basic services, with shelter and food to spare. Indeed, with a greater awareness of the chance that is involved in the amount of resources that any individual has access to, and the planetary commons that underpins them, the very notion of private property would have to be transformed. So if the Yamnaya gift of the wagon was one that had a fossil-fuelled sting in the tail, maybe another gift of the Yamnaya – the guest–host relation – can be a necessary antidote or 'counter-gift'.

In the following chapter, we pick up on the theme of the crude and violent disembedding of matter from its physical and cultural context. Turning to the colonial extractive frontier, we look at a case that involves not only the expropriation of minerals, but the unearthing and mobilization of the ancestral spirits who dwell in the ground that has been excavated. Looking at once at the problem of the disruption of biogeochemical cycles through intensive extraction and the issue of mobilizing 'spirit', we address the question of how the insights of Anthropocene science might converse with a range of Indigenous and traditional knowledge practices.

# 7

# Grounding Colonialism, Decolonizing Earth

## Introduction: Spirited Resistance

Anthropologist and artist Katerina Teaiwa recounts a story told by Kaiao Borerei, a member of a dancing group originally from the Pacific island of Banaba that had visited Rotorua, Aotearoa New Zealand in the 1970s:

> While on a bus trip through the nearby countryside, we saw an aerial topdressing plane putting fertiliser onto a farm. The bus driver told us it was superphosphate from Ocean Island and that made us feel sad and stirred our hearts. It seems that some of Banaba is in New Zealand. (cited in Teaiwa 2015: 103)

Twenty years later, activist Raobeia 'Ken' Sigrah made a similar point about the fate of his island, this time using a more explicitly political rhetoric: 'Where is Banaba? ... . Banaba's all over Australia, New Zealand and everywhere else in the world. Been used as phosphate. So where is my country? Where is my island?' (cited in Cushman 2013: 109).

Situated close to the equator in the West-Central Pacific, Banaba – also known as Ocean Island – was the source of much of the mineral phosphate that has been applied extensively to the pastoral farmland of Aotearoa New Zealand and Australia. So important was phosphorus-rich rock that informed observers foresaw the outcome for Banaba almost as soon as extraction commenced. Writing in 1909, colonial officer Arthur Mahaffy predicted that 'the island would become perfectly uninhabitable for men – and a mere desert of pointed coral rocks' (cited in Cushman 2013: 126–7). By 1980 an estimated twenty-two million tons of minerals had been removed from Banaba, and, like its fellow Pacific phosphate colony of Nauru, the bulk of the island had indeed been reduced to a lithic landscape so starkly lifeless that most observers compare it to an alien planet.

The mineral phosphate extracted from Banaba and Nauru is a smallish but significant fraction of the tens of billions of tons of material annually mined, quarried – and mobilized – that we spoke of in the previous chapter. And in many ways, the fate of these islands is paradigmatic of the 'blast: dump: crush: extract: exhaust' modern mentality indicted by Mumford (1934: 74). As Teaiwa reflects: 'what had taken millions of years to create, what had formed from the rubbing together of heaven and earth, was wiped out in just eighty years by the hands and machines of man' (2015: 40). Unable to sustain themselves amidst the ruins of their home island, most of the Banaban population was less-than-voluntarily relocated after World War II to the Fijian island of Rabi some 2,100 kilometres to the south – purchased on their behalf by the phosphate corporate actors from the proceeds of mining (2015: 141–2).

While we have often spoken in the book so far about reorganization of the physical stuff of the Earth in both logical and empirical terms, we have also touched upon the idea that matter might be imbued with meaning, and that 'force' and 'signification' may not be as distinct as Western thought often assumes them to be. Teaiwa, whose family background is Banaban, as well as I-Kiribati and African American, recognizes that the poignant experience of the travelling dancers in rural Aotearoa New Zealand is as much about the mobilization of culture and spirit as it is about a mineral resource or substance. For the people of Banaba, like most other Pacific societies, human life is inseparable from land, just as land and sea often merge into one another. '[T]he concept of te aba, or land, in the Kiribati language spoken by both I-Kiribati and Banabans unites the body of the land with the bodies of the people', Teaiwa observes (2012: 75). And as she also says, '[t]he body of the people is in that landscape so when it's mined and crushed and dug up, you're not just doing it with rock, you're also doing it with people, with the remains of people' (Theobold 2018).

For Teaiwa the story does not end *here* on the devastated island – where a world has literally come to an end – or even *there*, with resettlement on the ecologically unfamiliar and hurricane-prone Rabi Island. On the island of Rabi, she recounts, Banabans continue to perform and tell stories that both celebrate their survival in a new land and maintain vital lifelines to their home island – even as they lament its destruction (Teaiwa 2015). As we saw in chapter 5, the forces that destroyed the island of Banaba and severed its people from the sustenance of their ancestral land have had similar impacts across much of the colonized world. But just as vital elements of Banaban cultural and spiritual life have survived, so too have Indigenous peoples and their knowledge practices lived on in many other afflicted regions. As geographer Adam Bobbette recounts, Indonesian communities have retained their attunement to the multivocal messages of their environment. 'In this cosmos', he observes, 'the dead, unborn, distant humans, forests, lakes, groves, caves, murmur, yell, whisper, or scream, and demand to be deciphered, translated, and understood' (2019: 175–6).

Today, as extractive frontiers ceaselessly roam from exhausted sites like the Pacific phosphate colonies to new or underexploited zones, local cosmologies – and the figures that populate them – are increasingly asserting themselves in political arenas that once seemed hostile and impenetrable. Entities associated with earthly or cosmic processes that 'modernizing' forces had formerly disavowed or relegated to supernatural domains – spirits, deities, agential ancestors, sapient animals, sentient geological formations – are reappearing as worldly political actors. As anthropologist Marisol de la Cadena puts it, in reference to Latin America:

> The appearance of earth-beings in social protests may evince a moment of rupture of modern politics and … an insurgence of indigenous forces and practices with the capacity to significantly disrupt prevalent political formations. (2010: 336; see also 2015: 35–7)

Across the planet, in this way, a multitude of other-than-human figures are performing vital roles in ongoing encounters with radically uncertain conditions. This brings us back more explicitly to themes of planetary partiality that we raised in chapter 2, and the problematic of colonization that we addressed in chapter 5. Over the centuries of Euro-Atlantic colonization, vastly uneven power relations have enabled an onto-epistemological organization of reality native to Europe to be imposed upon much of the rest of the world. Consequently, a great multitude of other ontologies or cosmologies, and all the manifold beings they embrace, have been subjugated and marginalized. The recent resurgence of earthly and ancestral figures, in this sense, is bound up with projects of 'decolonizing' those modes of thought and practice that have been negatively – often catastrophically – impacted by the imperious advance of Western modernity.

But a sense of being poised, precariously, at a juncture between this and other possible worlds, we have been arguing throughout the book, is as much a part of modern Western experience as it is of a world of other peoples – if not as openly or explicitly. As the outsourcing of earthly precariousness to others, and the full force of the unworlding of other's worlds, rebound on the West or the North, here too the given-ness of physical existence and 'the everyday boundaries of the human' come ineluctably into question. As Teaiwa is well aware, the fate of Banaba and that of the Global West are quintessentially bound together. 'I felt like I was viewing the rise and fall of the industrial revolution on a tiny island in the very centre of the vast Pacific', she reflects (2011: 89). And just as the boundaries of Banaba, its people, its spirits have been utterly transfigured, so too are boundaries of very different kinds being threatened or infringed upon by excessive phosphate extraction from places like Banaba and Nauru. For as we will shortly see, disruption of phosphorus flows has been identified as one of the gravest threats to the current operating state of the Earth system.

What, then, should we make of the relationship between scientific accounts of the globally scaled biogeochemical cycling and those locally generated, spirit-infused cosmologies that increasingly demand to be heard on the global stage? This brings us to one of the thorniest issues of the Anthropocene 'moment' and of our own efforts to work up a planetary social thought. Is it possible, we ask in this chapter, to adopt a certain fidelity to the findings of predominantly Western 'Earth-oriented investigators' (Edgeworth et al. 2019: 338) while at the same time affirming an irreducible plurality of earthly practices, earth-beings and cosmologies? To put it another way, how does our invitation to think with and through a sense of planetary multiplicity equate with the rising call to decolonize the Earth?

We make no pretence of being ethnographers. Our approach in this chapter is one of concerned interdisciplinary interloping, or to borrow a phrase from anthropologist James Scott, 'trespasser's reconnaissance' (2017: ix). After briefly reviewing the scientific literature on the current state of the phosphorus cycle, we turn to recent discussions about the relationship between decolonizing thought and other approaches to the current environmental or planetary predicament. But just as questions of countering colonialism and its afterlives are inciting reactions to singular constructions of nature, confronting the Western imperium also draws us back into matters of the deep geohistory and dynamics of the Earth. We approach these issues through the example of pastoral economies and phosphate colonialism in the Pacific. This involves both looking in more detail at Teaiwa's account of the destratifying of the living earth of Banaba, and our own unpacking of the practice of airborne application of agricultural fertilizer.

What might it mean, we ask, to consider the mobilization of ancestral spirit and the use of aircraft to disperse superphosphate over vast acreages as two different ways of giving shape or form to the experience of living on the threshold between radically different worlds? This brings us more explicitly to the meeting grounds between Western science and the multitude of other ways of composing worlds. We ask what this encounter might look like once we loosen the assumption that Western thought is limited to a singular nature and acknowledge the importance of what we have been referring to as planetary multiplicity: the self-differentiation or other-worlding thematics we discern within science itself.

## Accelerating Fertilizer Use

Fertilizer use, we noted in chapter 3, features prominently among the precipitous curves that are key to the Great Acceleration thesis. In the planetary boundaries framework, phosphorus and nitrogen flows are now placed well inside the zone of high risk, meaning that the transformation of these cycles is rated alongside declining biodiversity as one of the most immediate threats to the Earth system (Steffen et al. 2015b: 6). The major culprit here is escalating global reliance on artificial fertilizer to maintain or increase the productivity of agro-ecosystems (Rockström et al. 2009). Unlike nitrogen, which can be captured from the air using the energy-intensive Haber-Bosch process (Cushman 2013: 346), phosphorus – like other mineral resources – can only be extracted from the solid ground. While there are concerns about passing 'peak phosphorus' availability, the bigger worry in the Earth systems literature is that phosphate-based fertilizer is adding phosphorus to natural cycling at a pace that in many places greatly exceeds background rates resulting from geological weathering (Carpenter and Bennett 2011; Rockström et al. 2009).

In the phosphorus cycle, the major human interference comes about as runoff from agricultural fertilization and sewage discharge enters water bodies. Here, the surplus of nutrients results in blooms of plants and algae that then consume oxygen as they eventually die and get degraded by bacteria (Carpenter and Bennett 2011). While this can result in abrupt changes at the ecosystem scale, the prevailing view has been that there are insufficient accessible phosphate reserves to bring ocean phosphorus to levels that would trigger a planet-wide shift to anoxic or oxygen-depleted oceans (Rockström et al. 2009). However, researchers have recently claimed that a planetary boundary for freshwater eutrophication has already been transgressed, while the potential for localized anoxia to merge into ocean-scaled anoxic events 'loom[s] in the future' (Carpenter and Bennett 2011: 8).

'Yet the crisis of eutrophication – like the looming crisis of phosphate rock scarcity that could overturn our whole industrial system', observe anthropologist Zachary Caple and environmental historian Gregory Cushman, 'is barely on our political radar' (2016). Even a cursory encounter with the science of biogeochemical cycles suggests the gravity of the current predicament – an impression backed up by energy theorist Vaclav Smil's calculation that, under current agro-ecological regimes, we could feed only about 40 per cent of the current global human population without intensive use of artificial fertilizer (2001: xv).

As we know well by now, it matters *how* an issue like the phosphorus crisis enters the political arena. While some researchers still speak of 'humanity's addiction to phosphate rock' (Cordell et al. 2009: 292), others have responded to the critique of universalizing human agency by disaggregating contributions to planetary risk. As with other Great Acceleration curves, trends in fertilizer consumption are now divided between OECD nations, the rising industrializing powers and the rest of the world (Steffen et al. 2015a). Though it gestures to issues of equity, the subdivided Great Acceleration graph does little to explain the global socioeconomic forces behind Banaba's devastation, and it certainly doesn't tell us about the destratified spirit of Banaban ancestors that may also be coursing through the accelerating phosphorus cycle.

Nevertheless, scientific efforts to gauge and represent shifts in biogeo-chemical cycling through the Earth system, as our planetary thinking would have it, open a window onto phenomena that not only exceed the grammars and genres in which they are expressed but reach beyond our own species. In terms of stratal analysis, the massive, ongoing release of phosphorus from lithic reservoirs and its accelerated circulation through water bodies and terrestrial and marine food webs constitute an event not only in human history but also in the history of the planet. We would do well to take emerging evidence of such reorganization of biospheric, lithospheric and hydrospheric processes very seriously indeed, as Teaiwa and many other decolonizing thinkers concur.

There are, however, aspects of this story that Western science may not be best positioned to relate. And this is not just a matter of whose voices and rights have historically been disavowed, we argue, but a question of how we might yet make sense of and respond to a future beyond our best predictions.

## Decolonization and the Cosmos

In chapter 5 we explored the connections in Western thought between a repressed sense of the radical uncertainty of the Earth, the vision of a unidirectional advance of 'man' out of a mute, unthinking nature, and the tendency to position non-Western peoples at lower or earlier development stages. This reasoning is closely associated with the modern 'settlement' discussed in chapter 2: the axiom that there is a single, universal nature conducive to being deciphered by the no-less singular endeavour of science. Or, as critical science studies scholars have put it, it is the hard-line division of the world into facts – the domain of the sciences – and beliefs – the realm of culture, politics and other forms of human expression and opinion (Shapin and Schaffer 1985; Latour 1993).

What the two sides of this definitively modern divide shared, however, was a commitment to the secularization or 'disenchantment' of the world. Just as operations of the physical world were purged of supernatural powers, so too was the sphere of self-conscious human action liberated from interfering gods, ghosts and demons. Consequently, in much the same way that belief in a nature animated by deities, spirits or ancestors was taken as indicative of failure to break out of nature's clutches and into purposive, knowledgeable agency, so too was any faith in divine or spiritual intervention in the social sphere seen to be symptomatic of immature lack of trust in the power of collective will. And on both sides, these markers of arrested development were emphatically mapped onto the racialized world order of the European imperium.

Eventually, however, the more cosmopolitan Euro-Atlantic social thinkers became aware of the oppressive implications of categorizing the beliefs of others as primitive or uncivilized, leading to a growing willingness to embrace the full diversity of knowledge systems. But the task of overturning racialized developmental hierarchies can be more demanding than it often appears. As Dipesh Chakrabarty (2000) proposes, even – or especially – critical thinkers who pursue the cause of justice and recognition for others have often sought to do this by way of explaining religious or supernatural beliefs in terms of the sociocultural contexts from which they are seen to have emerged. While this gesture at first seems respectful of the particularity of sundry spiritual, spectral and divine beings, he contends, its effect is actually to convert the unique and grounded powers of these entities – their 'radical untranslatability' – into the shared conceptual frameworks of the modern Western social sciences and humanities (2000: 75–6). In short, what in their own worlds are powerful, agential beings end up as colourful instantiations of cultural diversity.

Over recent decades, Western-trained critical thinkers and their non-Western interlocutors have been seeking a way out of this dilemma. An increasingly admissible alternative is the proposition that knowledge systems of 'Indigenous' or 'traditional' peoples are not so much culturally variegated ways of making sense of an ultimately commensurate reality as they are ways of constituting irreducibly different worlds. Detailed ethnographic accounts of the way that non-Western people conceive of rocks that listen (Povinelli 1995), sentient forests (Kohn 2013), interventionist mountains (de la Cadena 2015: 35), glaciers that are capable of moral judgement (Cruikshank 2005: 3), and dingoes that make us human (Rose 1992) have been presented as evidence that worlds can be ordered in ways otherwise than the Western model. In particular, varying attributions of intentionality, sentience and moral or political power in such stories have been marshalled to show how the Western division between an insensate nature and a restrictively human realm of reasoned activity is but one of many possibilities for apportioning worldly agency.

Over a longer timescale, theorists and activists from formerly colonized regions have been making the case that overcoming colonization is not simply a matter of transforming unequal power relations, but a task of reimagining subjectivities, identities and cultural formations distorted by oppressive colonial worldviews – sometimes shorthanded as 'decolonizing the mind' (Ngũgĩ 1986; see also Fanon 1965). Along with overturning racialized ontologies, this project sets out to undermine the assumption that the West does 'research' while those othered by Western knowledge practices only do 'culture' and thus remain objects of research. And in a closely related sense it also seeks to revitalize the multitude of ways of knowing self and world that were disavowed by globalizing Western thought (Smith 1999; Connell 2007; Mignolo 2011).

Still deeply concerned with globally structured socioeconomic inequality, the decolonization of knowledge practices and subject formation is often closely tied up with resistance to capitalist exploitation and the incursions of the state and other 'modernizing' institutions. In this regard, narrowly developmentalist logics – whether deployed by corporations, government agencies or nongovernmental organizations – are increasingly seen to be inhospitable to other ways of knowing and being. And it is in this context, as we saw earlier, that resurgent 'earth-beings' and kindred other-than-human entities are making insistent inroads into political arenas. Or to put it another way, the imperative to decolonize is increasingly being framed as a site where ontology – ideas about what kinds of things exist – and politics are inseparable endeavours.

The tight linkage between political projects of decolonization and the quest to subvert single authoritative claims to knowledge is now frequently expressed in terms of preference for 'multinaturalism' or 'pluriverses' over a 'universe' or 'one-world world' (see Law 2015; Blaser and de la Cadena 2018; Reiter 2018; Escobar 2018). For its contemporary exponents, a pluriverse or a 'many-world world' is one in which, in the words of sociologist and science studies scholar John Law, *different realities are enacted in different practices* (2015: 130). The claim that worlds are enacted, practised or performed by participating collectives of humans and other-than-humans is often taken to imply that there is no exterior, 'out-there', pre-existing nature that can be taken as the ultimate arbiter of the 'right' way of knowing and being in the world. As anthropologists Eduardo Vivieros de Castro and Déborah Danowski explain, this means that a pluriverse is 'the opposite of a "world without us" in the sense of a universe without anyone, a cosmos unified by the absence of experience' (2018: 183)

But it's worth keeping in mind that the notion that different human groups or collectives practise, perform or enact distinct worlds into existence, and the idea that they do so in concert with nonhuman entities, does not in itself require an encounter with Indigenous peoples, a point we return to at the close of this chapter. Over recent decades, as we've noted at several points in the book, critical social and philosophical thinkers have been developing complex and nuanced grammars precisely for dealing with 'nonconventional' forms of agency, different kinds of 'becoming' and heterogeneous processes of world-building. Many fields of inquiry now offer accounts of the way that insistent organisms confront their human counterparts, agential machines interface with conventional social actors, signifying objects rebound across global sociocultural divides. Defences of purity, fixed identity and bound-edness are ever more rare, and it is arguably the more-than-human, the assembled, the contaminated, the hybrid, the creolized that now predominate in mainstream social and cultural inquiry.

So while we should not underestimate the challenges posed by the question of 'ontology of the otherwise' (Povinelli 2014), many Western social thinkers seem to feel that they are already fairly well versed in the demands of staging encounters with other worlds, other peoples, other beings. Or at least they feel that they are somewhat better prepared to do so than their counterparts in the natural sciences – whose entry into the perplexing world of entangled anthropic and more-than-anthropic agency appears to have been shorter, sharper, less-rehearsed.

Recognizing that decolonization is increasingly hitched to the ontological contestation of 'a single scientifically knowable nature' (de la Cadena 2010: 359), that modern trends towards secularization are under revision, and that modes of knowing and being which mobilize a range of other-than-human beings are on the ascent, can help us to see why Anthropocene diagnoses of the planetary condition are meeting with 'spirited' resistance. But there are tensions, we want to suggest, between the drive to interrogate colonial legacies and the emphatic turning away from any understanding of the Earth or cosmos that doesn't fit with the model of co-enactment by humans and their immediate other-than-human collaborators. This comes back to our ongoing claim throughout this book that acknowledging the dynamics of planetary self-differenti-ating processes whether or not our own species is present is not the same thing as 'commitment to the idea of a *single* all-encompassing reality' (Law 2015: 127, our italics). This raises issues that we seek to tease out by revisiting the pastoral economies of the South-West Pacific and the phosphate colonialism upon which they were constructed.

## (Un)Grounding Colonialism

More than a matter of 'humanity's addiction to phosphate rock', the extractive colonialism that made the islands of Banaba and Nauru all-but-uninhabitable was driven by the specific dynamics of colonial development in Aotearoa New Zealand and Australia (Teaiwa 2015; Cushman 2013). The trans-global linkages that bound the Antipodean colonies to the metropolitan 'mother country' of Great Britain were from early on dominated by the export of agricultural produce. This flow of primary produce in turn depended on a prior movement in the other direction: the translocation from Europe to the temperate settler colonies of an entire assemblage of plants, animals and agricultural technologies and practices (Clark 1999). European colonizers thus sought to recon-struct the world they knew: to create what historian Alfred Crosby (1986) referred to as 'Neo-Europes'.

At first glance, this process would seem to epitomize the idea of a human-orchestrated but more-than-humanly composed enactment of a new reality – under conditions of oppressive colonial relations. In the case of Aotearoa New Zealand, with important parallels in Australia and other white settler colonies, farmable land was expropriated, often violently and with concerted resistance from Indigenous Māori inhab-itants – *tangata whenua* or 'people of the land'. Native biota were displaced, sometimes driven to extinction, by land-clearing and the intentional or incidental introduction of species, mostly comprised of plants, animals and insects long-adapted to intensively farmed European agro-ecosystems.

Aotearoa New Zealand's topographic and climatic resemblance to North-Western Europe, however, was deeply misleading, and European farming practices frequently had cataclysmic impacts. Crosby (1986: 267) cites local politician and naturalist William Travers, who in the 1860s observed that the islands 'had reached a point at which, like a house built of incoherent materials, a blow struck anywhere shakes and damages the whole fabric'. Or as Māori in the North Island's Waikato region chanted: 'Like a creeping thing,/The Land is moving;/When gone, where shall man/Find a dwelling?' (1986: 262).

As it turned out, much of the New Zealand soil lacked vital nutrients for sustained pastoral farming. Soil fertility often declined rapidly, and, especially on deforested hill country, the loss of vegetative cover resulted in severe erosion – to such an extent that by the late 1930s New Zealand agronomists feared the 'decline and fall' of the Antipodean 'empire of grass' (Cushman 2013: 131). While early European settlers tended to assume that the problem was the geological immaturity of the 'new' world (see Guthrie-Smith 1999: 24), the inverse is closer to the truth. Later environmental histories deduced that it was recent glaciation that gifted much of Europe with rich soils, and the fact that plants and animals – including humans – had recolonized the post-glacial terrain together meant that the European ecosystem was especially tolerant of disturbance (Flannery 1994: 304; Pyne 1997b: 34–9). Consequently, New Zealand's biota, like that of other temperate settler colonies, was frequently outcompeted by the versatile, rapidly proliferating plants and animals that had recolonized post-ice-age Europe, while local topsoil turned out to be especially vulnerable to the unfamiliar perturbation wrought by herds of hoofed animals.

This could be read as a textbook case of the hazards of universalist assumptions about nature and the need to only deploy 'partial knowledges' that are grounded in the context of particular times and places. But we would also stress that making sense of the specificities of nature in Europe and Aotearoa New Zealand is only possible within an understanding of the context of the planet-scaled geophysical and astronomical dynamics that drive glacial episodes and the tectonic processes that distribute landmasses across the Earth's surfaces – and their very long-term evolutionary consequences. To put it in our terms, *geohistorical analysis* helps us to grasp why different kinds of living things are predisposed towards certain physical conditions, whereas *stratal analysis* attunes us to the consequences of disembedding life forms from one planetary stratum or zone and transporting them to a very different one.

The state-led response to New Zealand's erosion crisis was a decisive intensification in the artificial supplementing of vital soil nutrients. Superphosphate – mineral phosphate treated with acid to speed its release into the soil – was the fertilizer of choice. From the 1840s, increasing demands for phosphate led to a booming international trade in guano – accumulated seabird excrement – sourced predominantly from coastal islands off Peru (Cushman 2013: 40–7). But pivotal to the rise of high-input, high-output agriculture in New Zealand and Australia was the discovery of a phosphate supply closer to home. Around 1900 it became apparent to colonial prospectors that the tiny Pacific islands of Nauru and Banaba were largely composed of high-grade phosphate rock (Cushman 2013: 117–19; Teaiwa 2015: 3). Under the auspices of the new and mostly British-owned Pacific Phosphates Company, mining began almost immediately. Post-World War I, administrative control of both islands passed into the conjoint hands of Australian, New Zealand and British governments. And with the formal colonization of Banaba and Nauru, the rural economies of New Zealand and Australia secured access to an apparently unlimited supply of phosphate (Cushman 2013: 129).

As extractive operations escalated, the people of Banaba began to protest the destruction of their island and way of life. Female elders from the islands, who were traditionally active participants in politics with equal land rights, were often at the forefront of resistance (Teaiwa 2015: 133–4; Cushman 2013: 125). But, as was the case over most of the colonized world, local sovereignty was decisively sacrificed to 'wider' economic interest. As an article in the *Sydney Morning Herald* of 1912 offered its appraisal: 'Naturally some think the native owners are right, yet it is inconceivable that less than 500 Ocean Island-born natives can be allowed to prevent the mining and export of a produc[t] of such immense value to all the rest of mankind' (cited in Teaiwa 2015: 17).

In combination with introduced grasses, application of now locally manufactured superphosphate saw remarkable productivity gains in pastoral farming, especially in the North Island of New Zealand and south-east Australia. As Gregory Cushman observes, acquisition of Pacific phosphate colonies became key to the Neo-European imperative, enabling 'parts of the Antipodes to become far more like their mother country in biological terms – if only skin deep' (2013: 129). The cautionary note is vital. Spurred by the hyperbolic promise that suffused superphosphate, some farmers in both Australia and New Zealand took advantage of cheap fertilizer to push land far beyond its carrying capacity. Moreover, much hill country, where the problem of soil erosion was most severe, remained beyond the reach of agrochemical improvement. The recurrent crises of the Neo-Europes were far from over.

In the years after World War II, agrochemical inputs literally went up a level. Making use of surplus military aircraft and veterans with wartime flying experience, New Zealand agronomists ran a series of trials in the late 1940s using light aircraft to spread fertilizer over large areas. Early success with sheep and dairy farms saw the rapid uptake of 'aerial topdressing' locally and in south-eastern Australia, followed by diffusion of the technique to other farming regions worldwide (Cushman 2013: 129–31). It was the early adopters of airborne superphosphate application that enjoyed some of the most impressive gains, as millions of acres of once-marginal land were engineered into export-oriented pastoral productivity. As Cushman concludes: 'This "Grasslands

Revolution" allowed Australians and New Zealanders to eat high on the food chain and enjoy some of the best living standards in the world' (2013: 131–2).

Writing just before the idea of the Anthropocene surfaced, environmental historian William Cronon described the ecological changes associated with European settler colonization as 'truly planetary in scope' (1999: xii). From our point of view, European colonialism – in all its forms – has been planetary not only in its reach and repercussions, but in its very constitution. Engaging with colonialism through geohistorical analysis directs our attention to the way that the trajectories of the planet, at every scale, condition the opportunities open to human agents, if often in inadvertent and misunderstood ways – an approach that historians of transcontinental interconnections, such as William McNeill (1976) and Alfred Crosby (1986), help open up. It can also prompt us to see that in many cases, globally mobile Euro-Western actors were able to capitalize on climatic rhythms and other Earth-system variability, using temporary environmental stress as an opportunity to insert themselves into local worlds, as we briefly considered in chapter 5 (see also Cruikshank 2005: ch. 1; Clark and Gunaratnam 2017).

But we need to insist that colonialism should never be seen simply as the following of pathways opened up by pre-existing planetary histories, however much pre-existing geophysical and evolutionary developments play a conditioning role. To understand the event of phosphate colonialism, and gain a sense of how localized superphosphate-powered agricultural 'improvements' were levered up to impact upon the global phosphorus cycle, we also need to see how entirely novel organizations of matter were worked into existence. We now take up our 'stratal' analysis of aerial topdressing, in order to track the specific linkages through which formerly distinct planetary compartments or strata came to be articulated into new and unprecedented modes of geological agency. Along the way, we will not forget that destratified and remobilized spirit also enters the topdressing assemblage.

## The Aerial Topdressing Assemblage

By the mid-1960s, almost half the agrochemical fertilizer used worldwide was dropped from aircraft (Techhistory n.d.), a statistic that may help us make the connection between localized innovation and global environmental change, but reveals little of the novelty or strangeness of the event it quantifies. It's worth noting that it took some eight millennia of farmers systematically applying fertilizer to their crops before the process became airborne. The earliest 'crop dusting' in the USA in the 1920s was restricted to insecticides or fungicides, and it was not until the experiments in New Zealand two decades later that fertilizer application too went aerial.

Prior to its development by humans in the early twentieth century, powered flight, as opposed to floating, gliding and other forms of 'drift' that we introduced in the previous chapter, evolved independently in four classes of organisms: a metapattern recurring in the divergent lineages of insects, birds, bats and the extinct pterosaurs. The origins of insect flight – which seems to have first appeared late in the Carboniferous period around 300 million years ago – remain obscure, though there is growing evidence that wings developed from ancestral gills (Grimaldi and Engel 2005: 155). One of the most significant consequences of early powered flight was not just the provision of a new way to move, but the coming together of flying animals and the reproductive processes of entirely unrelated forms of life: namely, the alliance of winged insects and flowering plants. Some 90 per cent of all terrestrial plant life belongs to the phylum of angiosperms or flowering plants, and the vast majority of this flora relies upon pollination by flying insects for its reproduction. Forged over 130 million years ago, the insect–angiosperm alliance has been the key to the planet-wide and Earth-shaping evolutionary success of both partners (Grimaldi and Engel 2005: 607; Clark 2013).

For Deleuze and Guattari this conjuncture of flying insects and flowering plants is a prime example of what they variously refer to as a rhizome or an assemblage: the meshing of two or more previously unrelated lineages to create an entirely new kind of functionality (Deleuze and Guattari 1987: 10). In their mutual transformative encounter, the coupling of wasp and orchid, as Deleuze and Guattari's version of stratal analysis would have it, opens a new line or direction of development that could not have been predicted from either of their individual trajectories. No less that the insect–flowering plant connection, we would add, the knotting together of the aircraft, agrochemical fertilizers and fossil fuels is a novel event in the geohistory of our planet.

Following the thematization of mobility in the previous chapter, we can think of human mechanized aviation – this planet's fifth and latest invention of powered flight – as having vital continuities with the ways in which other organisms have learned to channel certain opportunities or affordances within the Earth system. Powered flight in this regard is a working in concert of the energies of an organismic body and the fluid motions of the Earth's atmosphere. Because of the low density of air, flying requires lift as well as thrust and so it is more costly in terms of energy expended per unit of time than either swimming or terrestrial motion. However, the low viscosity of air allows faster speeds – so flying is more energetically efficient per unit of distance (Goldspink 1977:

164–5; Szerszynski 2016b). The challenge of getting airborne tends to limit the 'cargo' that a flying organism is able to carry (Haff 2012). However, the advantage of the energetic efficiency of flight, once on the wing, means that flying can be a highly effective way of transporting relatively small things over considerable distances.

The role of bird excrement in building up entire islands of phosphate-rich guano reminds us that combining flight and a freight of nutrient-rich chemicals has important precursors. But the modern human innovation of mechanized flight allows for an unprecedented scaling-up of the cargo or payload, alongside the heightened intentionality that delivers the load to specified targets. And crucial here is the tapping of an energy source external to the human or organismic body: namely the concentrated energy of fossil hydrocarbons combusted to generate motorized propulsion. In the artificial fertilizer-based agricultural development story we are telling, access to a huge stock of mineral phosphate is crucial – but regular flights over extensive areas carrying a considerable agrochemical cargo would not have been feasible without a ready supply of cheap hydrocarbons to power them (Cushman 2013: 131).

In order for the aerial topdressing assemblage to come into being, hydrocarbons, mineral phosphate and powered flight each had to be freed up from its existing consolidations or stratifications. That is to say, they had to be mobilized or made to flow. In an example of Feenberg's (1999) 'primary instrumentalization' that we discussed in the previous chapter, fossil hydrocarbons and phosphate needed to be prised out of their respective lithic strata – but also planes and their pilots had to be released from the constraints of military aviation. Furthermore, to grasp the inventive force of this new conjunction, we need to understand more of the composition of each of the components. We have already sketched out the planetary genealogy of mechanized aero-mobility. With regard to the mineral phosphate sourced from Banaba and Nauru, current thinking suggests that it derives from microscopic marine life in ancient reef ecosystems that were nourished by rich, nutrient-laden equatorial ocean upwellings. What eventually became rock, in this way, may well have begun as the waste products of dense mats of photosynthesizing cyanobacteria deposited over millions of years (Cushman 2013: 111, 120; Teaiwa 2015: 30–1). So too did the fossil hydrocarbons essential to the topdressing assemblage have organic origins. Affordable petroleum – funded largely by agricultural exports – was imported to New Zealand from vast Middle Eastern oil fields: subterranean energy-rich strata whose origin lay in the sedimentation of organic matter during the Jurassic and Cretaceous periods (see Cushman 2013: 131).

At this point, it's worth recalling what we said about excess in chapter 2. Any stratum of the Earth, we argued, embodies more potentiality than current human or nonhuman operations has actualized or set to work. With the threefold conjunction of powered flight, phosphates and fossilized hydrocarbons, as Deleuze and Guattari's own approach to stratal analysis would caution us, the uncertainty inherent in tapping into a single novel stratum is radically magnified. Indeed, events such as this in which the contents of multiple strata irrupt into one another tend to be disastrous, even unsurvivable (Deleuze and Guattari 1987: 503; Povinelli 2016: 55).

At the originary sites of aerial topdressing, human actors were strangely willing to risk their lives. With a 20 per cent chance of a fatal accident per decade of flying, New Zealand topdressing pilots experienced death rates that exceeded those of the nation's armed forces in all major conflicts since the 1950s, though only recently have there been efforts to commemorate these losses (Wilkinson 2017). As yet, this acknowledgement of loss appears detached from the associated sacrifice of entire Pacific worlds and the mourning and memorialization by Banabans and Nauruans that attend the geocide of their homelands. At another scale, as we saw earlier, injudicious application of mineral phosphate is triggering mass eutrophication – resulting in the destruction of entire ecosystems and threatening termination of the current operating state of the Earth's phosphorus cycle.

These crises can no longer be addressed as though they were separate. As the displaced people of Banaba appeal in international courts for redress over the destruction and desecration of their land, their ancestral spirits join other 'unconventional' entities in the political arena. Extrapolating from Deleuze and Guattari's warnings about the danger of 'too-sudden destratification' of existing organizations of matter, we might now envisage aerial topdressing as implicated in a too-sudden destratification or disorganization of spirit (Szerszynski 2017b).

But how does this alter or inspire the way we should think about the flight–phosphate–fossil fuel assemblage? And in a more general sense, how might a sense of the infusion of planetary biogeochemical cycles with ancestral spirits, gods or ghosts help us to reimagine the task of science in the time of radical transformation in the operation of the Earth system? These are questions that are pertinent not only to the issue of phosphate colonialism and the crisis of the phosphorous cycle, but to the relationship between planetary multiplicity and earthly multitudes that we have been developing throughout this book.

## Earth-Beings at the Threshold

We have seen how social critics make reference to the 'localized' worldview of 'real people, in real places' in order to take issue with the allegedly detached, global and placeless perspective of Anthropocene science. As Katerina Teaiwa makes clear, however, the components of 'place-based' existence can also be globally mobile.

> One can imagine the rock of Banaba split into twenty million tons of tiny particles that, over eighty years, must now be dispersed across the planet via the British colonial machine and the industries of mining, shipping, farming, food and clothing manufacturing ... . As the island fractures into pieces and moves across the ocean it creates and breaks countless relationships between peoples, places and products. (2011: 88–90)

What Teaiwa (2012: 86) refers to as 'literal cross-fertilizations', in this regard, are not only a matter of the worldly entanglement of resource economies, but a dynamic in which spirits, gods and ancestors travel extensively and enter into new relationships (2011: 86; 2015: 182; see also Povinelli 2016: 13). And this is more than just a footloose colonial or capitalist supplement to embedded Indigeneity, for Teaiwa reminds us that Pacific peoples – together with their plants, animals, treasured objects and spirits – have been active participants in far-reaching maritime networks for many thousands of years (2015: 25–6; see also Hau'ofa 1994).

Teaiwa's ready mobilization of spirit resonates with other ethnographic accounts that draw attention to the willingness of earth-beings and their human mediators to take advantage of modern technologies and infrastructures. Bobbette (2019: 175) speaks of the cosmos of Indonesian animists as 'one of excessive communications' in which mobile phones, radios and computers join trees, rocks, wombs and animals as spirit mediums, while anthropologist Alessandro Questa evokes the 'hyper-inhabited' world of Mexico's Indigenous Masewal people (Questa 2019: 36). More generally, a sense of grappling with an excess of meaning, force and potentiality characterizes recent readings of resurgent enspirited or sacred worlds. Whereas environmental thinkers and other sympathetic interlocutors with non-Western thought in the 1960s, 1970s and 1980s tended to stress Indigenous or traditional peoples' harmony with a sustaining natural order, contemporary researchers seem more inclined to focus on the way that earth-beings and the human agents who work with them are active participants in a world of potentially overwhelming physical and social forces. And it is the presence of danger, in so many cases, that makes the carefully modulated mutual exchanges between human collectives and other-than-human entities so crucial.

In conversation with the work of Vivieros de Castro, Bobbette proposes that the sharing of sentience and the shifting of identities between human and nonhuman beings are ways that human agents learn to experience their world from different points of view *within* that world. 'Because perspectives can circulate amongst this world of forms', he observes, 'humans can be possessed by other perspectives while maintaining their unique bodily form' (2019: 188): a circulation of standpoints that serves as a kind of experimental and constantly revisable infrastructure for living in the midst of volatile Earth processes. Or as we might put it in our own terminology, the ability to inhabit and move between different modes of being appears to be one of the enduring ways that earthly multitudes contend with the challenges of planetary multiplicity. Indeed, the capacity to move between and learn from multiple other-than-human perspectives appears so often where there are deep, intimate relations with Earth and life processes that we might consider it a kind of metapattern: a 'solution' that recurs in various forms across unrelated sites and lineages.

It is this multi-perspectivalism – or multinaturalism – that sympathetic commentators are wont to contrast with the singular, universalizing vantage of Western science in general and the propositions of the Anthropocene in particular – whether or not contemporary scientists commit themselves to protecting current planetary conditions. 'As a matter of planetary concern', reflect Mario Blaser and Marisol de la Cadena, 'the Anthropocene requires analyses and proposals that would reveal the inner workings of the one-world world so as to prevent their destructive capacity' (2018: 15). Or as Vivieros de Castro and Danowski attest, the scientific Anthropocene thesis offers a prematurely unified cosmos: 'the precocious cosmopolitical unification of the multiverse' (Viveiros de Castro and Danowski 2018: 178).

In keeping with the case we have been building throughout the book, we are less willing to unequivocally consign contemporary geoscience to the 'one-world' compartment, and more willing to discern wayward and insurgent traces of multiplicity *within* the sciences behind the Anthropocene. Without a certain fidelity to the threshold events disclosed by Earth and life sciences, we would find ourselves less informed and less empowered in our siding with those most vulnerable to shifts in the global climate and other Earth systems. And yet, we too feel that the emergent sciences of planetary multiplicity still tend to treat radical discontinuity or catastrophic shifting largely as an object of knowledge, rather than as a fundamental unsettling of the conditions of possibility of doing science or of knowing the Earth and cosmos. And it is Western science's unwillingness, as yet, to position itself *within* the threshold, we would suggest, that places profound limitations on its capacity to help us to live through transformations of such intensity that they threaten not only the worlds we know but our capacity to make sense of these worlds.

As a way of living with earthly uncertainty, our 'trespasser's reconnaissance' suggests, the aptitude of Indigenous peoples for circulating between multiple points of view shows strengths where Western science – even when it thematizes planetary multiplicity – is falling short. We should not forget, however, that as sciences concerned with the dynamics of complex systems propose, it is as thresholds are approached that matter-energy is at its most expressive, its most creative, its most potentially surprising. But whereas the earth-beings, telluric spirits and kindred other-than-human beings of which we have been speaking are at their most agential in the vicinity of the transformative event, Western science, we are proposing, remains relatively bereft of figures attuned to the fraught and wrenching passage between one world and another. And despite modern social or philosophical thought finding itself in the post-World War II years having to probe the question of how to speak through and from self-induced disaster, it has as yet not been especially forthcoming in ways and means to articulate the becoming-other of the Earth.

In recent years anthropologist Elizabeth Povinelli has been proposing new figures that might help us grapple both with the forcible interpolation of Indigenous peoples into colonial and capitalist regimes, and with the environmental catastrophes precipitated by the latest phase of global capitalism. What is especially inspiring for us in this conceptual and tactical figuration is Povinelli's foregrounding of the fraught, complex and shifting relationship between the living and the nonliving, or biology and geology (2015; 2016: 16–20). The Australian Aboriginal figure of Tjipel – at once a young woman and a tidal creek – Povinelli describes as 'a mixture, not a substance … a composite nonsovereign nonlife being – part biological, geological, and meteorological' (2015: 173). Povinelli's more generalized figures of the Desert, the Animist and the Virus are likewise multiple, biological-geological beings that serve both to diagnose the current crisis-ridden planetary trajectory and to hold open the possibility of organizing the fundamental componentry of existence 'otherwise' (2016: 16–20; 2012).

Read through Povinelli's figuration of composite living–nonliving beings and Teaiwa's mineral–spiritual cross-fertilizations, our aerial topdressing assemblage does more than just bring together previously unacquainted strata. If not yet a figure that offers spiritual inspiration, the fertilizer-dispensing aeroplane can help us throw into relief – and inhabit – troubling thresholds between worlds: the Indigenous and the colonial-capitalist, the human and machinic, the biologic and the geologic, strata and Earth system, Holocene and Anthropocene. And in particular, it can help us to sense and embody what might otherwise slip through our sensory registers. No less than the practice of dancing that is a key to Teaiwa's figuring of earthly and spiritual Pacific diasporas, low-level aerial topdressing entails an intricate choreography: one in which mechanically mobilized human bodies weave their way through wind-sheltered gullies, around trees, peaks and powerlines. And in this way, we begin to grasp how a performance geared to the optimization of productive life is bound up with the possibility of sudden death, the infliction of geocide, the precipitation of planetary eutrophication.

While conceiving of the aerial topdressing apparatus as an earth-being risks premature desecularization, it's worth recalling Teaiwa's canny observation that the enthralment of the productivity-enhancing power of superphosphate by state agronomists and entrepreneurs in the Antipodean pastoral economies itself 'walked a fine line between science and magic' (2015: 105–6). Likewise noteworthy is Caple and Cushman's swipe at the transubstantiation between the geos and the bios in the mineral phosphate agro-economies: 'the sin of turning stones into bread' with its threat to the entire terrestrial 'garden' (2016). But if experiencing the full force of the Anthropocene is beyond our current cognitive or affective reach, as Chakrabarty has suggested, then hitching a ride on the vehicle that welds together Jurassic hydrocarbons, Miocene lithic mineral phosphates and late-Holocene powered flight may be one way to multiply perspectives on a planet undergoing upheaval.

The intention of our stratal analysis of the aerial topdressing assemblage, then, is neither to 'scientize' its distinctive sociocultural dimensions, nor to fast-forward the practice into full earth-being status. Our aim has been to 'provincialize' fertilizer-bearing aero-mobility – to render it strange, or perhaps strangely familiar to those who already know it well – such that it might more easily converse or congregate with a world of other figures that dwell in the danger zones of a self-differentiating planet. We also like the idea that showing how low-level topdressing came to be – socioculturally, geohistorically, stratally – might at some point help us to imagine other ways of growing food, other ways of intervening in the phosphorus cycle, other ways of reckoning with the physical, social and spiritual devastations of extractive colonialism.

## On Decolonizing the Thinking of the World

'*Writing* about bodies', attests Teaiwa, 'is not the same as *imagining* or *experiencing* the world or history *from the perspective of* a writing or moving body' (2012: 72). And writing *about* the Earth, we would have it, is not the same as trying to imagine or experience our planet as a mobile, self-differentiating, self-investigative body. Thinking, writing, speculating *through* the Earth, however, do not come easily to those of us who fledged in worlds that were constituted with the very aim of raising the subject high above any merely material threat to its continued flourishing. It is in this sense that the proliferating earth-beings, telluric spirits and animate objects of Indigenous worlds offer incitements to Western thinkers: not just through their demonstration that other ways of composing realities are equally feasible, but because they offer practical lessons in enduring or thriving in the thick of life-threatening threshold events.

In our own writing, the current resurgence of category-bending, other-worlding entities has helped us to expand and enrich what we mean by earthly multitudes: showing us that an analysis of the human collectives who engage with the multiplicity of planetary form and force needs to reach far beyond the received empirical registers of the Western gaze. Whereas we argued earlier in the book that geologic forces work their way into our bodies, our communities, our worlds, the lines of reasoning we have pursued in this chapter prompt us to extend this logic to include the way that minerals infused with the ancestral spirit of other peoples have infiltrated our economic circuits, our soil strata and water bodies, our very flesh and blood. Along the way it became apparent that there is no totalling of global fertilizer consumption, no evidence of shifting phosphorus cycles that is not to some degree permeated by traces of ancestral spirit or earth-being – a rumbling presence that will not show up in instrument readings or laboratory tests but is nonetheless proving increasingly capable of intervening in global public life.

In conversation with Indigenous and other non-Western knowledge formations, as we have seen, critical thinkers have been advancing an ontological politics which proposes that different peoples and their associate beings enact their worlds, natures, cosmoses: realities that are irreducible to one another or to any unifying framework, yet may also be deeply – if partially – entangled (see de la Cadena 2010: 361; 2015: xxv). It's worth remembering, however, that prior to their harnessing to the imperative of decolonization, certain styles and practices of doing relational ontology were already well established in Western academia. The core precept of pluriversal thinkers that all collective existence is composed out of socio-natural associations, along with the claim that worlds are locally enacted or performed by humans and kindred nonhumans, did not await Indigenous confirmation to make significant inroads into mainstream social thought.

This suturing of the ontological and the political is not without its tensions. As we have seen, some theorists are quick to equate any reference to a 'world without us' with one-world universalism – and to counter with the claim that humans and nonhumans would better be conceived as mutually entangled all the way down or all the way out.

Others more readily affirm that human entanglement with other life forms has a geologic or cosmic subtending – or, in the words of Povinelli, that 'we were also rocks and sediment before we settled into this mode of existence' (Povinelli et al. 2017: 178). Some commentators appear affronted by any reference to regions or zones of fully inhuman nature, while others are comfortable with that idea that 'there is a tangible physical world out there that sometimes affirms but often mocks the representations we design to constrain it' (Cruikshank 2005: 7).

These are not simply matters of onto-epistemological musing, but have implications for the ways that social thinkers engage with natural scientists – and for the degree to which we allow ourselves to be lured, excited or shocked by the findings of science. How or whether we can conceive of worlds unpeopled by ourselves or our proxy beings colours our reception of the Anthropocene, and conditions what we choose to push away – or to push further and harder. In this regard, the tension we experience in relation to our own fidelity to much of the empirical evidence disclosed by the geosciences, if not always to the way it is presented, seems closely related to the quandary of which philosopher Isabelle Stengers speaks with characteristic candour and clarity:

> I think that we academics cannot ... deny that we 'know' something is coming with a rather awful speed that will put into question the ways of life of most inhabitants of this earth – while we also know that this knowledge situates us in our own temporality, which should not engulf other peoples. We cannot dream – let alone think – this tension away with sophisticated arguments about cosmopolitics or ontological politics. We have to accept and think with this perplexing situation. (2018: 97)

We share Stengers's willingness to turn the lens of political ontology back upon ourselves, to dwell on our own fears, and to think deeply about how we in the Global West might learn from those peoples who recognize that other-than-human entities must be respected, propitiated and nourished if they are not to turn on us (Stengers 2018: 97–100). So too do we affirm her call to acknowledge our own implication in the brutal suppression of those who have established and sustained cautious relations with the invisible or insensible aspects of existence (2018: 102–3).

But throughout this book, our main way of responding to the tension confronted by Stengers has been to probe and play up the moments *within* Western science that – sometimes in spite of itself – disclose multiplicity or self-differentiation in the constitution of the Earth itself. 'The multiverse, the antenomic or precosmic background state, remains nonunified, on the human *as well as on the world side*', observe Viveiros de Castro and Danowski (2018: 181, our italics), and it is the pluriversality in the world side just as much as the human side that we have chosen to explore, embellish and elaborate upon. While different knowledge practices offer their own pathways into the multiplicities proper to material existence, we see the willingness of Western 'planetary' sciences to acknowledge powers of self-differentiation in regions far beyond human influence not as an oversight but as a provocation.

What would it mean, then, for the imperative to decolonize an overly-Westernized world if we were to ask 'what kind of planet is this that enables multiple forms of human collective, that makes many-world worlds possible, that proliferates telluric spirits and earth-beings'? Attentive to the risks involved, we are prepared to wager on the possibility of affirming that 'divergent worlding practices' inhere in the world itself without giving Western science the first or last word in articulating these enactments.

One way of accounting for our planet's non-selfsameness is indeed to '[make] the earth human, all the way back to its beginning and all the way down to its molten core' (Bobbette 2019: 179). But another way is to insist that so much of what Western thought has restrictively assigned to the human – contingency, the will to make a difference, the capacity to communicate through and across those differences – might well be at work where we are not. Or to put it otherwise, if we are attentive to the lessons of Indigenous peoples, we may begin to move from 'an indifferent world to an intensely interested one' (Povinelli 2016: 77), but if we listen closely to Western science we may pick up hints and murmurings of a world that is non-indifferent and intensely interested in itself. How we recognize and work up that self-differentiating power is only part of the problem, however. Perhaps the greater challenge, as thinkers intent on decolonizing the thinking of the world seem to be saying, is what to do or how best to act when we find ourselves caught up in those wrenching self-transformations.

With no pretence of offering a plan, we want to close this chapter by briefly considering how further attention to composite, meaning-infused and threshold-dwelling entities might help us re-inflect the current crisis of biogeochemical cycling. Clearly, applying millions of tons of destratified minerals to certain regions to make their agro-ecological performance more like that of a very different region is an unsustainable strategy. A great many forms of extraction, Indigenous voices insist, impinge upon ground where gods, spirits or ancestors dwell, and the extent to which such entities are threatened or disturbed might well be taken as an alternative measure of disruption to vital Earth system flows. Moreover, it is only on a certain kind of planet that we can imagine such a multiplication and mobilization of 'geo-spiritual' entities (Szerszynski 2017b). For it takes a particular version of planetary multiplicity, we would tentatively suggest, to provide the conditions under which modes of sensing or investigation can acquire the suppleness to shift between different categories of body and being.

In our reading, Teaiwa's mineral–spiritual 'cross-fertilizations', for all her story bespeaks the brutality of the colonial extractive frontier, also admit of a cautious promise or at least an ethical incitement. Like the drift mobilities that we envisioned in chapter 6, Teaiwa's dispersions and refractions of spirit through global-planetary space invite us to think about careful, respectful and hospitable overtures to the destratified spirit of other worlds that finds its way into our lives. Even if the worst excesses of colonial and capitalist expropriation can be avoided, these are not challenges that are likely to recede. For under conditions of judicious carbon descent, many of us will remain dependent on 'enspirited materials': the minerals embedded in our solar panels, wind turbines and rechargeable batteries, the foods and fibres we turn to under changing climatic conditions – which are as likely as not to bear traces of the ancestral or sacral ground from which they have been sourced (see Childs 2020).

In the context of accelerating Earth system change, in a related sense, we might also ask about alternative ways of understanding piloted airborne vehicles and their capacity to traverse extensive and uneven terrain. This raises the possibility of seeing the powered flight–cargo assemblage not simply as a technological instrument or device, but as a 'figure' invested with meaning apposite to its role in negotiating unfolding threshold events. Perhaps anticipated by the growing role already played by aeroplanes of various types and sizes in disaster relief (Kraft 2019), we might more explicitly consider how to inflect aero-mobility with generosity and hospitality in times when lives are becoming ever more adrift.

In the final chapter, in lieu of a conclusion, we keep these kinds of questions coming. With an eye to the near future, we ask what the implications of planetary social thought might be for a series of challenges arising out of the current global environmental predicament, and point to some of the unresolved issues and the opportunities arising from the discussion so far.

# 8

# Earthly Multitudes and Planetary Futures: Ten Questions

## Introduction: On Time and Futurity

We began the book with a brief account of a surge of climate activism from youthful campaigners, many of whom were not yet born when the Anthropocene idea was first aired. In an important sense, the insights of the post-gradualist, nonlinear Earth sciences that help inform our notion of planetary multiplicity belong to the daily lived experience of this generation – for, as we suggested at the outset, they have never known what it is *not* to live in the shadow of climate tipping points. While justification is hardly necessary, we might see the urgency with which young activists have driven forward the agenda of meeting zero carbon targets as in part a reflection of this ineluctable presence of planetary thresholds in their lifeworld.

How is 'thought' – theory, research, strategy – responding to these challenges and the issues of time and futurity they raise? For several decades, discourses of sustainability have circled around the question of how to include generations-to-come in global environmental agenda-setting, along the way frequently stumbling over the dilemma of how to identify future people's needs or interests (Hannis 2017: 33). Recent additions to the field, informed by Earth systems thinking and the Anthropocene thesis, have offered more generalized thinking around the content of futurity while adding more precision to the issue of securing the planetary conditions to render such futures viable. Staking its claim for a 'Great Transformation towards Sustainability', a recent European report puts its weight behind 'development paths to sustainable societies that keep within the planetary guard rails and can offer all people, including future generations, a good life in dignity and a long-term future' (WBGU 2019: 7).

Likewise affirming the possibility of a 'good Anthropocene', interdisciplinary thinkers associated with the US-based Breakthrough Institute offer their own version of where to put the guard rails. These thinkers propose that new technologies and urban planning aimed at high-density living would enable significant areas of the Earth's surface to be freed from human intrusion and left to regenerate. As their manifesto explains: '[i]ntensifying many human activities – particularly farming, energy extraction, forestry, and settlement – so that they use less land and interfere less with the natural world is the key to decoupling human development from environmental impacts' (Asafu-Adjaye et al. 2015: 7). Numerous other Anthropocene-informed strategies provide variations on the theme of safeguarding vital ecological resources by delinking economic growth from environmental impacts, most often imagined in terms of some combination of technological innovation and novel financial instruments.

But do such attempts at reasoned manoeuvring out of the predicament of Earth system change – with their evocation of straightforward, linear paths from problem recognition to problem-solving – do justice to the depth of fear, anxiety, indignation expressed by young, climate science-savvy protestors? Do these attempts bear witness to or reckon with the concern that older generations increasingly have about the world they are leaving behind, what author Michael Chabon has described as 'the abyss of a parent's greatest fears ... the fear of knowing – as every parent fears – that you have left your children a world more damaged, more poisoned, more base and violent and cheerless and toxic, more doomed, than the one you inherited' (2007: 4)?

As we hardly need to say, few critical social thinkers have been convinced by the prospect of good, dignified or even tolerable Anthropocenes. For many left-leaning theorists, as we saw in chapter 2, climate crisis and 'the shock of the Anthropocene' serve as monstrous, insurmountable vindications of long-descried pathologies in the dominant global social order. Repeated citations of Fredric Jameson's vaguely attributed remark 'that it is easier to imagine the end of the world than to imagine the end of capitalism' (2003: 76), along with the updating of the old 'socialism or barbarism' slogan to 'socialism or extinction' (Reese 2019; Noor 2019), are indicative of the depth of feeling about futurity and the pivotal role the global environmental predicament has come to play in anticapitalist thought.

For the left, it should be added, capitalism's disdain for planetary limits is but the latest manifestation of its congenital contempt for guard rails of any description. But the idea that imminent climate catastrophe 'changes everything' (Klein 2014), and the corresponding call for swift action to curtail the Earth-threatening activities of corporate and state actors, also generate friction. For as we noted in chapter 2, progressive thinkers have also expressed concern about the way that declarations of emergency can impede that process of inclusive political debate and detract from mobilization for fundamental societal change.

For us, this tension between urgent and more deliberative responsive modes is indicative of a deeper set of questions about human action and its temporalities that attend all attempts to respond meaningfully to the planetary situation – whatever their political tenor. As we suggested in the introduction to this book, the imperative of speed and urgency – however vital demands for decisive action on climate change or other environmental threats may be – is not the only temporality of responsible human action. As Derrida (1992a) and others have reminded us, all considered responses to troubling situations are shot through with uncertainty and incomplete knowledge, this being the inescapable fate of political and ethical action. While the condition of being imperfectly informed is not an excuse for inaction or dithering, it *is* suggestive that – alongside urgency – responsibility also calls for patient, searching, reflective modes of operation. As well as and often bound up with the time of decisiveness there is the time it takes to delve into origins, to reckon with inheritances, to imagine possible futures, to weigh up multiple options, to listen to objections and to convince others of chosen pathways (Barnett 2004; 2005). There are times of prospection and retrospection, of trial and error, of revision and trying yet again.

If every attempt to respond in a caring and judicious way to matters of concern involves a juggling act of multiple temporalities of action, we would argue, addressing the challenge of inhabiting a volatile Earth draws us into an especially challenging array of durations and tempos. More than a case of extending the temporalities of the social into geological deep time, what we have been referring to as planetary multiplicity encompasses a wide range of rhythms, intervals, periodicities and singularities. While many changes undergone by our planet are indeed gradual – often imperceptibly slow from a human perspective – the idea that transitions in self-organized, far-from-equilibrium systems are often relatively rapid is a key component of the sciences with which we have been conversing. And it's important to note that we are not only talking about Western knowledge formations when we speak of scientific understandings of dynamic Earth, life and astronomical processes.

One of the main intentions behind our conceptualization of earthly multitudes is to begin to explore the manifold ways that human collectives negotiate with the varied temporalities of their physical worlds. We have been trying to do justice to the need for urgent responses to the challenges posed by Earth systems undergoing abrupt transition, while also accounting for the many other tempos and durations involved in Earth-oriented collective practices. Without presuming that all earthly multitudes can or should contribute directly to contemporary problem-solving, we have sought to foster a way of thinking that remains open to the potentiality of geographically and historically diverse bodies of material praxis under any conditions.

In the rest of this chapter, we raise some questions – far from exhaustively – about what our notions of planetary multiplicity and earthly multitudes might mean for thinking about social futures. In what ways are the past, present and future of the Earth interconnected or implicated, we ask, and how do the time signatures of human material practices relate to these planetary temporalities? Our aim here is not to resolve the questions raised by the 'Anthropocene', but to direct the curiosity of social scientists and fellow travellers to challenges, quandaries and opportunities that invite further consideration.

## Ten Questions

### 1. What are the implications of planetary multiplicity for thinking about the past and future?

Our concept of planetary multiplicity proposes that planets like the Earth are self-incompatible, always out of step with themselves. They are restless, held far from thermal and chemical equilibrium by constant dissipation, as energy from their hot interior and their parent star passes through the system, preventing any part of it from settling. It is this internal, explosive difference-as-such that allow planets to become creative, historical entities. Materially closed and energetically open, they self-differentiate on all spatial and temporal scales.

This view of 'planetary being' plays upon what we see as an auto-deconstructive moment in recent scientific thinking about life, Earth and the cosmos. Conventional Earth science accounts of our planet's history – incarnated in the International Chronostratigraphic Chart – appear to describe a single, unilinear trajectory. But we have been proposing that post-gradualist or neo-catastrophist scientific approaches have themselves been unsettling the monological tone of this way of thinking, through their disclosure of planetary systems that at any moment contain multiple possibilities; a turn that we identify as having much in common with certain philosophical discourses of multiplicity.

Along these lines, we conceive of planetary multiplicity not so much as acting in time, but as actively temporizing or *making* time. By this we refer to the very condition of futurity and the passing of time: the coming into being of a present discernibly different from what came before, or to put it another way, the departure from stasis or selfsameness. Or as Derrida intones: 'What there is to give, uniquely, *would be called time*' (1992b: 29). Following this logic, an astronomical body that self-organizes, self-differentiates, learns how to do new things, is one that 'gives' time by exiting from the closed circuit of the same or the self-identical.

In this sense, then, the kind of *geohistorical analysis* we have been doing throughout this book is less about locating planetary changes in one great sweep of time than it is about trying to grasp the dynamics through which planets generate their own futurity by breaking out of their past states – at every scale from the smallest molecular rearrangements to entire Earth system shifts. By the same logic, however, the opening of new possibilities is a break with what used to be – an undoing or unworlding that spells an end for pre-existing conditions and in some cases for whole categories of entities or beings. This is one lesson that can be taken from the encounter with the succession of rocky strata that compose the Earth's crust – and as we saw in chapter 5, it was a deeply disturbing possibility for those modern Western thinkers around the turn of the nineteenth century who were still struggling to get their heads around the idea of a world of constant *human* historical change.

But there is more to planetary multiplicity than irruptions of novelty or cascades of irrecoverable loss. At certain points in the book we have also talked about the way that the Earth constantly generates structurally or organizationally analogous solutions to similar problems that arise in very different contexts – or what have been termed *metapatterns*. This, as we saw, includes a range of ways of organizing volumes into shapes and compartments, of combining disparate components into new structures, clusters or assemblages. And so, although a far-from-equilibrium planet like the Earth may lurch from one operating state to another in the course of its geohistorical becoming, it maintains a certain repertoire for change, an enduring capacity to resolve problems that recur at a range of scales and in various domains. In this regard, while critical social thinkers rightly remind us that we do not have access to a placeless, disembodied 'god's-eye view' of reality, we should also recall that on this planet, complex, light-sensitive, image-forming eyes appear to have evolved independently on a number of occasions. As we pointed out in chapter 4, this means that entities and phenomena that have 'forgotten' how they once resolved a problem posed by planetary conditions can be 'reminded' when the planet throws up analogous challenges.

A vision that emphasizes planetary self-organization is one that fully affirms the anxiety, indignation and anticipatory grief of younger people – and many of their more time-served seniors – over the closure of future horizons. While there is much that can be learned from past proxies or analogues of the present state of the Earth system, as the planet itself seeks out possible solutions to unprecedented human 'forcings' there is simply no way to fully anticipate how it will reorganize its own flows, compartments, clusterings and couplings. But we also need to be clear that for all the unshakeability of some of the Earth's grander-scale metapatterning aptitudes, much of what is currently being rapidly degraded is our planet's more fined-tuned capacities for self-differentiation and the generation of novelty.

Such are current anthropogenic impacts that it is the very grounds, the very potentiality, of our planet to reorganize itself in productive ways that is being compromised. Or to express it in Vicki Kirby's terms, we could say that what is being diminished is the Earth's own propensity for self-investigation, its own powers of self-understanding and probing of possibility (2011: 34–40). Planets, we have noted, can also lose or 'forget' things they had once learned. So when protestors exclaim, 'Why the actual f*** are we studying for a future we won't have!' we might hear them railing at once against their own and their planet's contraction of futurity.

## 2. How does the concept of earthly multitudes help us to think about social futures?

Along with our fellow life forms, we humans are condemned to change by the variability of our planet, to which we have added our own not-inconsiderable surcharge. In a variety of ways – not all of which we would affirm – earthly multitudes respond to and play off the multi-scalar periodicities, patternings and singularities of a restless planetary body. By securing their own continuity in the face of change, by carving out blocks or parcels of time in which to operate, and by impacting back upon the temporal dynamics of their environment, self-organizing earthly multitudes, no less than their cosmic domicile, actively temporize as they extemporize. Provoked, excited, lured by the self-incompatibility of the Earth, they too generate futurity by outreaching any measure of self-identity.

Over the course of the book we have dwelled more on the *longue durée* of Earth-oriented practices than on the various more precise conjunctures that have been posited as Anthropocene commencement dates. This decision draws in part on the argument that the Anthropocene Working

Group's election of a precisely defined, geosynchronous end-point of the Holocene distracts attention from what archaeologist Matt Edgeworth and his interdisciplinary team see as the more gradual, patchy, discontinuous and incremental geological changes wrought by a range of human collectivities over multi-millennial time frames. Rather than splitting historical human activity into a before and an after through a punctilious, pan-global Anthropocene/Holocene cut, Edgeworth et al. propose a longer-term, more regionalized, 'ground-up' accounting for the manifold ways in which our species has acquired and expressed its Earth-altering agency (2019).

This resonates with our own predilection for moving back and forth between the multi-scalar time signatures of planetary dynamics and the variegated temporizing of earthly multitudes. It's worth recalling that scientists use the term 'catastrophic shift' to speak of regime changes in systems that may be as large as the biosphere or as minute as a single microbial ecosystem. Without wishing to diminish the significance of Earth-wide transformations, for us a cautious de-exceptionalizing of catastrophe serves as a reminder that our species – in all its diversity and differentiation – has a wealth of experience in negotiating planetary transition. In brief, the more encompassing our sense of planetary multiplicity, the less surprised we will be by further reorganization of the Earth. Similarly, the broader the spectrum of earthly multitudes we take seriously, the deeper our reservoir of potentiality for improvising responses to emergent ecological and geophysical conditions. Here we concur with anthropologist James Clifford when he reflects that '[t]he past, materialized in land and ancestors, is always a source of the new' (2013: 25). Clifford is speaking here of Indigenous cosmologies, but we cannot see any good reason why this should be different for other cosmologies, worldviews and knowledge formations – which we take to be his lesson.

What our earthly multitudes get up to includes responding to abrupt climate change, ecological collapse or megafire. In finding new ways to frame, enfold and elaborate upon elemental forces, earthly multitudes, as we have seen, can themselves add new capabilities to the repertoire of their planet. Their mode of operation, however, is most often mundane: waiting quietly for animal herds to arrive, pumping petrol into idling vehicles, making or mending fabric amidst a hubbub of talk and song. But so too, we have sought to show, can such everyday actions initiate or incubate changes that eventually shift entire worlds. As it is with the becoming or self-differentiation of the Earth, modest changes can, on occasion, diffuse, multiply and repercuss into much larger-scale transformations.

Taking the past as a pool or repository of possible ways that our species articulates with the Earth does not limit us to acts of salvage or resuscitation, however vital such actions may be. It can also inspire counterfactual imaginaries, a rolling back to earlier junctures to speculate how developmental trajectories could have taken very different pathways (Clark 2019). To return to an example from chapter 3, we might ask why so many 'globally modern' people ended up having internal combustion engines at their disposal but not kilns or furnaces – and what the consequences would be if it had been the other way round. Or, we might wonder, what if the programmable machines on our desktops had maintained their intimate connection with spun fibre – or some other substantive, tangible material – rather than gravitating towards purely digital, electronic processing (see Pickering 2009)?

Our notion of *stratal analysis* is intended to underscore the importance of locating earthly multitudes – and any other Earth-bound entity or phenomenon – within the strata, flows, compartments or spheres of the Earth from which they emerged. This helps us to identify the specific elements and properties that an existing earthly multitude has enfolded, connected or played variations upon – but it also points us towards the possibilities for constructing alternative social futures that are as yet unrealized or only partially actualized. We also need to keep in mind the Earth's own proclivity for working out analogous solutions when faced with similar kinds of problems in unrelated domains or contexts, which has its counterpart in the way that historically or geographically distinct earthly multitudes facing comparable challenges often appear to come up with decidedly similar responses. Metapatterns, we suggest, also show up in human Earth-oriented activities. Alongside stressing the importance of the situatedness of strategies, routines and know-how, then, we may also need to leave openings for material practices to move or vault across time and space. And for multitudes to 'remember' solutions to planetary problems that they may have neglected, forgotten, or overwritten.

Even when we consider the frightening prospect of a generalized diminishing of the Earth's capacity for further generative self-differentiation, we would still affirm that an expansive scoping of earthly multitudes holds potential for finding new collective ways of living with and through emergent planetary conditions. Like the previous questions, this task exceeds the scope of this book and all our own analytic and imaginative registers – though in a later section we gesture towards some potential points of departure. First, however, we need to consider the powerful forces that have been eroding the vigour and diversity of earthly multitudes.

### 3. What is the relationship between earthly multitudes and the dominant global social order?

As we noted in earlier chapters, the imposition of colonial regimes and the relentless advance of global capitalism have devastated Earth-oriented practices in many places. Narratives of unrelenting decline and loss have been out of fashion for some time, and we willingly acknowledge that earthly multitudes across the world have found ways of enduring, reinventing themselves, metamorphosizing, creolizing, hybridizing, modernizing. But we would caution that knowledges and ways of life keyed to the deep temporal dynamics of the Earth are not easily replaced, and in many cases that which has been lost or attenuated cannot be offset by even the most creative attunement to the tempos of global modernity.

Western modernity has seen the progressive contraction of the 'multi' in earthly multitudes in two related developments. First, human skill has been increasingly codified and routinized, in a shift that can be described as one from craft to technology, from artisanal labour to machinofacture. This involves the move from tools that surround and extend the human body, held in such a way as to be sensitive to the tendencies of the nonhuman world, to an arrangement in which the body of the human worker faces a machine, a 'technical individual', a body in its own right, that compels the human body to conform to its movements (Feenberg 1999: 219; see also Szerszynski 2017c). Second, as part of the same development, for some at least, environments have been made more smooth, frictionless and predictable, making the skills of earthly multitudes less necessary. Rivers have been canalized, roads tarmacked, buildings more effectively insulated and artefacts more standardized.

This selective erosion and marginalization of Earth-oriented collective practices was organized across multiple dimensions. It was organized *socially*, through class relations that ensured it was the working classes, such as the miners, who were most exposed to planetary threats that resisted smoothing over. It was organized *geospatially*, through conquest and colonialism, slavery and the plantation system, ensuring that it was racialized bodies that bore the impact of volatile Earth processes often made even more turbulent by colonial interventions. It was organized *energetically* – by tapping into a geological store of energy that was so vast that it could be taken for granted. But it was also organized *technologically*, through the construction of an artefactual milieu for social life that acted – for some at least – as a buffer against the vicissitudes of planetary variation.

For us, it is important to acknowledge too that social orders or socioeconomic systems that we do not affirm are also ways of engaging with the multiplicity of the Earth – a point deftly expressed in environmental historian Jason Moore's observation that 'Wall Street is a way of organizing nature' (Moore and Keefer 2011). We might see capitalist modernity as a kind of hyperbolic earthly multitude, a rampaging attempt to out-speed, out-grow, out-accumulate planetary multiplicity. But by pumping an excess of matter-energy into the Earth system and by globally degrading ecological systems, capitalism ultimately exacerbates the very uncertainty it seeks to overcome – while also driving material practices of multiplicity towards uniformity. Whereas global-change and planetary-boundary approaches still fantasize about passing over some kind of benign social tipping point that will bring deleterious socioeconomic development under control, it would be more accurate to see capitalism itself as a system whose axiomatic is incessant positive feedback – such that it is constitutively self-reinforcing, runaway and cascading from the outset. Or to put it another way, capitalism *is* the passage over a tipping point.

There is currently no clear 'subject of history' waiting in the wings to challenge the dominant global socioeconomic order. But the possible resurgence of diverse earthly multitudes that we speak of in the next section does not require head-on confrontation with capitalism to intervene decisively in its cycles of positive feedback. Not only every blockade, but each reclaiming of fields, flows, strata, clusters or compartments of the Earth, introduces friction or obstruction to a system that is already struggling to sustain self-augmenting growth on a finite astronomical body.

## 4. How might the protection and enhancement of earthly multitudes help us through the current planetary crisis?

Acknowledging that some thresholds in ecological and environmental systems are already being transgressed, Earth system governance theorists seek to identify sites from which effective practical and political responses might emerge. As political scientist Victor Galaz and his colleagues observe:

> dealing with incremental changes in 'planetary boundaries' require[s] coordinated action evolving around repeated interactions, predictability and execution by nations, regional organizations and international organizations. At the same time, dealing with ecological surprise and cascading effects of environmental change, requires multilevel and

adhoc responses, where a high degree of flexibility and experimentation is allowed. Intriguingly enough, these two capacities seem to be difficult to maintain within the same institutional architecture. (Galaz et al. 2012: 83)

This observation would hardly be 'intriguing' to Indigenous peoples and others with long place-based traditions who have been fighting to persist in their flexible, multifaceted responses to environmental dynamism for centuries (see Whyte 2018b). We should not underestimate how remarkable it is that after half a millennium of organized assault, so many earthly multitudes have endured in some form – and are, at numerous sites, regrouping and taking new directions. Just as researchers have noted the close correlation between protecting human cultural-linguistic diversity and safeguarding biological diversity (Maffi 2001), so too, we would suggest, are there often substantive connections between maintaining collective Earth-attuned practices and defending or enhancing ecosystemic capacities to absorb pressure or shocks. But while there are metrics – albeit imperfect – for assessing risks to languages and biodiversity, we lack measures for gauging the 'health' of earthly multitudes.

In the face of increasingly rapid Earth system change, we need to be very careful indeed in our crafting of responsive and responsible 'institutional architectures'. While the intensification of certain types of land use and productivity to lighten impacts on vital physical systems holds some appeal for us, we are sceptical of ecomodernist proposals for the generalized delinking of further economic development from environmental impacts (e.g. Asafu-Adjaye et al. 2015). This is not just because of the paucity of evidence that such decoupling is achievable, but because many of the greatest threats posed by Earth systems in transition have been exacerbated precisely by the interruption of deep social entanglement with dynamic Earth and life processes.

Thousand of years, sometimes tens or hundreds of thousands of years, of managing landscapes with fire, Stephen Pyne exhorts, leaves our species with profound responsibilities to maintain this task (1997b: 322–7). Similar claims could be made with regard to human interaction with watercourses, sediment, slope morphology, plant and animal life. Even, or especially, on a planet that is currently self-organizing in ways we cannot predict, it seems to us, recoupling rather than decoupling makes more sense: which is to say, renewing and reinvigorating our contact with what Tim Ingold refers to as 'the rough edges of the world' (2013: 72–3).

As these 'edges' roughen or fray still further, there are numerous contexts in which smarter devices and infrastructures and digitized information could assist our collective responses. But claims that 'machine intelligence' or 'autonomous technical systems' – or a generalized 'digital Anthropocene' – will lead the way to sustainability and secure planetary boundaries (WBGU 2019: 8–9) seem to us ill-advised. Historically and geographically wide-ranging evidence, some of which we touched upon in chapters 3 and 4, suggests that probing experimentation, improvisation and related cognitive shifts are most likely to occur through sustained contact with the 'friction of materials' (Ingold 2013: 72–3). Or in archaeologist Lambros Malafouris's reading, it is the coming together of brain, mind and culture through the manipulation of matter that serves as 'the missing link between neural and cultural plasticity' (2010: 41).

We should hardly need to repeat claims that under the increasingly precarious conditions of the current global socioeconomic order, capacities for individualized flexibility, adaptability and self-reliance are touted as attributes of the idealized resilient subject. But in their collective manifestation, such attributes should not be disavowed, for as we suggested in the previous section, they can also be the basis for severing the self-augmenting circuitry of capital from the energy, materials, life, labour and other feedstock upon which it remains utterly dependent.

## 5. What are the political or ethical challenges posed by earthly multitudes?

Channelling and extrapolating from earthly powers enables human actors to do things that they couldn't otherwise achieve. There is no political power that is not in some sense enabled, supported, augmented by the work of earthly multitudes. But that doesn't make earthly multitudes themselves immediately or inevitably political, let alone desirable. Only under certain circumstances, it has been observed, do materials and their manipulation become objects of explicit contention (Barry 2010: 109). Such situations are not infrequent, however. Earth-oriented practitioners have actively opposed the appropriation of their productions or offerings; they have resisted the co-option and codifying of their skills; they have defied rules that forbid or delimit their customary practices. In the last of these cases, when statutory restrictions are flouted and banned procedures are resumed, it can be difficult for outside observers to tell if this is an act of political resistance or simply a return to preferred livelihoods – or both at once (see Kull 2002).

The relationship between the temporalities of earthly multitudes and the times of politics are complex. While earthly multitudes from time to time find themselves responding to major systemic transitions, we have sought to 'dedramatize' such shifts by contextualizing them within a broader range of ongoing Earth system transformations. As we mentioned above, much critical political thought also invests deeply in the idea of ruptural events, raising tricky questions about the way that desired sociopolitical upheavals relate to undesired planetary upheavals. Here we take inspiration from political theorist Bonnie Honig (2009: xviii), who acknowledges the significance of extreme events in the realm of politics, but encourages us to 'de-exceptionalize the emergency'. While recognizing that there are decisive moments when the very framing of the political is stretched or fractured, Honig reminds us that efforts to extend, bend or break out of conventional limits are the very stuff of politics. Along these lines, she advocates forms of political thought and action that '[cut] across the binary of extraordinary versus ordinary, rupture versus procedural' (2009: xviii). In the *Broken Earth* series N. K. Jemisin expresses a similar intuition of the toing and froing between the mundane and the exceptional when her narrator notes that '[o]ne person's normal is another person's Shattering' (2017: 170).

Likewise, earthly multitudes may be oriented towards physical variability that ranges from the minutiae of circadian rhythms through to epochal Earth system reorganization. In this way, the more effective Earth-oriented practices tread pathways between the ordinary and the rare, the routine and the unanticipated, the local and the planetary. So when we think about those situations when earthly multitudes are politicized, we would do well to consider the multiple temporizations involved and what might be gained from de-exceptionalizing the emergency – and the event of emergence.

This sense that the recurrent flexing or fracturing of the frames through which we organize our lives is bound up with the not-so-extraordinary upheaving of the Earth also draws us into the demands of ethical relating. Just as earthly multitudes are on occasion politicized, so too from time to time will they be faced with requests or entreaties from others – or will themselves make such appeals. As well as more mundane questions about how and when to share spaces, materials, know-how or productions, any collective of Earth-oriented practitioners will sooner or later find itself overwhelmed, undermined or wrong-footed by changing planetary conditions. Earthly multitudes, we shouldn't forget, fall short and make mistakes. In such contexts, ethical initiatives about what to offer others who are in need or what to ask of others when under duress can be as much a part of dealing with the challenges of planetary multiplicity as the material practices that provide things that can be given or requested.

In chapter 6, we offered some speculations about inherited and emergent relations of hospitality in the context of new 'possibility spaces' for mobility on a fast-changing Earth. As global populations are evicted from settled Holocene climates, we can anticipate that distinctions between hosts and guests will grow increasingly fluid and unstable, suggesting that ethical improvisation will be one of the foremost challenges and excitations of earthly multitudes-to-come.

## 6. What is the relationship between forging new planetary futures and the task of decolonization?

As with political power more generally, colonization is always, among other things, a strategy for coping with planetary multiplicity. As an appropriation and overwriting of the capacities of others to live with the variability of their physical worlds, colonizing imperatives at once jeopardize existing earthly multitudes and exacerbate the threats of environmental uncertainty. This means that dealing with the legacies of colonization in general, and the last half millennium of Euro-Atlantic colonialism in particular, is inseparable from any attempt to think futurity through the lens of earthly multitudes.

The fact that colonized people endured the 'end of the world' – or indeed repeated 'endings' – is a reminder that even the most unthinkably cataclysmic events are not necessary terminal and should not be used to consign those who suffered them to a superseded social or geological past (Whyte 2017; 2018b; Bold 2019). For empathetic interlocutors, the capacity of Indigenous peoples and other long-term dwellers-in-place to live on through successive upheavals makes their knowledge and experience seem less a 'remnant of the past' than a 'figuration of the future' (Danowski and Viveiros de Castro 2016: 123). Or as Kyle Whyte's (2018a: 228–9) 'Anishinaabe perspective on intergenerational time' would have it, we might conceive of Indigenous ancestors as having already offered speculative or imaginary visions of the dystopian realities that their descendants are now living through. Outdoing our own attempts to conjure the multiple temporalities of earthly multitudes, Whyte's account of Indigenous temporization includes 'narratives of cyclicality, reversal, dream-like scenarios, simultaneity, counter-factuality, irregular rhythms, ironic un-cyclicality, slipstream, parodies of linear pragmatism, eternality' (2018a: 229).

But as critical scholars – Indigenous and otherwise – have made clear, acknowledgement of the efficacy of customary knowledge practices comes with the risk of perpetuating appropriative and extractive colonial relations. Drawing on Indigenous studies scholars Eve Tuck and Wayne Yang's critique of the expropriation of aspects of Indigenous material culture to 'rescue settler futurity' by assuaging colonial guilt and anxiety

(2012: 3), we might consider the broader temptation to salvage white Western futurity through the embrace of ecological Indigeneity in the face of the ever-more globally uneven impacts of Earth system destabilization. We are also conscious that affirmation of customary lifeways has the possible side effect of delegitimizing the activities of compatriot cultural practitioners that appear more compromised or less conspicuously 'earthly', a point that grates uncomfortably with our comment above about the possible non-substitutability of time-served practices.

Just as legacies of colonialism ensure there is no innocent cultural borrowing, so too can the political ascent of earth-beings and other more-than-secular agents complicate what may otherwise appear to be environmentally desirable developments. Katerina Teaiwa's account of ancestral spirit bound up in agrochemical fertilizer application alerts us to other cases in which the extraction of minerals essential to renewable energy technologies turns out to impinge upon the domain of land- or sea-based spiritual beings held in high esteem by local people (see Childs 2020). And so, while Whyte (2018a: 238) reminds us that contemporary Indigenous communities, in the quest for liveable futures, 'are always in dialogue with our ancestors as dystopianists and fantasizers', we must be aware that broader explorations of new planetary futures may be stretching these dialogues along far-reaching and tortuous pathways. While such eventualities remind us that the challenges of decolonization are profound and interminable, they can also serve as prompts to press forward the equally unending project of 'provincializing Europe' (Chakrabarty 2000). We take this to imply that any staging of encounters between the earthly multitudes of the West and those of the majority world requires not only concerted efforts to de-exoticize the latter, but also the comprehensive making strange of the former (Szerszynski 2017b).

## 7. What is the role of creative or aesthetic sensibilities in shaping new planetary futures?

One of the strangest and most destructive characteristics of capitalist modernity, from the point of view of the Earth system, is an entrainment to positive feedback loops so totalizing that it manages to reprocess negative or self-corrective counter-actions back into self-augmenting circuits. 'The social realm ... has let loose an unnatural growth, so to speak, of the natural', as Hannah Arendt (1958: 47) observed, perceptively viewing this process not simply as anti-natural but as a hyperbolization of the dynamics of the biotic world. As a result, Arendt (1958: 124–6) and many others have subsequently noted, the economic system is obliged to constantly maximize the amount of Earth resources it puts to productive use.

In response, some styles of environmentalism have sought to render this cycling even tighter and more efficient. By contrast, we observe, earthly multitudes with time-served understandings of the inherent variability and occasional extremity of their physical milieu tend to value a certain looseness of fit – what early systems theorist Gregory Bateson referred to as 'uncommitted potentiality for change' (1972: 497). 'Lodge yourself on a stratum, experiment with the opportunities it offers', advise Deleuze and Guattari, before reminding would-be-experimenters of the need for some spare or fallow ground: 'have a small plot of new land at all time' (1987: 161). Or perhaps not so small. In the Indigenous perspective of Kyle Whyte, '[r]edundancy is a quality that refers to states of affairs of having multiple options for adaptation when changes occur', which he links not only to material sufficiency but to opportunities for education and awareness-raising of community members. 'Redundancy', Whyte adds, 'is similar to buffering in resilience or systems theory' (2018b: 132).

While scientific accounts of the way the Earth learned to do new things identify some big leaps in the efficiency of cycling matter-energy, we might bear in mind the contribution of a certain excess or superfluity to the opening of these opportunities, just as we should recall how much gratuitous beauty and exuberance permeate the living world. Likewise, our deep if conjectural dive into the history of earthly multitudes was suggestive that significant breakthroughs in harnessing life, matter and energy emerged less from need than from open-ended experimentation. In the words of metallurgist Cyril Stanley Smith: 'discovery requires aesthetically motivated curiosity, not logic, for new things can acquire validity only by interaction in an environment that has yet to be' (1981: 325).

Smith's reflections resonate with our own sense of the value of non-purposive generativity in all future-facing activity on an inherently unpredictable planet. While capitalist imperatives tend to concentrate innovation in specialist pockets, our expansive scoping of earthly multi-tudes suggests that creativity attuned to earthly variability is more likely to be distributed across broad fronts or networks of adaptive practice. It is not easy to fully appreciate or even recognize such emergent Earth-oriented innovation from a distance. Moreover, as we suggested in the previous section, under the prevailing order it is also extremely difficult to shield nascent accomplishments from appropriative or extractive logics.

To cite Smith again: '[a]ll big things grow from little things, but new little things will be destroyed by their environment unless they are cherished for reasons more like love than purpose' (1981: 331). How to furnish the conditions that might nurture new earthly multitudes remains a formidable challenge, a task made still more demanding by the knowledge that there is nothing stopping incipient Earth-oriented practices from being cruel, ugly or destructive.

### 8. What contribution might earthly multitudes make to technical regime change?

However appealing or lovable we might find emergent Earth-oriented practices, their conversion into larger-scale infrastructures can face huge challenges. As we touched upon earlier, large networked technological systems – in particular those premised upon superfluities of energy – can at least provisionally smooth out the rough edges of planetary multiplicity. However, especially where such systems or regimes attain high degrees of path-dependence, longer-term prognoses point to proneness to disruption from both internal disrepair and extreme events (Graham 2010). To these undesirable outcomes we would add the attenuation and loss of diversity of earthly multitudes.

On the other hand, for us, acts of infrastructural maintenance and repair (Graham and Thrift 2007) exhibit aspects of Earth-oriented practice, as do emergency technological improvisations and the more endemic practices of assembly and requisitioning typical of informal urban spaces (McFarlane 2011). So too under conditions in which urban infrastructure is intermittent or discontinuous can people themselves – by way of their networks, collaborations, mobilities – provide many of the services of physical infrastructure (Simone 2004). In a related sense, temporary settlements – such as protest encampments, occupied sites and refugee camps – often generate what political theorist Angela Mitropolous (2012: 229) refers to as 'promiscuous infrastructures': experimental and improvised provisioning arrangements that both are enabled by and further promote generous collective existence.

It's worth recalling that acts of generosity and hospitality are vital 'load-bearing structures of society' (Vaughan 2002: 98), an intuition that coping with the COVID-19 pandemic has driven home, as voluntary, self-organized groups in so many places stepped into the breach of overstretched and unravelling infrastructure. And as we were abruptly reminded of the utter irreplaceability of the human components of our 'technical' regimes, so too should we keep in mind that much of what became modern infrastructure is assembled out of techniques and knowledges – such as ceramics, glass-making, welding, metal extrusion, tunnelling, pipe-laying, hydraulic engineering – that bear the signatures of earthly multitudes. Under conditions of post-carbon power-down, coupled with accelerating Earth system change, we anticipate seeing much of the 'withdrawn' contribution of collective, hands-on material practices returning to visibility, together with outbursts of 'disruptive technology' that provide more accessible, tinker-able, improvisable alternatives to standardized infrastructural regimes (see Tyfield 2014b).

So while we are cautiously affirmative about the role that digitality might play in sharing innovations and linking niche activities (see Geels 2012), we are dubious about the conjecture that in the face of escalating planetary turbulence 'machine intelligence [will] help us where human intelligence obviously fails' (WBGU 2019: 3; see also Lovelock 2019). Our inclination is to scan the horizon – or rather, the interstices of existing technical regimes – for signs of emergent 'infrastructuring practices' (Blok et al. 2016) that grapple explicitly with the material frictions and roughening edges of planetary change. For under planetary conditions increasingly likely to involve runaway, cascading change, it would seem to us that viable infrastructural futures lie less in automated delegation than in multiplicitous capacities for grubby-fingered repair, impromptu innovation, widely distributed experimentation and 'promiscuous' sharing.

## 9. What is the relationship between human earthly multitudes and other living things in the context of planetary multiplicity?

'Well trampled places do not resist me but support me', observes philosopher Emmanuel Levinas (1969: 138). We would do well to take this literally, for a great deal of what earthly multitudes have been able to achieve has been subtended or inspired by the activities of other-than-human life forms. Our hands have been more than full in this book dealing with the way our species – in all its diversity – has played variations on the theme of planetary dynamism and self-differentiation. But before we close, we want to stress just how crucial other creatures have been in the making of earthly multitudes – and how vital they still are in mediating between human material practices and the variability of the Earth.

Writing about sheep, philosopher of science Vinciane Despret and ecologist Michel Meuret describe how the animals collectively extend the capacity of the Earth to sense and express itself: 'The memory of the flock', they write, 'gives to the land a part of its existence. By the concrete memory of the mouths, the eyes, the guts, the bodies, the legs, and the feet, the flock multiplies the ways lands, paths, bushes, springs, and rocks exist' (2016: 33). With careful stewardship, observe Despret and Meuret, the presence of these animals reduces fire risk and enhances biodiversity. In a vastly expanded register, we would add, living communities have frequently been at the forefront of the Earth's evolving capacity to do new things, just as they have recolonized ground that has been seared and churned – and in this way they have helped the planet negotiate its own catastrophic upheavals.

It hardly needs to be said that, whereas Indigenous or other time-served inhabitation most often nurture the diversity of the nonhuman life with which they see their lives as utterly entangled, Western modernity has been instrumental in the reduction and rendering uniform of other living things (and indeed of the 'nonorganic life' produced by material self-organization – see DeLanda 1992). And, once triggered, Earth system change perpetuates and intensifies this diminishment. Geographer Susan Ruddick reminds us that climate change impacts upon the means by which living creatures make sense of their worlds, by disrupting the 'visual, auditory, olfactory, electromagnetic and other cues in the landscape [that] influence the behaviours of animals and organisms in broadly defined geosystems' (2017: 133). In this way, the Earth's own powers of knowing or self-investigation are diminished. To lose a species or to narrow its options is to lessen the capacity of the Earth to learn new things or to absorb shocks: it is to empty out some of the richest pockets of information anywhere in the planetary body. As environmental humanities scholar Thom van Dooren (2010: 285) reflects, '[w]hen species disappear from the world they leave a tear in the biosocial relational field that is life; an absence and a wound that can never be filled, but must nonetheless be "repaired" in some way, lest the patterns of amplification continue and the dead keep piling up'.

Van Dooren's acknowledgement of the need to actively work towards redressing the loss or rending of living worlds – however exacting and interminable – resonates with our recognition that any viable path to geosocial futurity lies in deeper immersion in the organic and inorganic fabric of the planet rather than in withdrawal. For earthly multitudes both existing and to come, this is more than a matter of seeking to recompose relationships that support our own lifeworlds. It is also about nurturing ways of inhabiting the world from which we can take insight and inspiration, modes of embodied and sensory being that can multiply our perspectives on our planetary existence and enhance the Earth's own self-investigation. But at a time when many species endure only by scraping out new niches in the interstices of human worlds, a time when temporization itself seems to be contracting, we cannot overestimate the magnitude of this task.

## 10. How might thinking planetary multiplicity and multiple planetarity together help us imagine alternative futures?

At the heart of our book is the idea that Earth is characterized by an inherent capacity to become other than it is. This planetary multiplicity is a feature that our planet shares with other planets: it is but one variation on a theme of self-differentiation or self-inconsistency that astronomical thinkers observe in an ever-expanding register of planetary bodies in and beyond our solar system. While we agree that the vast majority of our species and other Terran life forms will be likely to remain 'earthbound' for the foreseeable future (Latour 2017), we have argued that *comparative and speculative planetology* helps us to probe future possibilities open to us and our planet. And in this sense we seek to extend the entwined thematics of planetary multiplicity and multiple planetarity that can already be discerned in the Gaia hypothesis and other tributaries of Anthropocene thought (see Olson and Messeri 2015).

It is not coincidental that, in the post-World War II years, ideas of planetary multiplicity and multiplanetarity emerged together, for as we saw in chapter 2, the view of the Earth as an integrated system emerged in a context of viewing our home planet as one amongst many planetary bodies. If we are interested in what new things the Earth might yet be capable of doing, it helps to gain some distance from the existing state of our planet and its geohistory to date. Knowledge of what other planets can do or have become, we have argued, helps us to avoid 'planetary chauvinism' and to expand our sense of what it is possible for astronomical bodies to do (Szerszynski 2017c).

This relates to the current renewed interest in extraterrestrial exploration. Here, planetary social thought can help us to shift discussion from the question of how to extend terrestrial operations into the cosmos to the issue of how we 'Terrans' might be transformed by the conditions that we encounter beyond our own planet. In this sense, we concur with anthropologist David Valentine's suggestion that, for all its familiar entrepreneurial and frontier-extending rhetoric, much 'NewSpace' thinking 'exceeds the demands, fantasies, or time frames of capitalism' (2012: 1062). And indeed, the question Valentine goes on to ask of the possible futures that might emerge from revitalized efforts to venture beyond Earth – that is, 'How do we take this cosmology seriously without thinking that we already know the answer?' (2012: 1064) – is one that captures the animating impulse of our own engagement with planetary multiplicity.

It is interesting to observe how much of today's science fiction – an increasingly transnational genre – moves back and forth between the question of what is becoming of the Earth, and the question of what 'we' might encounter and be transformed by in our venturing beyond our planet. Well aware that we are neither science fiction writers nor planetary scientists, in *Planetary Social Thought* we have asked a lot of questions about what might become of our planet and its human contingent of playful, experimental, most often mundane, sometimes reckless or cruel, occasionally desperate earthly multitudes. We have generally avoided giving precise or programmatic answers. This has primarily been a work of theory, and neither the Earth nor its human and nonhuman collectives await the findings of theory before responding to problems or opportunities. Here we heed the counsel of Clive Barnett, who maintains that 'theory matters not because it guides our actions but because it helps to direct our curiosity to issues that deserve further attention' (2017: 1).

Both the Earth and its sub-componentry of human Earth-oriented multitudes are currently working on the problem of what to do about a surge of carbon dioxide in the atmosphere and oceans, how to deal with the material consequences of turning the Earth's crust inside out in the search for useful materials, how to respond to the accelerating loss of the diversity of living things, and what to make of a proliferation of new channels for disseminating living and nonliving matter. The challenge is never simply to resolve a problem, to identify and stick to a pathway, for the constant reorganization of planetary forces will keep throwing up new problems, opening up new pathways and closing down old ones. New things, new practices, new earthly multitudes will coalesce and gather support 'only by interaction in an environment that has yet to be'. There are indeed very urgent global and local problems we currently face – but forging new planetary futures is also a matter of making time. And that, we have been suggesting, requires a deep, explorative and imaginative approach to the varied ways in which our species has joined forces with the Earth, together with an appreciation of the way our planet goes about its own, active, temporizing.

# Bibliography

Aitchison, Leslie (1960) *A History of Metals*, Vol. 1, London: MacDonald & Evans.

Allewaert, Monique (2013) *Ariel's Ecology: Plantations, Personhood, and Colonialism in the American Tropics*, Minneapolis: University of Minnesota Press.

Alley, Richard B. (2000) *The Two-Mile Time Machine: Ice Cores, Abrupt Climate Change, and Our Future*, Princeton, NJ: Princeton University Press.

Anderson, Kay (2007) *Race and the Crisis of Humanism*, London: Routledge.

Anderson, Kevin (2015) 'Talks in the city of light generate more heat', *Nature*, 528(7583), 437.

Anderson, Kevin and Alice Bows (2011) 'Beyond "dangerous" climate change: emission scenarios for a new world', *Philosophical Transactions of the Royal Society A: Mathematical, Physical and Engineering Sciences*, 369(1934), pp. 20–44.

Anthony, David W. (2007) *The Horse, the Wheel, and Language: How Bronze-Age Riders from the Eurasian Steppes Shaped the Modern World*, Princeton, NJ: Princeton University Press.

Anthropocene Working Group (2019) *Working Group on the 'Anthropocene'*, Subcommission on Quaternary Stratigraphy, <http://quaternary.stratigraphy.org/working-groups/anthropocene/>.

Appadurai, Arjun (1990) 'Disjuncture and difference in the global cultural economy', *Theory, Culture & Society*, 7(2–3), pp. 295–310.

Arendt, Hannah (1951) *The Origins of Totalitarianism*, New York: Harcourt, Brace.

Arendt, Hannah (1958) *The Human Condition*, Chicago: University of Chicago Press.

Arnold, David (1999) 'Hunger in the garden of plenty: the Bengal famine of

1770', in *Dreadful Visitations: Confronting Natural Catastrophe in the Age of Enlightenment*, ed. Alessa Johns, New York: Routledge, pp. 81–112.

Asafu-Adjaye, John, Linus Blomqvist, Stewart Brand, Barry Brook, Ruth de Fries, Erle Ellis, Christopher Foreman, David Keith, Martin Lewis et al. (2015) *An Ecomodernist Manifesto*, Oakland, CA: Breakthrough Institute.

Bachelard, Gaston (1964) *The Psychoanalysis of Fire*, London: Routledge & Kegan Paul.

Baldwin, Andrew and Giovanni Bettini (eds.) (2017) *Life Adrift: Climate Change, Migration, Critique*, London: Rowman & Littlefield International.

Baldwin, James (1963) *The Fire Next Time*, New York: Dial Press.

Barber, Elizabeth Wayland (1994) *Women's Work: The First 20,000 Years: Women, Cloth, and Society in Early Times*, New York: Norton.

Barfield, Owen (1954) *History in English Words*, new edition, London: Faber and Faber.

Barnett, Clive (2004) 'Deconstructing radical democracy: articulation, representation, and being-with-others', *Political Geography*, 23(5), pp. 503–28.

Barnett, Clive (2005) 'Ways of relating: hospitality and the acknowledgement of otherness', *Progress in Human Geography*, 29(1), pp. 5–21.

Barnett, Clive (2017) *The Priority of Injustice: Locating Democracy in Critical Theory*, Athens, GA: University of Georgia Press.

Barnosky, Anthony D., Elizabeth A. Hadly, Jordi Bascompte, Eric L. Berlow, James H. Brown, Mikael Fortelius, Wayne M. Getz, John Harte, Alan Hastings et al. (2012) 'Approaching a state shift in Earth's biosphere', *Nature*, 486(7401), pp. 52–8.

Barry, Andrew (2010) 'Materialist politics: metallurgy', in *Political Matter: Technoscience, Democracy, and Public Life*, ed. Bruce Braun and Sarah Whatmore, Minneapolis: University of Minnesota Press, pp. 89–118.

Basalla, George (1988) *The Evolution of Technology*, Cambridge: Cambridge University Press.

Bataille, Georges (1988) *The Accursed Share: An Essay on General Economy*, Vol. I, tr. Robert Hurley, New York: Zone Books.

Bataille, Georges (1993) *The Accursed Share: An Essay on General Economy*, Vols. II and III, tr. Robert Hurley, New York: Zone Books.

Bataille, Georges (2013) 'The economy equal to the universe', tr. Stuart Kendall, *Scapegoat*, 5, pp. 34–7.

Bateson, Gregory (1972) *Steps to an Ecology of Mind: Collected Essays in Anthropology, Psychiatry, Evolution, and Epistemology*, New York: Ballantine.

Bateson, Gregory (1979) *Mind and Nature: A Necessary Unity*, New York: Dutton.

Behringer, Wolfgang (2017) 'Climate and history: hunger, anti-semitism, and reform during the Tambora crisis of 1815–1820', in *German History in Global and Transnational Perspective*, ed. David Lederer, London: Palgrave Macmillan, pp. 9–41.

Bennett, Jane (2010) *Vibrant Matter: A Political Ecology of Things*, Durham, NC: Duke University Press.

Bhabha, Homi K. (1998) 'Anxiety in the midst of difference', *Political and Legal Anthropology Review*, 21(1), pp. 123–37.

Binford, Lewis R. (1980) 'Willow smoke and dogs' tails: hunter-gatherer settlement systems and archaeological site formation', *American Antiquity*, 45(1), pp. 4–20.

Blaser, Mario and Marisol de la Cadena (2018) 'Introduction. Pluriverse: proposals for a world of many worlds', in *A World of Many Worlds*, ed. Marisol de la Cadena and Mario Blaser, Durham, NC: Duke University Press, pp. 1–22.

Blok, Anders, Moe Nakazora and Brit Ross Winthereik (2016) 'Infrastructuring environments', *Science as Culture*, 25(1), pp. 1–22.

Blomberg, S. P. and T. Garland (2002) 'Tempo and mode in evolution: phylogenetic inertia, adaptation and comparative methods', *Journal of Evolutionary Biology*, 15(6), pp. 899–910.

Bloodworth, Andrew (2014) 'A once and future extractive history of Britain', in *Proceedings of the 17th Extractive Industry Geology Conference*, Warwick: EIG Conferences Ltd, 1–6.

Bobbette, Adam (2019) 'Cosmological reason on a volcano', in *Political Geology: Active Stratigraphies and the Making of Life*, ed. Adam Bobbette and Amy Donovan, London: Palgrave Macmillan, pp. 169–99.

Bold, Rosalyn (ed.) (2019) *Indigenous Perceptions of the End of the World: Creating a Cosmopolitics of Change*, London: Palgrave Macmillan.

Bonneuil, Christophe (2015) 'The geological turn: narratives of the Anthropocene', in *The Anthropocene and the Global Environmental Crisis*, ed. Clive Hamilton, Christophe Bonneuil and François Gemenne, London: Routledge, pp. 17–31.

Bonneuil, Christophe and Jean-Baptiste Fressoz (2016) *The Shock of the Anthropocene: The Earth, History, and Us*, tr. David Fernbach, London: Verso.

Braudel, Fernand (1981) *Civilization and Capitalism, 15th–18th Century, Volume I: The Structures of Everyday Life*, tr. Miriam Kochan and Sian Reynolds, New York: Harper & Row.

Braudel, Fernand (1982) *Civilization and Capitalism, 15th–18th Century, Volume II: The Wheels of Commerce*, tr. Sian Reynolds, New York: Harper & Row.

Brennan, Teresa (2000) *Exhausting Modernity: Grounds for a New Economy*, London: Routledge.

Bridge, Gavin (2009) 'The hole world: spaces and scales of extraction', *New Geographies*, 2, pp. 43–8.

Broecker, Wallace S. (1987) 'Unpleasant surprises in the greenhouse?', *Nature*, 328(6126), pp. 123–6.

Broecker, Wallace S. (2008) *How to calm an angry beast*, CBC News, <https://www.cbc.ca/news/technology/wallace-broecker-how-to-calm-an-angry-beast-1.714719>.

Brooke, John L. (2014) *Climate Change and the Course of Global History: A Rough Journey*, New York: Cambridge University Press.

Buchanan, Mark (2000) *Ubiquity: The Science of History, or Why the World Is Simpler Than We Think*, London: Weidenfeld & Nicolson.

Butterfield, Nicholas J. (2007) 'Macroevolution and macroecology through deep time', *Palaeontology*, 50(1), pp. 41–55.

Butterfield, Nicholas J. (2011) 'Animals and the invention of the Phanerozoic Earth system', *Trends in Ecology & Evolution*, 26(2), pp. 81–7.

Caple, Zachary and Gregory T. Cushman (2016) *The phosphorus apparatus*, Technosphere Magazine, <https://technosphere-magazine.hkw.de/p/1-The-Phosphorus-Apparatus-czfdPRXcpUj4nxj8aQQ1GZ>.

Carpenter, Stephen R. and Elena M. Bennett (2011) 'Reconsideration of the planetary boundary for phosphorus', *Environmental Research Letters*, 6(1), 014009.

CAST (2018) *Aerocene*, MIT Center for Art, Science & Technology (CAST), <https://arts.mit.edu/aerocene/>.

Castells, Manuel (2000) *The Rise of the Network Society*, Oxford: Blackwell.

Césaire, Aimé (1995) *Notebook of a Return to My Native Land – Cahier D'un Retour Au Pays Natal*, tr. Mireille Rosello and Annie Pritchard, Newcastle upon Tyne: Bloodaxe Books.

Césaire, Aimé (2001) *Discourse on Colonialism*, tr. Joan Pinkham, New York: Monthly Review Press.

Chabon, Michael (2007) 'After the apocalypse', *New York Review of Books*, 54(2), https://www.nybooks.com/articles/2007/02/15/after-the-apocalypse.

Chakrabarty, Dipesh (2000) *Provincializing Europe: Postcolonial Thought and Historical Difference*, Princeton, NJ: Princeton University Press.

Chakrabarty, Dipesh (2014) 'Climate and capital: on conjoined histories', *Critical Inquiry*, 41(1), pp. 1–23.

Childs, John (2020) 'Performing "blue degrowth": critiquing seabed mining in Papua New Guinea through creative practice', *Sustainability Science*, 15(1), pp. 117–29.

Clark, Nigel (1999) 'Wild life: ferality and the frontier with chaos', in *Quicksands: Foundational Histories in Australia & Aotearoa New Zealand*, ed. Klaus Neumann, Nicholas Thomas and Hilary Ericksen, Sydney: University of New South Wales Press, pp. 133–52.

Clark, Nigel (2011) *Inhuman Nature: Sociable Life on a Dynamic Planet*, London: Sage.

Clark, Nigel (2012) 'Moving and shaking: mobility on a dynamic planet', in *Atlas: Geography, Architecture and Change in an Interdependent World*, ed. Renata Tyszczuk, Joe Smith, Nigel Clark and Melissa Butcher, London: Black Dog, pp. 22–9.

Clark, Nigel (2013) 'Mobile life: biosecurity practices and insect globalization', *Science as Culture*, 22(1), pp. 16–37.

Clark, Nigel (2014) 'Geo-politics and the disaster of the Anthropocene', *The Sociological Review*, 62(S1), pp. 19–37.

Clark, Nigel (2015) 'Fiery arts: pyrotechnology and the political aesthetics of the Anthropocene', *GeoHumanities*, 1(2), pp. 266–84.

Clark, Nigel (2016) 'Anthropocene incitements: toward a politics and ethics of ex-orbitant planetarity', in *The Politics of Globality since 1945: Assembling the Planet*, ed. Rens van Munster and Casper Sylvest, London: Routledge, pp. 126–44.

Clark, Nigel (2018a) 'Earth, fire, art: pyrotechnology and the crafting of the social', in *Inventing the Social*, ed. Noortje Marres, Michael Guggenheim and Alex Wilkie, Manchester: Mattering Press, pp. 173–94.

Clark, Nigel (2018b) 'Infernal machinery: thermopolitics of the explosion', *Culture Machine*, 17, <https://culturemachine.net/vol-17-thermal-objects/infernal-machinery/>.

Clark, Nigel (2019) 'Enflamed imaginations: of fire and futurity', in *Culture and Climate Change: Scenarios*, ed. Renata Tyszczuk, Joe Smith and Robert Butler, Cambridge: Shed, pp. 30–6.

Clark, Nigel and Yasmin Gunaratnam (2013) 'Sustaining difference: climate change, diet and the materiality of race', in *Geographies of Race and Food: Fields, Bodies, Markets*, ed. Rachel B. Slocum and Arun Saldanha, Farnham: Ashgate, pp. 157–73.

Clark, Nigel and Yasmin Gunaratnam (2017) 'Earthing the Anthropos? From "socializing the Anthropocene" to geologizing the social', *European Journal of Social Theory*, 20(1), pp. 146–63.

Clark, Nigel and Kathryn Yusoff (2014) 'Combustion and society: a fire-centred history of energy use', *Theory, Culture & Society*, 31(5), pp. 203–26.

Clark, Nigel and Kathryn Yusoff (2017) 'Geosocial formations and the Anthropocene', *Theory, Culture & Society*, 34(2–3), pp. 3–23.

Clarke, Bruce and Mark B. N. Hansen (eds.) (2009) *Emergence and Embodiment: New Essays on Second-Order Systems Theory*, Durham, NC: Duke University Press.

Clayton, Philip and Paul Davies (eds.) (2006) *The Re-Emergence of Emergence: The Emergentist Hypothesis from Science to Religion*, Oxford: Oxford University Press.

Cleal, Christopher J. and Barry A. Thomas (1996) *British Upper Carboniferous Stratigraphy*, London: Chapman and Hall.

Clifford, James (2013) *Returns: Becoming Indigenous in the Twenty-First Century*, Cambridge, MA: Harvard University Press.

Colebrook, Claire (2017a) 'Fragility, globalism and the end of the world', *Ctrl-Z: New Media Philosophy*, 7, <http://www.ctrl-z.net.au/articles/issue-7/colebrook-fragility-globalism-and-the-end-of-the-world/>.

Colebrook, Claire (2017b) 'Transcendental migration: taking refuge from climate change', in *Life Adrift: Climate Change, Migration, Critique*, ed. Andrew Baldwin and Giovanni Bettini, London: Rowman & Littlefield International, pp. 115–30.

Colebrook, Claire (2019) 'A cut in relationality: art at the end of the world', *Angelaki*, 24(3), pp. 175–95.

Coleman, William (1973) 'Limits of the recapitulation theory: Carl Friedrich Kielmeyer's critique of the presumed parallelism of Earth history, ontogeny, and the present order of organisms', *Isis*, 64(3), pp. 341–50.

Colling, A., N. Dise, P. Francis, N. Harris and C. Wilson (1997) *The Dynamic Earth*, Milton Keynes: Open University.

Connell, Raewyn (2007) *Southern Theory: Social Science and the Global Dynamics of Knowledge*, Cambridge: Polity.

Conner, Clifford D. (2005) *A People's History of Science: Miners, Midwives, and 'Low Mechanicks'*, New York: Nation Books.

Cooper, Melinda (2010) 'Turbulent worlds: financial markets and environmental crisis', *Theory, Culture & Society*, 27(2–3), pp. 167–90.

Cordell, Dana, Jan-Olof Drangert and Stuart White (2009) 'The story of phosphorus: global food security and food for thought', *Global Environmental Change*, 19(2), pp. 292–305.

Cronon, William (1999) 'Foreword', in *Tutira: The Story of a New Zealand Sheep Station*, Herbert Guthrie-Smith, Auckland: Godwit, pp. xi–xv.

Crosby, Alfred W. (1986) *Ecological Imperialism: The Biological Expansion of Europe, 900–1900*, Cambridge: Cambridge University Press.

Cruikshank, Julie (2005) *Do Glaciers Listen? Local Knowledge, Colonial Encounters, and Social Imagination*, Vancouver & Seattle: UBC Press & University of Washington Press.

Crutzen, P. J. and E. F. Stoermer (2000) 'The "Anthropocene"', *IGBP Newsletter*, 41, pp. 17–18.

Crutzen, Paul (2004) 'Anti-Gaia', in *Global Change and the Earth System: A Planet Under Pressure*, Will Steffen, Jill Jäger, Pamela Matson, Berrien Moore, Frank Oldfield, Katherine Richardson, Angelina Sanderson, H. John Schellnhuber, B. L. Turner, Peter Tyson and Robert J. Wasson, Berlin: Springer, p. 72.

Crutzen, Paul J. (2002) 'Geology of mankind', *Nature* 415, p. 23.

Cushman, Gregory T. (2013) *Guano and the Opening of the Pacific World: A Global Ecological History*, Cambridge: Cambridge University Press.

Danowski, Déborah and Eduardo Viveiros de Castro (2016) *The Ends of the World*, Cambridge: Polity.

Darwin, Charles (1859) *On the Origin of Species by Means of Natural Selection, or the Preservation of Favoured Races in the Struggle for Life*, London: John Murray.

David, Paul A. (1985) 'Clio and the economics of QWERTY', *American Economic Review*, 75, pp. 332–7.

Davies, Jeremy (2016) *The Birth of the Anthropocene*, Oakland, CA: University of California Press.

Davis, Heather and Zoe Todd (2017) 'On the importance of a date, or, decolonizing the Anthropocene', *ACME: An International Journal for Critical Geographies*, 16(4), pp. 761–80.

Davis, Mike (1996) 'Cosmic dancers on history's stage? The permanent revolution in the Earth sciences', *New Left Review*, 217, pp. 48–84.

Davis, Mike (2001) *Late Victorian Holocausts: El Niño Famines and the Making of the Third World*, New York: Verso.

de la Cadena, Marisol (2010) 'Indigenous cosmopolitics in the Andes: conceptual reflections beyond "politics"', *Cultural Anthropology*, 25(2), pp. 334–70.

de la Cadena, Marisol (2015) *Earth Beings: Ecologies of Practice across Andean Worlds*, Durham, NC: Duke University Press.

DeLanda, Manuel (1992) 'Nonorganic life', in *Zone 6: Incorporations*, ed. Jonathan Crary and Sanford Kwinter, New York: Urzone, pp. 129–67.

DeLanda, Manuel (2002) *Intensive Science and Virtual Philosophy*, London: Continuum.

Delany, Samuel R. (2012) *Starboard Wine: More Notes on the Language of Science Fiction*, revised edition, Middletown, CN: Wesleyan University Press.

Deleuze, Gilles (1988a) *Bergsonism*, tr. Hugh Tomlinson and Barbara Habberjam, New York: Zone Books.

Deleuze, Gilles (1988b) *Foucault*, tr. Seán Hand, Minneapolis: University of Minnesota Press.

Deleuze, Gilles and Félix Guattari (1987) *A Thousand Plateaus: Capitalism and Schizophrenia*, tr. Brian Massumi, Minneapolis: University of Minnesota Press.

Deleuze, Gilles and Félix Guattari (1994) *What Is Philosophy?*, tr. H. Tomlinson and G. Burchell, New York: Columbia University Press.

Derrida, Jacques (1981) *Dissemination*, tr. Barbara Johnson, London: Athlone.

Derrida, Jacques (1992a) 'Force of law: the "mystical foundation of authority"', in *Deconstruction and the Possibility of Justice*, ed. Drucilla Cornell, Michel Rosenfeld and David Carlson, New York: Routledge, pp. 3–67.

Derrida, Jacques (1992b) *Given Time: I. Counterfeit Money*, tr. Peggy Kamuf, Chicago: University of Chicago Press.

Derrida, Jacques (1994) *Specters of Marx: The State of the Debt, the Work of Mourning, and the New International*, tr. Peggy Kamuf, New York: Routledge.

Derrida, Jacques (1995) *Points ...: Interviews, 1974–1994*, tr. Peggy Kamuf and others, Stanford, CA: Stanford University Press.

Despret, Vinciane and Michel Meuret (2016) 'Cosmoecological sheep and the arts of living on a damaged planet', *Environmental Humanities*, 8(1), pp. 24–36.

Edgeworth, Matt, Erle C. Ellis, Philip Gibbard, Cath Neal and Michael Ellis (2019) 'The chronostratigraphic method is unsuitable for determining the start of the Anthropocene', *Progress in Physical Geography: Earth and Environment*, 43(3), pp. 334–44.

Edwards, Kasey (2016) *Why are we still ironing our husband's shirts?*, Sydney Morning Herald, <https://www.smh.com.au/lifestyle/life-and-relationships/why-are-we-still-ironing-our-husbands-shirts-20160902-gr7sq6.html>.

Edwards, Paul N. (2010) *A Vast Machine: Computer Models, Climate Data, and the Politics of Global Warming*, Cambridge, MA: MIT Press.

Eger, Martin (1993) 'Hermeneutics and the new epic of science', in *The Literature of Science: Perspectives on Popular Scientific Writing*, ed. Murdo William McRae, Athens, GA: University of Georgia Press, pp. 187–209.

Eiseley, Loren C. (1978) *The Star Thrower*, New York: Times Books.

Engels, Friedrich (2009) *The Condition of the Working Class in England*, tr. Florence Wischnewetzky, Oxford: Oxford University Press.

Escobar, Arturo (2018) *Designs for the Pluriverse: Radical Interdependence, Autonomy, and the Making of Worlds*, Durham, NC: Duke University Press.

Fabian, Johannes (1983) *Time and the Other: How Anthropology Makes its Object*, New York: Columbia University Press.

Fairlie, Simon (2009) 'A short history of enclosure in Britain', *The Land*, 7, pp. 16–31.

Fanon, Frantz (1965) *The Wretched of the Earth*, tr. Constance Farrington, New York: Grove Press.

Feenberg, Andrew (1999) *Questioning Technology*, London: Routledge.

Ferreira da Silva, Denise (2011) 'Notes for a critique of the "Metaphysics of Race"', *Theory, Culture & Society*, 28(1), pp. 138–48.

Ferreira da Silva, Denise (2014) 'Toward a Black feminist poethics: the quest(ion) of Blackness toward the end of the world', *The Black Scholar*, 44(2), pp. 81–97.

Flannery, Tim F. (1994) *The Future Eaters: An Ecological History of the Australasian Lands and People*, Sydney: Reed.

Folke, Carl (2004) 'Enhancing resilience for adapting to global change', in *Global Change and the Earth System: A Planet Under Pressure*, ed. Will Steffen, Jill Jäger, Pamela Matson, Berrien Moore, Frank Oldfield, Katherine Richardson, Angelina Sanderson, H. John Schellnhuber, B. L. Turner, Peter Tyson and Robert J. Wasson, Berlin: Springer, pp. 287.

Forbes, R. J. (1950) *Metallurgy in Antiquity: A Notebook for Archaeologists and Technologists*, Leiden: E. J. Brill.

Fortey, Richard A. (2005) *The Earth: An Intimate History*, London: HarperPerennial.

Foster, John Bellamy and Paul Burkett (2016) *Marx and the Earth*, Leiden: Brill.

Foucault, Michel (2002) *The Order of Things: An Archaeology of the Human Sciences*, London: Routledge.

Francis, Lisbeth (1991) 'Sailing Downwind: Aerodynamic Performance of the *Velella* Sail', *Journal of Experimental Biology*, 158(1), pp. 117–32.

Frank, Adam, Axel Kleidon and Marina Alberti (2017) 'Earth as a hybrid planet: the Anthropocene in an evolutionary astrobiological context', *Anthropocene*, 19(Supplement C), pp. 13–21.

Fraser, James Angus, Melissa Leach and James Fairhead (2014) 'Anthropogenic dark earths in the landscapes of Upper Guinea, West Africa: intentional or inevitable?', *Annals of the Association of American Geographers*, 104(6), pp. 1222–38.

Freese, Barbara (2016) *Coal: A Human History*, revised and updated edition, London: Arrow Books.

Galaz, Victor, Frank Biermann, Beatrice Crona, Derk Loorbach, Carl Folke, Per Olsson, Måns Nilsson, Jeremy Allouche, Åsa Persson et al. (2012) '"Planetary boundaries": exploring the challenges for global environmental governance', *Current Opinion in Environmental Sustainability*, 4(1), pp. 80–7.

Gasché, Rodolphe (2014) *Geophilosophy: On Gilles Deleuze and Félix Guattari's What is Philosophy?*, Evanston, IL: Northwestern University Press.

Geels, Frank W. (2012) 'A socio-technical analysis of low-carbon transitions: introducing the multi-level perspective into transport studies', *Journal of Transport Geography*, 24, pp. 471–82.

Ghosh, Amitav (2016) *The Great Derangement: Climate Change and the Unthinkable*, Chicago: University of Chicago Press.

Gilmore, Mary (1986) *Old Days, Old Ways: A Book of Recollections*, North Ryde: Angus & Robertson.

Gilroy, Paul (1993) 'Living memory: a meeting with Toni Morrison', in *Small Acts: Thoughts on the Politics of Black Cultures*, New York: Serpent's Tail, pp. 175–82.

Gilroy, Paul (2000) *Against Race: Imagining Political Culture Beyond the Color Line*, Cambridge, MA: Belknap Press of Harvard University Press.

Goddard, Michael (2011) 'From the multitudo to the multitude: the place of Spinoza in the political philosophy of Toni Negri', in *Reading Negri: Marxism in the Age of Empire*, ed. Pierre Lamarche, Max Rosenkrantz and David Sherman, Chicago: Open Court, pp. 171–92.

GoIroning (2018) *Why ironing clothes is important*, GoIroning, <https://goironing.co.uk/why-ironing-clothes-is-important/>.

Goldspink, G. (1977) 'Energy cost of locomotion', in *Mechanics and Energetics of Animal Locomotion*, ed. R. McNeill Alexander and G. Goldspink, London: Chapman and Hall, pp. 153–67.

Goody, Jack (2012) *Metals, Culture and Capitalism: An Essay on the Origins of the Modern World*, Cambridge: Cambridge University Press.

Goucher, Candice L. (1993) 'African metallurgy in the Atlantic world', *African Archaeological Review*, 11(1), pp. 197–215.

Graham, Stephen (2010) 'When infrastructures fail', in *Disrupted Cities: When Infrastructure Fails*, ed. Stephen Graham, New York: Routledge, pp. 1–26.

Graham, Stephen and Nigel Thrift (2007) 'Out of order: understanding repair and maintenance', *Theory, Culture & Society*, 24(3), pp. 1–25.

Grant, Iain Hamilton (2000) 'Kant after geophilosophy: the physics of analogy and the metaphysics of nature', in *The Matter of Critique: Readings in Kant's Philosophy*, ed. Andrea Rehberg and Rachel Jones, Manchester: Clinamen Press, pp. 37–60.

Grant, Iain Hamilton (2006) *Philosophies of Nature after Schelling*, London: Continuum.

Gretton, Lel (n.d.) *History of ironing*, Old and Interesting, <http://www.oldandinteresting.com/antique-irons-smoothers-mangles.aspx>.

Grimaldi, David A. and Michael S. Engel (2005) *Evolution of the Insects*, Cambridge: Cambridge University Press.

Grosz, Elizabeth (2008) *Chaos, Territory, Art: Deleuze and the Framing of the Earth*, New York: Columbia University Press.

Grosz, Elizabeth (2011) *Becoming Undone: Darwinian Reflections on Life, Politics, and Art*, Durham, NC: Duke University Press.

Grosz, Elizabeth, Kathryn Yusoff and Nigel Clark (2017) 'An interview with Elizabeth Grosz: geopower, inhumanism and the biopolitical', *Theory, Culture & Society*, 34(2–3), pp. 129–46.

Guerts, Anna (2015) *Are we done with ironing?*, History Matters, <http://www.historymatters.group.shef.ac.uk/ironing/>.

Guthrie-Smith, Herbert (1999) *Tutira: The Story of a New Zealand Sheep Station*, Auckland: Godwit.

Haaland, Randi (2007–8) 'Say it in iron: symbols of transformation and reproduction in the European iron age', *Current Swedish Archaeology*, 15–16, pp. 91–110.

Haberl, Helmut, K. Heinz Erb, Fridolin Krausmann, Veronika Gaube, Alberte Bondeau, Christoph Plutzar, Simone Gingrich, Wolfgang Lucht and Marina Fischer-Kowalski (2007) 'Quantifying and mapping the human appropriation of net primary production in earth's terrestrial ecosystems', *Proceedings of the National Academy of Sciences*, 104(31), pp. 12942–7.

Haff, Peter K. (2010) 'Hillslopes, rivers, plows, and trucks: mass transport on Earth's surface by natural and technological processes', *Earth Surface Processes and Landforms*, 35(10), pp. 1157–66.

Haff, Peter K. (2012) 'Technology and human purpose: the problem of solids transport on the Earth's surface', *Earth System Dynamics*, 3(2), pp. 149–56.

Haff, Peter K. (2014) 'Technology as a geological phenomenon: implications for human well-being', *Geological Society, London, Special Publications*, 395(1), pp. 301–9.

Hallam, Sylvia J. (1975) *Fire and Hearth: A Study of Aboriginal Usage and European Usurpation in South-Western Australia*, Canberra: Australian Institute of Aboriginal Studies.

Hamilton, Clive (2015) *Can humans survive the Anthropocene?*, <https://clive hamilton.com/can-humans-survive-the-anthropocene/>.

Hamilton, Clive and Jacques Grinevald (2015) 'Was the Anthropocene anticipated?', *The Anthropocene Review*, 2(1), pp. 59–72.

Hannis, Mike (2017) 'After development? In defence of sustainability', *Global Discourse*, 7(1), pp. 28–38.

Haraway, Donna (1988) 'Situated knowledges: the science question in feminism and the privilege of partial perspective', *Feminist Studies*, 14(3), pp. 575–99.

Haraway, Donna (1991a) 'A Cyborg Manifesto', in *Simians, Cyborgs and Women: The Reinvention of Nature*, Donna Haraway, London: Routledge, pp. 149–81.

Haraway, Donna (1991b) *Simians, Cyborgs and Women: The Reinvention of Nature*, London: Routledge.

Haraway, Donna (1992) 'The promises of monsters: a regenerative politics for inappropriate/d others', in *Cultural Studies*, ed. Lawrence Grossberg, Cary Nelson and Paula A. Treichler, New York: Routledge, pp. 295–336.

Hardt, Michael and Antonio Negri (2000) *Empire*, Cambridge, MA: Harvard University Press.

Hardt, Michael and Antonio Negri (2004) *Multitude: War and Democracy in the Age of Empire*, London: Penguin.

Hardt, Michael and Antonio Negri (2009) *Commonwealth*, Cambridge, MA: Belknap Press of Harvard University Press.

Harvey, David (2008) 'The right to the city', *New Left Review*, 53, pp. 23–40.

Hau'ofa, Epeli (1994) 'Our sea of islands', *The Contemporary Pacific*, 6(1), pp. 148–61.

Hazen, Robert M. (2012) *The Story of Earth: The First 4.5 Billion Years, from Stardust to Living Planet*, New York: Viking.

Head, Lesley (2016) *Hope and Grief in the Anthropocene: Re-Conceptualising Human–Nature Relations*, London: Routledge.

Hegel, Georg Wilhelm Friedrich (1970) *Hegel's Philosophy of Nature: Being Part Two of the Encyclopaedia of the Philosophical Sciences (1830)*, tr. Arnold V. Miller, Oxford: Clarendon Press.

Hegel, Georg Wilhelm Friedrich (2001) *The Philosophy of History*, tr. J. Sibree, Kitchener, Ontario: Batoche Books.

Hermann, Weston A. (2006) 'Quantifying global exergy resources', *Energy*, 31(12), pp. 1685–702.

Holder, Josh, Niko Kommenda and Jonathan Watts (2017) 'The three-degree world: the cities that will be drowned by global warming', *Guardian*, 3 November.

Honig, Bonnie (2009) *Emergency Politics: Paradox, Law, Democracy*, Princeton, NJ: Princeton University Press.

Howell, Elizabeth (2013) *On giant blue alien planet, it rains molten glass*, Space.com, <https://www.space.com/22614-blue-alien-planet-glass-rain.html>.

Huber, Matthew T. (2013) *Lifeblood: Oil, Freedom, and the Forces of Capital*, Minneapolis: University of Minnesota Press.

Ingold, Tim (2013) *Making: Anthropology, Archaeology, Art and Architecture*, London: Routledge.

Ingold, Tim and Jo Lee Vergunst (2008) 'Introduction', in *Ways of Walking: Ethnography and Practice on Foot*, ed. Tim Ingold and Jo Lee Vergunst, Aldershot: Ashgate, pp. 1–19.

Jablonka, Eva and Marion J. Lamb (2005) *Evolution in Four Dimensions: Genetic, Epigenetic, Behavioral, and Symbolic Variation in the History of Life*, Cambridge, MA: MIT Press.

Jameson, Fredric (2003) 'Future city', *New Left Review*, 21, pp. 65–79.

Jarvis, A. J., S. J. Jarvis and C. N. Hewitt (2015) 'Resource acquisition, distribution and end-use efficiencies and the growth of industrial society', *Earth System Dynamics*, 6(2), pp. 689–702.

Jasanoff, Sheila (2010) 'A new climate for society', *Theory, Culture & Society*, 27(2–3), pp. 233–53.

Jemisin, N. K. (2016a) *The Fifth Season*, New York: Orbit.

Jemisin, N. K. (2016b) *WIRED Book Club: fantasy writer N.K. Jemisin on the weird dreams that fuel her stories*, WIRED, <https://www.wired.com/2016/06/wired-book-club-nk-jemisin/>.

Jemisin, N. K. (2017) *The Stone Sky*, New York: Orbit.

Johns, Alessa (1999) 'Introduction', in *Dreadful Visitations: Confronting Natural Catastrophe in the Age of Enlightenment*, ed. Alessa Johns, New York: Routledge, pp. xi–xxv.

Jonas, Hans (2001) *The Phenomenon of Life: Toward a Philosophical Biology*, Evanston, IL: Northwestern University Press.

Judson, Olivia P. (2017) 'The energy expansions of evolution', *Nature Ecology & Evolution*, 1, 0138.

Kant, Immanuel (1993) *Opus Postumum*, tr. Eckart Förster, Cambridge: Cambridge University Press.

Kant, Immanuel (2005) *Critique of Judgment*, tr. J. H. Bernard, Mineola, NY: Dover.

Kant, Immanuel (2012) *Universal Natural History and Theory of the Heavens*, in *Natural Science*, tr. Olaf Rienhardt, Cambridge: Cambridge University Press, pp. 190–308.

Karera, Axelle (2019) 'Blackness and the pitfalls of Anthropocene ethics', *Critical Philosophy of Race*, 7(1), pp. 32–56.

Kelly, Robert L. (2013) *The Lifeways of Hunter-Gatherers: The Foraging Spectrum*, 2nd edition, Cambridge: Cambridge University Press.

Kember, Sarah (2017) 'After the Anthropocene: the photographic for earthly survival?', *Digital Creativity*, 28(4), pp. 348–53.

King, Geoffrey and Geoff Bailey (2015) 'Tectonics and human evolution', *Antiquity*, 80(308), pp. 265–86.

Kirby, Vicki (2011) *Quantum Anthropologies: Life at Large*, Durham, NC: Duke University Press.

Kleidon, Axel (2010) 'A basic introduction to the thermodynamics of the Earth system far from equilibrium and maximum entropy production', *Philosophical Transactions of the Royal Society B: Biological Sciences*, 365(1545), pp. 1303–15.

Kleidon, Axel (2016) *Thermodynamic Foundations of the Earth System*, Cambridge: Cambridge University Press.

Klein, Naomi (2014) *This Changes Everything: Capitalism Vs. the Climate*, New York: Simon & Schuster.

Knoll, Andrew H. and Richard K. Bambach (2000) 'Directionality in the history of life: diffusion from the left wall or repeated scaling of the right?', *Paleobiology*, 26(sp4), pp. 1–14.

Kohn, Eduardo (2013) *How Forests Think: Toward an Anthropology Beyond the Human*, London: University of California Press.

Kolb, David (2008) 'Darwin rocks Hegel: does nature have a history?', *Hegel Bulletin*, 29(1–2), pp. 97–117.

Kraft, Mike (2019) *The changing face of disaster relief: how general aviation (and social media) is making a huge impact*, OPS Group, <https://ops.group/blog/the-changing-face-of-disaster-relief-flying/>.

Kull, Christian A. (2002) 'Madagascar aflame: landscape burning as peasant protest, resistance, or a resource management tool?', *Political Geography*, 21(7), pp. 927–53.

Land, Nick (2012) 'Barker speaks: the CCRU interview with Professor D.C. Barker', in *Fanged Noumena: Collected Writings 1987–2007*, Nick Land, Falmouth & New York: Urbanomic & Sequence Press, pp. 493–505.

Langton, Marcia (1998) *Burning Questions: Emerging Environmental Issues for Indigenous Peoples in Northern Australia*, Darwin: Centre for Indigenous Natural and Cultural Resource Management, Northern Territory University.

Langton, Marcia (2019) *Fire, water and astronomy: Aboriginal and Torres Strait Islander culture comes to life in the classroom*, Guardian, <https://www.theguardian.com/commentisfree/2019/apr/11/fire-water-and-astronomy-aboriginal-and-torres-strait-islander-culture-comes-to-life-in-the-classroom>.

Last, Angela (2015) 'Fruit of the cyclone: undoing geopolitics through geopoetics', *Geoforum*, 64, pp. 56–64.

Latour, Bruno (1993) *We Have Never Been Modern*, tr. Catherine Porter, Hemel Hempstead: Harvester Wheatsheaf.

Latour, Bruno (2004) *Politics of Nature: How to Bring the Sciences into Democracy*, tr. Catherine Porter, Cambridge, MA: Harvard University Press.

Latour, Bruno (2005) *Reassembling the Social: An Introduction to Actor-Network-Theory*, Oxford: Oxford University Press.

Latour, Bruno (2017) *Facing Gaia: Eight Lectures on the New Climatic Regime*, tr. Catherine Porter, Cambridge: Polity.

Latour, Bruno (2018) *Down to Earth: Politics in the New Climatic Regime*, tr. Catherine Porter, Cambridge: Polity.

Laudan, Rachel (1987) *From Mineralogy to Geology: The Foundations of a Science, 1650–1830*, Chicago: University of Chicago Press.

Law, John (2015) 'What's wrong with a one-world world?', *Distinktion: Journal of Social Theory*, 16(1), pp. 126–39.

Lenton, Tim (2016) *Earth System Science: A Very Short Introduction*, Oxford: Oxford University Press.

Lenton, Timothy M., Hermann Held, Elmar Kriegler, Jim W. Hall, Wolfgang Lucht, Stefan Rahmstorf and Hans Joachim Schellnhuber (2008) 'Tipping elements in the Earth's climate system', *Proceedings of the National Academy of Sciences*, 105(6), pp. 1786–93.

Lenton, Timothy M., Peter-Paul Pichler and Helga Weisz (2016) 'Revolutions in energy input and material cycling in Earth history and human history', *Earth System Dynamics*, 7(2), pp. 353–70.

Lenton, Timothy M. and Andrew J. Watson (2011) *Revolutions that Made the Earth*, Oxford: Oxford University Press.

Lenton, Timothy M. and Hywel T. P. Williams (2013) 'On the origin of planetary-scale tipping points', *Trends in Ecology & Evolution*, 28(7), pp. 380–2.

Lesure, Richard G. (1997) 'Figurines and social identities in early sedentary societies', in *Women in Prehistory: North America and Mesoamerica*, ed. Cheryl Claassen and Rosemary A. Joyce, Philadelphia: University of Pennsylvania Press, pp. 227–48.

Levinas, Emmanuel (1969) *Totality and Infinity: An Essay on Exteriority*, tr. Alphonso Lingis, Pittsburgh: Duquesne University Press.

Levinson, Stephen C. (2003) *Space in Language and Cognition: Explorations in Cognitive Diversity*, Cambridge: Cambridge University Press.

Lewis, Simon L. and Mark A. Maslin (2015) 'Defining the Anthropocene', *Nature*, 519(7542), pp. 171–80.

Liberman, Anatoly (2015) *Crossing the threshold: why 'thresh ~ thrash'?*, OUPblog, <https://blog.oup.com/2015/02/thresh-thrash-etymology-word-origin/>.

Liebenberg, Louis (1990) *The Art of Tracking: The Origin of Science*, Claremont: D. Philip.

Liebenberg, Louis (2006) 'Persistence hunting by modern hunter–gatherers', *Current Anthropology*, 47(6), pp. 1017–26.

Lineweaver, Charles H. and Chas A. Egan (2008) 'Life, gravity and the second law of thermodynamics', *Physics of Life Reviews*, 5(4), pp. 225–42.

Lorch, Mark (2017) 'The chemistry of ironing', *American Scientist*, 105(3), p. 142.

Lövbrand, Eva, Silke Beck, Jason Chilvers, Tim Forsyth, Johan Hedrén, Mike Hulme, Rolf Lidskog and Eleftheria Vasileiadou (2015) 'Who speaks for the future of Earth? How critical social science can extend the conversation on the Anthropocene', *Global Environmental Change*, 32(Supplement C), pp. 211–18.

Lövbrand, Eva, Johannes Stripple and Bo Wiman (2009) 'Earth system governmentality: reflections on science in the Anthropocene', *Global Environmental Change*, 19(1), pp. 7–13.

Lovelock, James (1979) *Gaia: A New Look at Life on Earth*, Oxford: Oxford University Press.

Lovelock, James (2019) *Novacene: The Coming Age of Hyperintelligence*, London: Allen Lane.

Lovins, Amory B. (1977) *Soft Energy Paths: Toward a Durable Peace*, San Francisco, CA: Friends of the Earth International.

Maffi, Luisa (ed.) (2001) *On Biocultural Diversity: Linking Language, Knowledge, and the Environment*, Washington, DC: Smithsonian Institution Press.

Malafouris, Lambros (2010) 'Grasping the concept of number: how did the sapient mind move beyond approximation?', in *The Archaeology of Measurement: Comprehending Heaven, Earth and Time in Ancient Societies*, ed. Iain Morley and Colin Renfrew, Cambridge: Cambridge University Press, pp. 35–42.

Malm, Andreas (2016) *Fossil Capital: The Rise of Steam-Power and the Roots of Global Warming*, London: Verso.

Malm, Andreas and Alf Hornborg (2014) 'The geology of mankind? A critique of the Anthropocene narrative', *The Anthropocene Review*, 1(1), pp. 62–9.

Margulis, Lynn (1998) *The Symbiotic Planet: A New Look at Evolution*, London: Weidenfeld & Nicolson.

Margulis, Lynn (2001) 'Bacteria in the origins of species: demise of the neo-Darwinian paradigm', in *A New Century of Biology*, ed. W. John Kress and Gary W. Barrett, Washington, DC: Smithsonian Institution Press, pp. 9–27.

Margulis, Lynn and Dorion Sagan (1995) *What Is Life?*, New York: Simon & Schuster.

Marx, Karl and Friedrich Engels (1975) *The Holy Family, or, Critique of Critical Criticism*, London: Lawrence & Wishart.

Marx, Karl and Friedrich Engels (2002) *The Communist Manifesto*, London: Penguin.

Masco, Joseph (2010) 'Bad weather: on planetary crisis', *Social Studies of Science*, 40(1), pp. 7–10.

Mauss, Marcel (1954) *The Gift: Forms and Functions of Exchange in Archaic Societies*, Glencoe, IL: Free Press.

Mbembe, Achille (2017) *Critique of Black Reason*, tr. Laurent Dubois, Durham, NC: Duke University Press.

McFarlane, Colin (2011) 'Assemblage and critical urbanism', *City*, 15(2), pp. 204–24.

McKittrick, Katherine (2013) 'Plantation futures', *Small Axe*, 17(3 (42)), pp. 1–15.

McKittrick, Katherine (2015) 'Axis, bold as love: on Sylvia Wynter, Jimi Hendrix, and the promise of science', in *Sylvia Wynter: On Being Human as Praxis*, ed. Katherine McKittrick, Durham, NC: Duke University Press, pp. 142–63.

McKittrick, Katherine (2016) 'Rebellion/invention/groove', *Small Axe*, 20(1 (49)), pp. 79–91.

McNeill, William Hardy (1976) *Plagues and Peoples*, Garden City, NY: Anchor Press.

McPhee, John (1989) *The Control of Nature*, New York: Farrar, Strauss and Giroux.

Michaels, Anne (1997) *Fugitive Pieces*, New York: A. A. Knopf.

Mignolo, Walter (2011) *The Darker Side of Western Modernity: Global Futures, Decolonial Options*, Durham, NC: Duke University Press.

Mitchell, Timothy (2011) *Carbon Democracy: Political Power in the Age of Oil*, London: Verso.

Mitropoulos, Angela (2012) *Contract and Contagion: From Biopolitics to Oikonomia*, Brooklyn, NY: Minor Compositions.

Moore, Jason W. (2015) *Capitalism in the Web of Life: Ecology and the Accumulation of Capital*, London: Verso.

Moore, Jason W. and Tom Keefer (2011) 'Wall Street is a way of organizing nature', *Upping the Anti: A Journal of Theory and Action*, 12, pp. 39–53.

Morgan, Robin (2014) *Going Too Far: The Personal Chronicle of a Feminist*, New York: Open Road.

Morton, Timothy (2018) 'Third stone from the sun', *SubStance*, 47(2), pp. 107–18.

Moten, Fred (2018) *Stolen Life*, Durham, NC: Duke University Press.

Mumford, Lewis (1934) *Technics and Civilization*, New York: Harcourt, Brace.

Nakashima, Douglas (2000) 'Burning questions: shaping landscapes with aboriginal fire. Interview with Professor Marcia Langton', *Natures Sciences Sociétés*, 8(1), pp. 50–6.

Nealson, Kenneth H. (2011) 'Early sensibilities', in *Chimeras and Consciousness: Evolution of the Sensory Self*, ed. Lynn Margulis, Celeste A. Asikainen and Wolfgang E. Krumbein, Cambridge: MA: MIT Press, pp. 45–52.

Nef, John U. (1964) *The Conquest of the Material World*, Cleveland: Meridian Books.

Negarestani, Reza (2014) 'The labor of the inhuman, part I: human', *e-flux*, 52.

Neiman, Susan (2002) *Evil in Modern Thought: An Alternative History of Philosophy*, Princeton, NJ: Princeton University Press.

New, Mark, Diana Liverman, Heike Schroder and Kevin Anderson (2011) 'Four degrees and beyond: the potential for a global temperature increase of four degrees and its implications', *Philosophical Transactions of the Royal Society A: Mathematical, Physical and Engineering Sciences*, 369(1934), pp. 6–19.

Ngũgĩ, wa Thiong'o (1986) *Decolonising the Mind: The Politics of Language in African Literature*, London: James Currey.

Nixon, Rob (2011) *Slow Violence and the Environmentalism of the Poor*, Cambridge, MA: Harvard University Press.

Noor, Dharna (2019) *Socialism or extinction*, Jacobin, <https://jacobinmag.com/2019/06/biodiversity-species-extinction-united-nations-report>.

Nye, David E. (1990) *Electrifying America: Social Meanings of a New Technology, 1880–1940*, Cambridge, MA: MIT Press.

Öberg, Stefan and Klas Rönnbäck (2016) *Mortality among European Settlers in Pre-Colonial West Africa: The 'White Man's Grave' Revisited. Göteborg*

*Papers in Economic History*, *20*, Göteborg: University of Gothenburg, Department of Economic History.

Odling-Smee, F. John, Kevin N. Laland and Marcus W. Feldman (2003) *Niche Construction: The Neglected Process in Evolution*, Princeton, NJ: Princeton University Press.

Olsen, Tillie (1961) 'I stand here ironing', in *Tell Me a Riddle*, Tillie Olsen, New York: Dell, pp. 9–21.

Olson, Valerie and Lisa Messeri (2015) 'Beyond the Anthropocene: un-earthing an epoch', *Environment and Society*, 6(1), pp. 28.

Pacey, Arnold (1990) *Technology in World Civilization: A Thousand-Year History*, Cambridge, MA: MIT Press.

Parisi, Luciana and Tiziana Terranova (2000) 'Heat-death: emergence and control in genetic engineering and artificial life', *CTheory*, <http://www.ctheory.net/articles.aspx?id=127>.

Pickering, Andrew (2009) 'Beyond design: cybernetics, biological computers and hylozoism', *Synthese*, 168(3), pp. 469–91.

Piggott, Stuart (1992) *Wagon, Chariot, and Carriage: Symbol and Status in the History of Transport*, London: Thames and Hudson.

Plant, Sadie (1997) *Zeroes + Ones: Digital Women + the New Technoculture*, New York: Doubleday.

Povinelli, Elizabeth A. (1995) 'Do rocks listen?', *American Anthropologist*, 97(3), pp. 505–18.

Povinelli, Elizabeth A. (2012) 'The will to be otherwise/The effort of endurance', *South Atlantic Quarterly*, 111(3), pp. 453–75.

Povinelli, Elizabeth A. (2014) *Geontologies of the otherwise*, Society for Cultural Anthropology: Fieldsights, <https://culanth.org/fieldsights/geontologies-of-the-otherwise>.

Povinelli, Elizabeth A. (2015) 'Transgender creeks and the three figures of power in late liberalism', *differences*, 26(1), pp. 168–87.

Povinelli, Elizabeth A. (2016) *Geontologies: A Requiem to Late Liberalism*, Durham, NC: Duke University Press.

Povinelli, Elizabeth A., Mathew Coleman and Kathryn Yusoff (2017) 'An interview with Elizabeth Povinelli: geontopower, biopolitics and the Anthropocene', *Theory, Culture & Society*, 34(2–3), pp. 169–85.

Prigogine, Ilya and Isabelle Stengers (1984) *Order Out of Chaos: Man's New Dialogue with Nature*, Toronto: Bantam Books.

Protevi, John (2009) *Political Affect: Connecting the Social and the Somatic*, Minneapolis: University of Minnesota Press.

Protevi, John (2013) *Life, War, Earth: Deleuze and the Sciences*, Minneapolis: University of Minnesota Press.

Pyne, Stephen J. (1986) *The Ice: A Journey to Antarctica*, Iowa City: University of Iowa Press.

Pyne, Stephen J. (1994) 'Maintaining focus: an introduction to anthropogenic fire', *Chemosphere*, 29(5), pp. 889–911.

Pyne, Stephen J. (1997a) *Vestal Fire: An Environmental History, Told through Fire, of Europe and Europe's Encounter with the World*, Seattle: University of Washington Press.

Pyne, Stephen J. (1997b) *World Fire: The Culture of Fire on Earth*, Seattle: University of Washington Press.

Pyne, Stephen J. (2001) *Fire: A Brief History*, Seattle: University of Washington Press.

Pyne, Stephen J. (2014) 'Moved by fire: history's Promethean moment', *The Appendix*, 2(4), pp. 92–6.

Questa, Alessandro (2019) 'Broken pillars of the sky: Masewal actions and reflections on modernity, spirits, and a damaged world', in *Indigenous Perceptions of the End of the World: Creating a Cosmopolitics of Change*, ed. Rosalyn Bold, London: Palgrave Macmillan, pp. 29–49.

Raichlen, David A., Brian M. Wood, Adam D. Gordon, Audax Z. P. Mabulla, Frank W. Marlowe and Herman Pontzer (2014) 'Evidence of Lévy walk foraging patterns in human hunter-gatherers', *Proceedings of the National Academy of Sciences*, 111(2), pp. 728–33.

Rajchman, John (2000) *The Deleuze Connections*, Cambridge, MA: MIT Press.

Ray, Gene (2004) 'Reading the Lisbon earthquake: Adorno, Lyotard, and the contemporary sublime', *The Yale Journal of Criticism*, 17(1), pp. 1–18.

Reese, Ted (2019) *Socialism or Extinction: Climate, Automation and War in the Final Capitalist Breakdown*, Toronto: Rakuten Kobo.

Rehder, J. E. (2000) *The Mastery and Uses of Fire in Antiquity*, Montreal: McGill-Queen's University Press.

Reiter, Bernd (ed.) (2018) *Constructing the Pluriverse: The Geopolitics of Knowledge*, Durham, NC: Duke University Press.

Reynolds, Andy, Eliane Ceccon, Cristina Baldauf, Tassia Karina Medeiros and Octavio Miramontes (2018) 'Lévy foraging patterns of rural humans', *PLOS ONE*, 13(6), e0199099.

Roberts, Benjamin W., Christopher P. Thornton and Vincent C. Pigott (2015) 'Development of metallurgy in Eurasia', *Antiquity*, 83(322), pp. 1012–22.

Roberts, J. Timmons and Bradley C. Parks (2007) *A Climate of Injustice: Global Inequality, North–South Politics, and Climate Policy*, Cambridge, MA: MIT Press.

Rockström, Johan, Will Steffen, Kevin Noone, Asa Persson, F. Stuart Chapin, Eric F. Lambin, Timothy M. Lenton, Marten Scheffer, Carl Folke et al. (2009) 'Planetary boundaries: exploring the safe operating space for humanity', *Ecology and Society*, 14(2), pp. 32.

Rose, Deborah Bird (1992) *Dingo Makes Us Human: Life and Land in an Aboriginal Australian Culture*, Cambridge: Cambridge University Press.

Rossi, Paolo (1984) *The Dark Abyss of Time: The History of the Earth & the History of Nations from Hooke to Vico*, Chicago: University of Chicago Press.

Roy, Arundhati (1997) *The God of Small Things*, London: Flamingo.

Ruddick, Susan M. (2017) 'Rethinking the subject, reimagining worlds', *Dialogues in Human Geography*, 7(2), pp. 119–39.

Ruddiman, William F. (2003) 'The Anthropogenic greenhouse era began thousands of years ago', *Climatic Change*, 61(3), pp. 261–93.

Rudwick, Martin J. S. (2005) *Bursting the Limits of Time: The Reconstruction of Geohistory in the Age of Revolution*, Chicago: University of Chicago Press.

Ruffin, Kimberly N. (2010) *Black on Earth: African American Ecoliterary Traditions*, Athens, GA: University of Georgia Press.

Scheffer, Marten, Steve Carpenter, Jonathan A. Foley, Carl Folke and Brian Walker (2001) 'Catastrophic shifts in ecosystems', *Nature*, 413(6856), pp. 591–6.

Schellnhuber, H. J. (1999) '"Earth system" analysis and the second Copernican revolution', *Nature*, 402(6761), pp. C19–C23.

Scotese, Chistopher R. and Charles R. Denham (1988) *User's Manual for Terra Mobilis™: Plate Tectonics for the Macintosh®*, Houston, TX: Earth in Motion Technologies.

Scott, James C. (2017) *Against the Grain: A Deep History of the Earliest States*, New Haven: Yale University Press.

Scranton, Roy (2015) *Learning to Die in the Anthropocene: Reflections on the End of a Civilization*, San Francisco, CA: City Lights.

Self, Steve and Mike Rampino (2012) *The crust and lithosphere*, Geological Society of London, <https://www.geolsoc.org.uk/flood_basalts_2>.

Serres, Michel (1995) *The Natural Contract*, tr. Elizabeth MacArthur and William Paulson, Ann Arbor, MI: University of Michigan Press.

Shapin, Steven and Simon Schaffer (1985) *Leviathan and the Air-Pump: Hobbes, Boyle, and the Experimental Life*, Princeton, NJ: Princeton University Press.

Sheets-Johnstone, Maxine (1999) *The Primacy of Movement*, Philadelphia: John Benjamins.

Shoba, Sandisiwe, Zoë Postman, Thamsanqa Mbovane and Masixole Feni (2019) *South Africans come out in support of #ClimateStrike*, Ground Up, <https://www.groundup.org.za/article/south-africans-comes-out-support-climatestrike/>.

Simondon, Gilbert (1992) 'The genesis of the individual', in *Zone 6: Incorporations*, ed. Jonathan Crary and Sanford Kwinter, tr. Mark Cohen and Sanford Kwinter, New York: Urzone, pp. 297–319.

Simone, AbdouMaliq (2004) 'People as infrastructure: intersecting fragments in Johannesburg', *Public Culture*, 16(3), pp. 407–29.

Sinclair, Upton (1927) *Oil! A Novel*, New York: A. & C. Boni.

Sloterdijk, Peter (2013) *In the World Interior of Capital: Towards a Philosophical Theory of Globalization*, tr. Wieland Hoban, Cambridge: Polity.

Smil, Vaclav (2001) *Enriching the Earth: Fritz Haber, Carl Bosch, and the Transformation of World Food Production*, Cambridge, MA: MIT Press.

Smith, Cyril Stanley (1981) *A Search for Structure: Selected Essays on Science, Art, and History*, Cambridge, MA: MIT Press.

Smith, Linda Tuhiwai (1999) *Decolonizing Methodologies: Research and Indigenous Peoples*, London: Zed Books.

Smith, S. D. (2012) 'Storm hazard and slavery: the impact of the 1831 Great Caribbean Hurricane on St Vincent', *Environment and History*, 18(1), pp. 97–123.

Soffer, O., J. M. Adovasio and D. C. Hyland (2000) 'The "Venus" figurines: textiles, basketry, gender, and status in the Upper Paleolithic', *Current Anthropology*, 41(4), pp. 511–37.

Soffer, Olga (2004) 'Recovering perishable technologies through use wear on tools: preliminary evidence for Upper Paleolithic weaving and net making', *Current Anthropology*, 45(3), pp. 407–13.

Soffer, Olga and J. M. Adovasio (2014) '"Their fingers were too fat to weave": ancient textiles and academic politics today', *North American Archaeologist*, 35(4), pp. 419–37.

Spinoza, Benedictus de (1994) *A Spinoza Reader: The Ethics and Other Works*, tr. Edwin Curley, Princeton, NJ: Princeton University Press.

Spivak, Gayatri Chakravorty (1994) 'Responsibility', *boundary 2*, 21(3), pp. 19–64.

Spivak, Gayatri Chakravorty (1999) *A Critique of Postcolonial Reason: Toward a History of the Vanishing Present*, Cambridge, MA: Harvard University Press.

Spivak, Gayatri Chakravorty (2003) 'Planetarity', in *Death of a Discipline*, Gayatri Chaksavorty Spivak, New York: Columbia University Press, pp. 71–102.

Steffen, Will, Wendy Broadgate, Lisa Deutsch, Owen Gaffney and Cornelia Ludwig (2015a) 'The trajectory of the Anthropocene: the Great Acceleration', *The Anthropocene Review*, 2(1), pp. 81–98.

Steffen, Will, Paul J. Crutzen and John R. McNeill (2007) 'The Anthropocene: are humans now overwhelming the great forces of nature?', *Ambio*, 36(8), pp. 614–21.

Steffen, Will, Jacques Grinevald, Paul Crutzen and John McNeill (2011a) 'The Anthropocene: conceptual and historical perspectives', *Philosophical Transactions of the Royal Society A*, 369(1938), pp. 842–67.

Steffen, Will, Jill Jäger, Pamela Matson, Berrien Moore, Frank Oldfield, Katherine Richardson, Angelina Sanderson, H. John Schellnhuber, B. L. Turner et al. (2004) *Global Change and the Earth System: A Planet Under Pressure*, Berlin: Springer.

Steffen, Will and Eric Lambin (2006) 'Earth system functioning in the Anthropocene: human impacts on the global environment', *Scripta Varia*, 106, pp. 112–44.

Steffen, Will, Reinhold Leinfelder, Jan Zalasiewicz, Colin N. Waters, Mark Williams, Colin Summerhayes, Anthony D. Barnosky, Alejandro Cearreta, Paul Crutzen et al. (2016) 'Stratigraphic and Earth System approaches to defining the Anthropocene', *Earth's Future*, 4(8), pp. 324–45.

Steffen, Will, Åsa Persson, Lisa Deutsch, Jan Zalasiewicz, Mark Williams, Katherine Richardson, Carole Crumley, Paul Crutzen, Carl Folke et al. (2011b) 'The Anthropocene: from global change to planetary stewardship', *AMBIO*, 40(7), pp. 739–61.

Steffen, Will, Katherine Richardson, Johan Rockström, Sarah E. Cornell, Ingo Fetzer, Elena M. Bennett, Reinette Biggs, Stephen R. Carpenter, Wim de Vries et al. (2015b) 'Planetary boundaries: guiding human development on a changing planet', *Science*, 347(6223), 1259855.

Stengers, Isabelle (2018) 'The challenge of ontological politics', in *A World of Many Worlds*, ed. Marisol de la Cadena and Mario Blaser, Durham, NC: Duke University Press, pp. 83–111.

Sterjova, Milica (2017) *Liquid fuel irons: a 19th century invention that is still being used when electricity isn't available*, Walls with Stories, <http://www.wallswithstories.com/

uncategorized/liquid-fuel-irons-a-19th-century-invention-that-is-still-being-used-when-electricity-isnt-available.html>.

Stone, Alison (2005) *Petrified Intelligence: Nature in Hegel's Philosophy*, Albany: State University of New York Press.

Strasser, Susan (2000) *Never Done: A History of American Housework*, New York: Henry Holt.

Summers, Michael E. and James Trefil (2017) *Exoplanets: Diamond Worlds, Super-Earths, Pulsar Planets, and the New Search for Life Beyond Our Solar System*, Washington, DC: Smithsonian Books.

Swyngedouw, Erik (2010) 'Apocalypse forever? Post-political populism and the spectre of climate change', *Theory, Culture & Society*, 27(2–3), pp. 213–32.

Szathmáry, Eörs and John Maynard Smith (1995) 'The major evolutionary transitions', *Nature*, 374(6519), pp. 227–32.

Szerszynski, Bronislaw (2012) 'The end of the end of nature: the Anthropocene and the fate of the human', *Oxford Literary Review*, 34(2), pp. 165–84.

Szerszynski, Bronislaw (2016a) 'Out of the Metazoic? Animals as a transitional form in planetary evolution', in *Thinking about Animals in the Age of the Anthropocene*, ed. Morten Tønnessen, Silver Rattasepp and Kristin Amstrong Oma, Lexington, MA: Lexington Books, pp. 163–79.

Szerszynski, Bronislaw (2016b) 'Planetary mobilities: movement, memory and emergence in the body of the Earth', *Mobilities*, 11(4), pp. 614–28.

Szerszynski, Bronislaw (2017a) 'The Anthropocene monument: on relating geological and human time', *European Journal of Social Theory*, 20(1), pp. 111–31.

Szerszynski, Bronislaw (2017b) 'Gods of the Anthropocene: geo-spiritual formations in the Earth's new epoch', *Theory, Culture & Society*, 34(2–3), pp. 253–75.

Szerszynski, Bronislaw (2017c) 'Viewing the technosphere in an interplanetary light', *The Anthropocene Review*, 4(2), pp. 92–102.

Szerszynski, Bronislaw (2019a) 'Drift as a planetary phenomenon', *Performance Research*, 23(7), pp. 136–44.

Szerszynski, Bronislaw (2019b) 'How the Earth remembers and forgets', in *Political Geology: Active Stratigraphies and the Making of Life*, ed. Adam Bobbette and Amy Donovan, London: Palgrave Macmillan, pp. 219–36.

Szerszynski, Bronislaw (2019c) 'A planetary turn for the social sciences?', in *Mobilities and Complexities*, ed. Morten Tønnessen, Silver Rattasepp and Kristin Amstrong Oma, London: Routledge, pp. 223–7.

Szerszynski, Bronislaw (forthcoming) 'How to dismantle a bus: planetary mobilities as method', in *Handbook of Methods and Applications for Mobilities Research*, ed. Monika Büscher, Malene Freudendal-Pedersen and Sven Kesselring, Cheltenham: Edward Elgar.

Szerszynski, Bronislaw, Matthew Kearnes, Phil Macnaghten, Richard Owen and Jack Stilgoe (2013) 'Why solar radiation management geoengineering and democracy won't mix', *Environment and Planning A*, 45(12), pp. 2809–16.

Szerszynski, Bronislaw and John Urry (2010) 'Changing climates: introduction', *Theory, Culture & Society*, 27(2–3), pp. 1–8.

Tavares, Paulo (2013) 'The geological imperative: on the political ecology of the Amazonia's deep history', in *Architecture in the Anthropocene: Encounters Among Design, Deep Time, Science and Philosophy*, ed. Etienne Turpin, Ann Arbor, MI: Open Humanities Press, pp. 209–39.

Teaiwa, Katerina Martina (2011) 'Recovering Ocean Island', *Life Writing*, 8(1), pp. 87–100.

Teaiwa, Katerina Martina (2012) 'Choreographing difference: the (body) politics of Banaban dance', *The Contemporary Pacific*, 24(1), pp. 65–94.

Teaiwa, Katerina Martina (2015) *Consuming Ocean Island: Stories of People and Phosphate from Banaba*, Bloomington: Indiana University Press.

Techhistory (n.d.) *Aerial fertilizer*, Techhistory, <http://www.techhistory.co.nz/OntheLand/aerial_top-dressing.htm>.

Theobold, Simon (2018) *Mining Banaba: Katerina Teaiwa talks mining phosphate & decolonising modern anthropology*, The Familiar Strange, <https://thefamiliarstrange.com/2018/11/12/ep-26-katerina-teaiwa/>.

Thrasher, Steven W. (2020) *I study prisons and AIDS history. Here's why self-isolation really scares me*, <https://slate.com/news-and-politics/2020/03/social-distancing-coronavirus-aids-prisons.html>.

Toulmin, Stephen and June Goodfield (1967) *The Discovery of Time*, Harmondsworth: Penguin.

Travis, Merle (1947a) 'Dark as a dungeon', on *Folk Songs of the Hills*, Los Angeles: Capitol.

Travis, Merle (1947b) 'Sixteen tons', on *Folk Songs of the Hills*, Los Angeles: Capitol.

Tsing, Anna Lowenhaupt (2015) *The Mushroom at the End of the World: On the Possibility of Life in Capitalist Ruins*, Princeton, NJ: Princeton University Press.

Tuck, Eve and K. Yang (2012) 'Decolonization is not a metaphor', *Decolonization*, 1(1), pp. 1–40.

Tyfield, David (2014a) '"King Coal is dead! Long live the king!" The paradoxes of coal's resurgence in the emergence of global low-carbon societies', *Theory, Culture & Society*, 31(5), pp. 59–81.

Tyfield, David (2014b) 'Putting the power in "socio-technical regimes": e-mobility transition in China as political process', *Mobilities*, 9(4), pp. 585–603.

Ulmer, Jasmine Brooke (2019) 'The Anthropocene is a question, not a strategic plan', *Philosophy and Theory in Higher Education* 1(1), pp. 65–84.

Urry, John (2007) *Mobilities*, Cambridge: Polity.

Valenti, Philip (1979) 'Leibniz, Papin, and the steam engine', *Fusion*, pp. 27–46.

Valentine, David (2012) 'Exit strategy: profit, cosmology, and the future of humans in space', *Anthropological Quarterly*, 85(4), pp. 1045–67.

van Dooren, Thom (2010) 'Pain of extinction: the death of a vulture', *Cultural Studies Review*, 16(2), pp. 271–89.

Vandiver, Pamela B., Olga Soffer, Bohuslav Klima and Jiři Svoboda (1989) 'The origins of ceramic technology at Dolni Věstonice, Czechoslovakia', *Science* 246(4933), pp. 1002–8.

Vaughan, Genevieve (2002) 'Mothering, communication and the gifts of language', in *The Enigma of Gift and Sacrifice*, ed. Edith Wyschogrod, Jean-Joseph Goux and Eric Boynton, New York: Fordham University Press, pp. 91–113.

Vernadsky, Vladimir (1998) *The Biosphere*, tr. David B. Langmuir, New York: Springer.

Virilio, Paul (1994) *Bunker Archeology*, tr. G. Collins, Princeton, NJ: Princeton Architectural Press.

Viswanathan, G. M., E. P. Raposo and M. G. E. da Luz (2008) 'Lévy flights and superdiffusion in the context of biological encounters and random searches', *Physics of Life Reviews*, 5(3), pp. 133–50.

Viveiros de Castro, Eduardo and Déborah Danowski (2018) 'Humans and terrans in the Gaia war', in *A World of Many Worlds*, ed. Marisol de la Cadena and Mario Blaser, Durham, NC: Duke University Press, pp. 172–203.

Vogel, Steven (1994) *Life in Moving Fluids: The Physical Biology of Flow*, 2nd edition, Princeton, NJ: Princeton University Press.

Volk, Tyler (1995) *Metapatterns across Space, Time, and Mind*, New York: Columbia University Press.

Volk, Tyler, Jeffrey W. Bloom and John Richards (2007) 'Toward a science of metapatterns: building upon Bateson's foundation', *Kybernetes*, 36(7/8), pp. 1070–80.

Walcott, Rinaldo (2009) 'Reconstructing manhood; or, the drag of black masculinity', *Small Axe*, 13(1 (49)), pp. 75–89.

Waltham, David (2014) *Lucky Planet: Why Earth Is Exceptional – and What That Means for Life in the Universe*, London: Icon Books.

Waltner-Toews, David, Annibale Biggeri, Bruna De Marchi, Silvio Funtowicz, Mario Giampietro, Martin O'Connor, Jerome R. Ravetz, Andrea Saltelli and Jeroen P. van der Sluijs (2020) *Post-normal pandemics: why COVID-19 requires a new approach to science*, Discover Society, <https://discoversociety.org/2020/03/27/post-normal-pandemics-why-covid-19-requires-a-new-approach-to-science/>.

Wang, Zhongshu (1982) *Han Civilization*, tr. Kwang-Chih Chang, New Haven: Yale University Press.

Waters, Colin N. (2009) 'Carboniferous geology of Northern England', *Open University Geological Society Journal*, 30(2), pp. 5–16.

WBGU (2019) *Towards Our Common Digital Future: Flagship Report*, Berlin: WBGU.

Weber, Max (2012) *The Protestant Ethic and the Spirit of Capitalism*, tr. Stephen Kalberg, London: Routledge.

Wertime, Theodore A. (1973) 'Pyrotechnology: man's first industrial uses of fire', *American Scientist*, 61(6), pp. 670–82.

Westbroek, Peter (1991) *Life as a Geological Force: Dynamics of the Earth*, New York: Norton.

White, Stephen K. (2000) *Sustaining Affirmation: The Strengths of Weak Ontology in Political Theory*, Princeton, NJ: Princeton University Press.

Whitehouse, David (2000) *Woven cloth dates back 27,000 years*, BBC News, <http://news.bbc.co.uk/1/hi/sci/tech/790569.stm>.

Whyte, Kyle (2017) 'Indigenous climate change studies: indigenizing futures, decolonizing the Anthropocene', *English Language Notes*, 55(1–2), pp. 153–62.

Whyte, Kyle (2018a) 'Indigenous science (fiction) for the Anthropocene: ancestral dystopias and fantasies of climate change crises', *Environment and Planning E: Nature and Space*, 1(1–2), pp. 224–42.

Whyte, Kyle (2018b) 'Settler colonialism, ecology, and environmental injustice', *Environment and Society*, 9(1), pp. 125–44.

Widlok, Thomas (2008) 'The dilemmas of walking: a comparative view', in *Ways of Walking: Ethnography and Practice on Foot*, ed. Tim Ingold and Jo Lee Vergunst, Aldershot: Ashgate, pp. 51–66.

Wilkinson, Jeremy (2017) *Crashes 'part of the job' says former top-dressing pilot Bruce Aitken*, Stuff, <https://www.stuff.co.nz/business/farming/88299889/crashes-part-of-the-job-says-former-topdressing-pilot-bruce-aitken>.

Wood, Gillen D'Arcy (2014) *Tambora: The Eruption That Changed the World*, Princeton, NJ: Princeton University Press.

Woods, Clyde (1998) *Development Arrested: The Blues and Plantation Power in the Mississippi Delta*, New York: Verso.

Wrangham, Richard W. (2009) *Catching Fire: How Cooking Made Us Human*, New York: Basic Books.

Wynter, Sylvia (1995) '1492: a new world view', in *Race, Discourse, and the Origin of the Americas: A New World View*, ed. Vera Lawrence Hyatt and Rex M. Nettleford, Washington, DC: Smithsonian Institution Press, pp. 5–57.

Wynter, Sylvia (2003) 'Unsettling the coloniality of being/power/truth/freedom: towards the human, after man, its overrepresentation – an argument', *The New Centennial Review*, 3(3), pp. 277–337.

Yener, K. Aslihan (2000) *The Domestication of Metals: The Rise of Complex Metal Industries in Anatolia*, Leiden: Brill.

Yusoff, Kathryn (2013) 'Geologic life: prehistory, climate, futures in the Anthropocene', *Environment and Planning D: Society and Space*, 31(5), pp. 779–95.

Yusoff, Kathryn (2016) 'Anthropogenesis: origins and endings in the Anthropocene', *Theory, Culture & Society*, 33(2), pp. 3–28.

Yusoff, Kathryn (2018) *A Billion Black Anthropocenes or None*, Minneapolis: University of Minnesota Press.

Zalasiewicz, Jan (2008) *The Earth after Us: What Legacy will Humans Leave in the Rocks?*, Oxford: Oxford University Press.

Zalasiewicz, Jan, Will Steffen, Reinhold Leinfelder, Mark Williams and Colin Waters (2017) 'Petrifying earth process: the stratigraphic imprint of key Earth System parameters in the Anthropocene', *Theory, Culture & Society*, 34(2–3), pp. 83–104.

Zalasiewicz, Jan, Colin N. Waters, Mark Williams, Anthony D. Barnosky, Alejandro Cearreta, Paul Crutzen, Erle Ellis, Michael A. Ellis, Ian J. Fairchild et al. (2015) 'When did the Anthropocene begin? A mid-twentieth century boundary level is stratigraphically optimal', *Quaternary International*, 383, pp. 196–203.

Zalasiewicz, Jan, Mark Williams, Alan Haywood and Michael Ellis (2011) 'The

Anthropocene: a new epoch of geological time?', *Philosophical Transactions of the Royal Society A*, 369(1938), pp. 835–41.

Zalasiewicz, Jan, Mark Williams, Will Steffen and Paul Crutzen (2010) 'The new world of the Anthropocene', *Environmental Science & Technology*, 44(7), pp. 2228–31.

Zalasiewicz, Jan, Mark Williams, Colin N. Waters, Anthony D. Barnosky, John Palmesino, Ann-Sofi Rönnskog, Matt Edgeworth, Cath Neal, Alejandro Cearreta et al. (2016) 'Scale and diversity of the physical technosphere: a geological perspective', *The Anthropocene Review*, 4(1), pp. 9–22.

# Index